Pink Floyd and Philosophy

Popular Culture and Philosophy®
Series Editor: George A. Reisch

Popular Culture and Philosophy®

Pink Floyd and Philosophy

Careful with that Axiom, Eugene!

Edited by

GEORGE A. REISCH

OPEN COURT
Chicago and La Salle, Illinois

Volume 30 in the series, Popular Culture and Philosophy®, edited by George A. Reisch

To order books from Open Court, call 1-800-815-2280, or visit our website at www.opencourtbooks.com.

Open Court Publishing Company is a division of Carus Publishing Company.

Library of Congress Cataloging-in-Publication Data

Pink Floyd and philosophy : careful with that axiom, Eugene! / edited by George A. Reisch.
     p. cm. — (Popular culture and philosophy)
     Summary: "Essays critically examine philosophical concepts and problems in the music and lyrics of the band Pink Floyd" — Provided by publisher.
    Includes bibliographical references and index.
    ISBN-13: 978-0-8126-9636-3 (trade pbk. : alk. paper)
    ISBN-10: 0-8126-9636-0 (trade pbk. : alk. paper)
    1. Pink Floyd (Musical group) 2. Rock music—History and criticism 3. Music—Philosophy and aesthetics. I. Reisch, George A., 1962-
ML421.P6P54 2007
782.42166092'2—dc22

2007034981

Contents

One of the opening shots from Adrian Maben's film, Pink Floyd Live at Pompeii: The Director's Cut *(1972; Hip-O Records, 2003)*

Pink Floyd: From Pompeii to Philosophy

By 1971, Pink Floyd had set the controls for the heart of philosophy. That year, Adrian Maben made his extraordinary concert film, *Pink Floyd at Pompeii*. It begins with the desolate, lonely strains of "Echoes" as Maben's camera—impossibly high above the ancient Roman amphitheatre at Pompeii—descends slowly into the circular theatre of stone. The band, its truckloads of equipment, and miles of cables are set up in the middle of the enormous circle below.

Pink Floyd had just begun writing and recording *Dark Side of the Moon* and had yet to be jolted by the international stardom that would propel them through the 1970s and culminate in their second monster album, *The Wall*, in 1979. That's why the setting and venue could not be more perfect—or ironic. For this enormous stone amphitheatre *is* a circular wall, built up long ago brick by brick, isolating Roger Waters, Nick Mason, David Gilmour, and Rick Wright from the outside world. It was originally designed to hold a live audience, of course. But there's none in this film. Pink Floyd simply plays—to themselves, to each other, to a handful of sound technicians—with the seriousness and concentration for which they were becoming famous. There is no public performance, no on-stage banter, no corporate sponsorship, no advertising. Those who might have come expecting to see Pink Floyd "in the flesh," to get drunk, stoned, or rowdy (or all three), might have felt that something was eluding them. But no audience was present, so the film shows no trace of the slowly growing discord between Roger Waters, in particular, and the enormous audiences that Pink Floyd would soon be playing to.

By the end of the 1970s, things had turned around completely. The very first song of *The Wall* has the album's protagonist, Pink, interrogating a stadium-sized crowd of inebriated teenagers:

So ya thought ya might like to go to the show.
To feel the warm thrill of confusion
That space cadet glow.
Tell me, is something eluding you, Sunshine?

His anger culminated in 1977 during a show in Montreal, Waters recalls in interviews. Noisy, disruptive fans so annoyed him that he spit on them from the stage. He was appalled at his behavior, he admits, and began to think seriously about how and why large audiences had become so disconnected from the music they had paid to hear, and from the musicians they had come to see "in the flesh." Soon, he was toying with the concept of a rock band separated from its audience by a huge brick wall. But even that idea did not assuage his sarcasm and bitterness. Early drafts of Waters's screenplay for the film version (released in 1982) included military airplanes dive bombing the audience.[1]

Here in the ruins of Pompeii, however, Waters and the band play without a hint of the frustration or bitterness that was to come. They are happy playing alone, behind their wall, without any suggestion that this is some psychotic confinement or retreat from a cruel, unbearable world. Those themes and messages had not yet become real and pressing for Waters. The event Maben's cameras capture is noncommerical, artistic, and musical.

The Weight of the Stone

And philosophical. Pink Floyd seems natural and comfortable in this setting not simply because they play so well or because Maben's cameras glide so gracefully around them. It is because the themes and ideas they had just begun to explore musically on *Meddle* and *Dark Side*—such as time, death, madness, loss, and empathy—have a well-known history in this and nearby venues. Over two thousand years ago, these concepts and the questions raised by them were first scrutinized by ancient Greek and Italian thinkers not far from the volcano Vesuvius that erupted and stripped away all but the stones of this once bustling Italian village. Even the philosophical and cultural

---

[1] What survived of that idea is merely the final stanza of "In the Flesh"— "Lights! Turn on the sound effects! Action!" "Drop it, drop it on 'em! Drop it on them!"

metaphor of Enlightenment that would soon help catapult the band to international stardom—the battle between the light and clarity of understanding and the darkness of shadows, mystery, and madness—is unmistakeable as the band plays alternately in the bright afternoon sun and the murky darkness.

These coincidences are not superficial, for a kind of philosophical consciousness and deliberateness had begun to take center stage in Pink Floyd's music and recordings by this time. Philosophy, after all, is an attempt to understand the underlying realities of the world and ourselves by stripping away our confusions and prejudices so that the light of understanding can reach the objective, permanent truth of things—like those naked blocks of stone encircling the band. Only a few years before, Pink Floyd was immersed in the swirling, amorphous, and ever-distracting psychedelia of the 1960s. But now they were cultivating a different approach, more formal and minimal, that replaced paisely musical ornamentation and whimsical experimentation with a laser-like focus on the elemental structures of reality (being, time and finitude), of economics (money), and modern psychology (prejudice, fear, and madness). In its own, distinctive musical way, that is, Pink Floyd set out to illuminate the truth of things.

This is not to say that the band's earlier music written by Syd Barrett had no philosophical point or significance. Obvious jokes about altered consciousness aside, Barrett's music was often inspired by a sense of wonder about one of the most vexing philosophical problems, namely "other minds" and the nature of alien experience. Barrett's first hit, "Arnold Layne," was controversial at the BBC probably not just because it was about a cross dresser who stole women's clothes from washing lines. It was because Barrett's song exudes wide-eyed fascination with Arnold and his private, subjective point of view. Trying them on in front of his mirror, Arnold's new clothes "suit him fine."

On *The Piper at the Gates of Dawn*, Pink Floyd's first album, Barrett wrote about how the world might look to us if we were gnomes ("The Gnome"), or scarecrows ("The Scarecrow"), or— most puzzling of all, it appears—his impenetrable siamese cat (in "Lucifer Sam") who kept confounding his imagination: "That cat's something I can't explain." Careers in academic philosophy can be made of this kind of puzzlement. Thomas Nagel's famous philosophical essay is not titled "What is it like to be a cat?" but it could have been (it's "What is it like to be a Bat?" in the *Philosophical Review,* 1974, and easily available online). Of course, Nagel's account attempts to spell out why it is that there will always be aspects of alien experience that we "can't explain." Barrett's doesn't, but it sounds better.

If Barrett was Aristotle—fascinated by the odd particulars and the strange details he encountered in the world around him—Waters, who gradually became the band's main songwriter in Barrett's absence, had Plato's very different interest in the regular, monolithic structures (or "forms," Plato called them) that control the general features of the world and our experience. With *Dark Side,* Waters's head for metaphysics and his growing talent as a songwriter combined to create an album that indicts Being itself: "Everything under the sun is in tune. . . ," *Dark Side* concludes, "But the sun is eclipsed by the moon." Borrowing the ancient astronomical notion of madness as lunacy, Waters says that Being has been conquered by darkness and madness. Life does not just *happen* to be difficult, sad, and tragic for so many. Because it is controlled by these underlying metaphysical structures, it is essentially and therefore permanently tragic. As the very first and last interlocking lyrics of *The Wall* suggest—"we came in?" and "Isn't this where. . ."—these structures have a maze-like, ultimately circular and reinforcing logic that made the eclipse of the sun, and Pink's retreat behind his wall, inevitable.

Pink Floyd and Philosophy

After playing in the amphitheatre at Pompeii, Pink Floyd released *Dark Side of the Moon* and rapidly became one of the most popular rock bands ever. As the authors of these chapters show, the band created a body of work that seriously addresses many of the experiences, concepts, and theories that philosophers have long analyzed and contemplated. These include the nature and causes of alienation, the metaphysics of Being, the absurdity of existence, the nature of perception, of identity, of artistic and commercial authenticity and, of course, madness. Along the way, these chapters never lose sight of the music, the band, and the personalities that so effectively wove metaphysics, epistemology, and a critical view of modern life into Pink Floyd's music. In some cases, these philosophers even shed light on debates that have long stymied fans and critics, such as how many Pink Floyds there really are, whether Syd Barrett was genuinely insane (and what that might mean), and whether our habit of organizing Pink Floyd's work by its main leader and songwriter—first Barrett, then Waters, and finally Gilmour—makes good sense. One argues forcefully that the band's most compelling and creative music is its adventurous compositions from the late 1960s, as leadership was passing from Barrett to Waters, which are usually overlooked as belonging to a merely transitional, formative period. Two others suggest (entirely independently of each other) that the only way to properly understand Barrett's rise and fall is to compare Barrett to Friedrich Nietzsche, philosophy's own crazy diamond who shone like the sun in his youth but succumbed, possibly for similar reasons as Barrett, to madness.

These authors are due an enormous thank-you not only for their intellectual contributions, but also their personal honesty. Many put their hearts and minds into revisiting the Pink Floyd albums of their youth (now on their iPods) that helped form their interests in Being, perception, alienation and other topics. As you read these chapters, you may therefore detect (as I did while editing them) the youthful spark of all those hours spent in the dark, lying on the floor halfway between the stereo speakers with black light posters gleaming from the walls (I was not the only one, I was relieved to learn). Not every professor or Ph.D. candidate can so easily put aside his or her seminar-room persona and reveal that Syd Barrett or *Wish You Were Here* matter just as much to them as Ludwig Wittgenstein or *Being and Nothingness*.

So even if you didn't play "Brain Damage" forty times in a row, as Randall Auxier did one dark, existential night in 1982; even if you didn't write bad poems after listening to *Wish You Were Here* as Sue Mroz confesses, you may appreciate that these authors have bared parts of their souls in writing about the albums and concepts that helped forge their aspirations and themselves. Along with the many insights that these chapters contain, this aspect of *Pink Floyd and Philosophy* has been the most surprising and rewarding. For alienation from others and the obstacles to genuine communication are dominant themes in Pink Floyd's music. So it's both ironic and uplifting that serious intellectual study of Pink Floyd can be a kind of antidote—an occasion, at least, for personal communication among fans, colleagues, and complete strangers about the structure of Being, the structure of Dave Gilmour's guitar solos, and everything in between.

Instead of noting the year of publication of each album or song mentioned in every essay, a selected discography of Pink Floyd's recordings is included as an appendix. For permission to quote from Pink Floyd's lyrics, I would like to thank Alfred Music Publishing. Images used in the interior of this book are from the film *Pink Floyd Live at Pompeii*, Pink Floyd performing on *Top of the Pops*, a promotional film for "Arnold Layne," and unknown photographers.

Pink Floyd in Popular Culture

1

"I Hate Pink Floyd," and other Fashion Mistakes of the 1960s, '70s, and Beyond

GEORGE A. REISCH

If you wanted to be hip in the late 1970s, you could be like Johnny Rotten and wear a T-shirt that declared "I hate Pink Floyd." Punk rockers hated many things, but they were right that during that decade rock music seemed to have lost its way. By the mid-1960s, Dylan had brought the liberal progressivism of Woody Guthrie to pop music's table and everyone from folk singers like Joni Mitchell to psychedelic art-house bands like the Velvet Underground felt more independent, vocal, and willing to take musical and political chances. For the most cosmically minded, the "Age of Aquarius" was on its way. Yet even those whose tastes were more grounded in surfboards or black leather agreed that pop music had become more than entertainment or a melodic diversion from life's boredom or disappointments. It was now a force for good, a unifying soundtrack for a new generation that aimed to save us the screw-ups and misplaced values of middle-aged technocrats, corporate suits, and cold warriors.

But anyone with a copy of *London Calling* can tell you that it didn't turn out that way. Depending whom you ask, the end of this musical idealism was either the violence at Altamont, John Lennon's musical opt-out on the White Album's "Revolution," or perhaps the revelation—Joe Boyd's or Kurt Cobain's, for example—that pop music for many is nothing more than a catchy tune or "pretty song" embraced without a clue to "what it means."[1] For me, the wake-up call was on the

---

[1] Boyd writes of "fighter pilots [who] could machine-gun Vietnamese farmers for sport while listening to Dylan and Hendrix on cockpit headphones" (*White*

local news one evening in 1978 (I think) as the Sex Pistols worked their way across the United States. Their call for musical anarchy was apt, for American airwaves once carried genuinely jarring, existential critiques of contemporary culture (think The Beatles' "A Day in the Life" or Simon and Garfunkel's "Seven O'clock News/Silent Night") or anthems for social equality (like "Respect"). But pop music had lately become bland and uniform. It seemed part of a corporate design to keep happy, uncritical consumers humming along (with Tony Orlando, Peter Frampton, or The Eagles) until the next advertisement. There were exceptions, of course, like Bruce Springsteen, Frank Zappa, and Punk's American forebears. But pop music as a whole drifted in the 1970s toward light, happy, feel-good songs that even Archie Bunker might enjoy whistling. And then, at the end of the decade, when it seemed impossible for pop to become thinner and *more* inconsequential, it actually did. Zappa called disco a "social disease" and tens of thousands agreed when they frisbeed their Bee Gees albums into the flames at Chicago's "Disco Demolition" in 1979.

But disco was not the only symptom of rock's failed aspirations. According to many critics and music journalists, the bands most responsible for driving pop music into the ditch belonged to art-rock or progressive rock and were more interested in Mozart than Motown. Bands like Emerson, Lake, and Palmer, Yes, and Genesis often eschewed the formalities of verses, choruses, and 4/4 beats and produced compositions featuring abstract and cryptic lyrics set to bizarre time signatures. In Yes's epic "Close to the Edge," Jon Anderson sang, "Guessing problems only to deceive the mention / Passing paths that climb halfway into the void." Critics were at the edge of their patience. Disco, at least, had no pretentions of being more than music for dancing and (euphemistically) rocking and rolling.

For many, Pink Floyd was at the very top of the progressive rock pile. In the mid-1970s, it was riding high on the record-setting success of *Dark Side of the Moon,* and was proving with *Wish You Were Here* and *Animals* that it had mastered the art of long, elaborate, and meticulously produced songs that often

---

Bicycles: Making Music in the 1960s, London, 2006, p. 271). Cobain mocked hormone-addled fans happy to sing along in "In Bloom" (*Nevermind*).

ignored pop's rules and conventions. By the end of 1979, the band had produced a *second* record-setting album, *The Wall*, and were poised to translate that success into film with Alan Parker and Roger Waters's film adapation.

But that doesn't explain why Johnny Rotten singled out Pink Floyd for that famous T-shirt. In fact, Pink Floyd climbed the charts as an *exception* to the rule that rock and pop contained few serious ideas or criticisms of culture or "the thin ice of modern life" (as Roger Waters put it in *The Wall*). Far from contributing to the post-Sixties musical malaise, Pink Floyd helped prevent pop music from becoming saturated with the soap-opera soundtracks of "California Rock" or the grunting repetition of disco. So, if you were a musician seeking to stand out as the next big thing, there wouldn't be much point in declaring "I hate Styx" or "I hate Disco." Lots of people hated them, too. Much better to stick a safety pin through your cheek, call the Queen of England a fascist, and insult as many fans and music critics as possible. Johnny Rotten's T-shirt declared "I hate Pink Floyd" because he (or perhaps his fashionista-handler Malcolm McLaren) figured that it would annoy the greatest number of people. He was right. In the 1970s, everyone loved Pink Floyd.

The Four Lads from Cambridge

For most, the love affair began in 1973, when *Dark Side of the Moon* started its historic ascent. If you didn't live through the 1970s, or just don't remember them, the *Dark Side* juggernaut might be hard to imagine. "Money," now a mainstay on classic rock stations, was a hit even on AM radio. And the luminescent prism floating in its empty, black world refracted its lonely ray of light on album covers, posters, T-shirts, macrame rugs, hand-painted cars and wall murals throughout North America and Europe. Even today, you can see *Dark Side of the Moon* T-shirts in coffee shops and classrooms, worn by fans decades younger than the album itself. Laser show aficionados still go "straight to the dark side of the moon" (as Fountains of Wayne put it) and the entire album has been re-recorded by reggae musicians as *Dub Side of the Moon*.[2]

---

[2] "Laser Show" from Fountains of Wayne's *Welcome Interstate Managers*. *Dub Side of the Moon* is discussed in Cari Callis's chapter of this book.

In the music trade, the album is one of the few for which "legendary" is not hype or exaggeration. Insiders will tell you that there's a CD pressing plant in Germany that exclusively presses *Dark Side* CD's, while nearly every article about the history of pop music (such as one I recently found in an in-flight magazine) will genuflect to its "591 weeks on the Billboard 200—a feat equaled by no other record in history" or point out that it continues to generate more revenue than major album releases by classic hip-hop artists.[3]

The prism stamped the popular culture of the Seventies much as the cover of the Beatles' *Sergeant Pepper* stamped the 1960s. Both bands are British quartets who did their most famous work at EMI's Abbey Road Studios. And both perfected their craft over the course of several albums before creating sonic masterpieces that took very large musical steps ahead of their predecessors. One difference, though, is that it took Pink Floyd about six years to find its way to *Dark Side* after they first hit the airwaves (with the single "Arnold Layne") in 1967. The Beatles needed only about four years to arrive at *Sergeant Pepper* after their first singles, but they did not have to grapple with the decline of their founder and main songwriter.

Syd Barrett first propelled Pink Floyd to success, but then quickly succumbed to . . . something. The consensus holds that Syd was done in by a combination of lurking mental illness (perhaps schizophrenia) and an over-indulgence in LSD. But some (and some writing in this book) think that Barrett was more in control of his withdrawal than the acid-casualty story suggests. Everyone *wants* to be a rock star, right? We assume that anyone who opts out after a few singles, a well-received album, and appearances on "Top of the Pops" must have been derailed by something outside of their control. Maybe. But Syd had a way of seeing things differently, as his music suggests. Pending a more definitive biographical or cinematic study of his life, there will perhaps always be room to wonder whether Syd was at least content, if not positively relieved, to find himself no longer the leader of an up-and-coming rock band.

---

[3] "The Abbey Road Sessions," *American Way* (June 1st, 2007); David Browne, "For Rap Pioneers, Paydays Are Measured in Pocket Change," *New York Times* (December 17th, 2006).

Whatever the truth about Syd, his bandmates had no doubt in 1968 that he could no longer effectively lead the band. His behavior and performances became unpredictable, and his personality and appearance changed dramatically. "Arnold Layne"'s producer Joe Boyd, seeing Syd for the first time after a few months at Club UFO, recalled being shocked to see that Syd's eyes had suddenly lost their famous sparkle.[4] The crazy diamond stopped shining and the songs he wrote for his band now seemed tossed off. One, Roger Waters and others recall, featured chord progressions that changed every time the song was played (it was titled, appropriately, "Have You Got It Yet?"). With live dates scheduled, and hopes high for success, the band recruited one of Barrett's oldest friends, Dave Gilmour, to back up Barrett on stage with singing and guitar playing. But he soon replaced Barrett altogether. All of them—Gilmour, drummer Nick Mason, keyboardist Richard Wright, and bassist Waters—began to write songs on their own.

Waters's talents and passions as a songwriter eventually provided a new rudder and vision for the band to follow. But for a couple of years, the band floundered. Sometimes they traded in Syd's penchant for psychedelic explorations like "Interstellar Overdrive" or "Astronomy Domine" (from *Piper at the Gates of Dawn*) for something more like Beethoven or Karlheinz Stockhausen. *Atom Heart Mother*, for example, sets the band against a choir and symphony. They also turned to modern electronic music, specifically the techniques of *musique concrète* for building compositions out of recorded sounds of everyday life. Sound effects and spontaneous recordings would become part of the band's signature sound, but not before they learned the hard way (through "Alan's Psychedelic Breakfast" at the close of *Atom Heart Mother*, for example) that adding the sounds of dripping faucets and frying eggs to a recording does not automatically

---

[4] Joe Boyd, interview, "Syd Barrett: A True Rock Legend," *The Guardian* (June 11th, 2006). See also Boyd's *White Bicycles* where he describes Syd "as if someone had reached inside his head and turned off a switch" (p. 141). Other general information about the history of Pink Floyd mentioned here, if not cited specifically, comes from Nicholas Schaffner's *Saucerful of Secrets: The Pink Floyd Odyssey* (New York, 1991); Phil Rose's *Which One's Pink* (Ontario, undated); and Mike Watkinson and Pete Anderson, *Crazy Diamond: Syd Barrett and the Dawn of Pink Floyd* (Omnibus, 1991).

make it more interesting or compelling. The band even tried their hand at a singer-songwriter approach, writing three-minute, acoustic songs often for film soundtracks. Some of their contemplative songs for filmmakers Barbet Schroeder (*More*, *The Valley*) and Michelangelo Antonioni (*Zabriskie Point*) would not sound too out of place on an early Crosby, Stills and Nash album.

Some thought that Pink Floyd without Barrett was doomed. Even their original managers thought so. The band's future seemed precarious, especially on the double album *Ummagumma*, for which—White Album–style—they recorded songs as individuals, each controlling one half of an LP side. Gilmour admitted later that his contribution was a picture of "desperation" and "waffling about, tacking bits and pieces together" in the recording studio.[5]

From Waffling to Meddling

Things turned around with *Meddle*, released in 1971. Like *Atom Heart Mother*, it featured both a long, album-side composition, "Echoes," as well as a handful of individual songs. Yet each was more developed, more distinctive, and more risk-taking than its predecessor. "One of These Days," for example, is an ominous, thunderous portrait of pure rage, its only lyric distorted and obscured deeply within the mix—"one of these days I'm going to cut you into little pieces." Gilmour's slide guitar evokes a roiling anger anticipating Pink's violent hotel-room tantrum in *The Wall*'s "One of My Turns."[6] The band also began to arrange its songs into coherent, dynamic albums (with "One of These Days" mercifully cross-fading into the quiet, calming "A Pillow of Winds.")

"Echoes" can be understood as something like Pink Floyd's proof of concept—a demonstration that a fairly simple song with three verses and an instrumental break can be stretched, magnified, broken-apart, rearranged, and greatly slowed-down to create an exhilarating twenty-minute musical experience.

---

[5] David Gilmour, quoted in *Sounds "Guitar Heroes" Magazine* (May 1983). But for a defense of *Ummagumma* as one of the band's creative high points, see Chapter 9 in this volume.

[6] Or one of Tony Soprano's bad days. "One of These Days" plays over the closing credits of "The Fleshy Part of the Thigh" (*The Sopranos*, Season 6, Episode 4).

"Echoes" ebbs and flows, and sometimes changes dramatically and suddenly. Yet it retains a sense of unity and purpose as it gradually circles back to its last, final verse.

Thematically, "Echoes" was a milestone, as well. Lines from the second verse—

> Strangers passing in the street
> By chance two separate glances meet
> And I am you and what I see is me—

laid the framework for what Roger Waters would later say was the political and philosophical question driving *Dark Side of the Moon* (and posed most clearly in "Us and Them"): can human beings identify and sympathize with each other, instead of antagonizing, mistrusting, or exploiting each other?[7]

Still, Pink Floyd remained in the shadow of The Beatles. "Echoes" nods self-consciously to "I Am the Walrus" ("I am he as you are me . . .") and "Across the Universe" (". . . exciting and inviting me"). But after several months inside Abbey Road studios, they emerged with a new album that accepted the method of *Sergeant Pepper* and other so-called concept albums—that a collection of songs should intertwine and support each other as a thematic whole—and took things a few steps farther. Most concept albums of the early 1970s used an idea or concept, such as a rock star from Mars, or a deaf and blind boy-prophet, to organize an album and tell some kind of story. But on *Dark Side of the Moon*, abstract concepts and ideas become more than tools. They themselves have become the subjects of the songs. Waters and the rest of the band stepped to the back of the stage—after *Meddle*, no photos of the band members appeared on major albums—to let the spotlight illuminate some of the metaphysical and phenomenological furniture of modern life, such as death, fear, time, alienation, and anxiety.

The Crazy Diamond

And madness. Madness haunts *Dark Side*. It gets closer and closer with each verse of "Brain Damage":

---

[7] Waters explains this in the interview in "Classic Albums: The Making of *The Dark Side of the Moon*" (DVD, 1997).

> The lunatic is on the grass . . .
> the lunatic is in the hall . . .
> the lunatic is in my head . . .

Syd continued to live in London and Cambridge and, for the first years after leaving the band, cross paths with his former bandmates. Both Gilmour and Waters continued to work with Syd occasionally and helped him produce two solo albums, *The Madcap Laughs* and *Barrett* (both 1970).[8] After that, the band fell completely out of touch with Syd until, some five years later, he turned up at Abbey Road studios while they were recording *Wish You Were Here*. Nick Mason recalled noticing a stranger kicking around in the control room—some bald, overweight man with "a fairly benign, but vacant, expression on his face." "More than twenty years later," Mason writes, "I can still remember that rush of confusion" upon being told that this seeming stranger was Syd Barrett, a man he remembered so differently "seven years earlier, six stone lighter, with dark curly hair and an ebullient personality." One aspect of that "rush of confusion," Mason admitted, was guilt. "We all played some part in bringing Syd to his present state, either through denial, a lack of responsibility, insensitivity, or downright selfishness."[9]

Regardless of how these and other feelings played out within the band, Syd is in plain sight in *Dark Side*'s lines about lunacy and estrangement ("if the band you're in starts playing different tunes"). And he is the addressee of *Wish You Were Here*'s musical postcard that seems to ask, How exactly did things go so wrong?:

> Did they get you to trade
> your heroes for ghosts?
> Hot ashes for trees?

---

[8] With its false starts and take-overs in some cases preserved, *Madcap Laughs* can be heard both as a tragic portrait of an artist who is no longer fully as present or disciplined as Syd obviously once was, or as an album by a prototypical "indie" musician who rejects expensive sonic sheen and wants his listeners to hear the lo-fi truth about what recording sessions are actually like. Brandon Forbes explores this (via philosopher and critic Walter Benjamin) in Chapter 17 of this volume.

[9] Nick Mason, *Inside Out: A Personal History of Pink Floyd* (San Francisco, 2005), pp. 211–12.

Hot air for a cool breeze?
Cold comfort for change?
And did you exchange a walk on part in the war
for a lead role in a cage?

"Have a Cigar" and "Welcome to the Machine" both describe the ugly guts inside the music industry's beast. The protagonist in both is an individual, "a dear boy," a "son," a genius *Wunderkind* who is lured into the industry's machine only to be caged, commodified, and controlled by executives happily "riding the gravy train." Pop stardom, the album would have us believe, is something like a very nasty trick.

Barrett makes less of an appearance in "Animals," but perhaps only incidentally. Waters's main focus here is a quasi-Orwellian world inhabited by pacifist sheep, backstabbing dogs, and greedy capitalist pigs. But he returns in *The Wall* as an amalgamation of Waters himself, "Pink" the fictional drug-addled, alienated rock star, and that once sparkling diamond that strolled into Abbey Road studios on June 4th, 1975. Syd's legendary status was ratcheted higher by the album's success and the film by Alan Parker in which Bob Geldof portrayed "Pink" in all his Barrett-like eccentricities and outbursts.

Syd had become a recluse and, as far as the music business goes, a has-been. Yet his legend and his talent continued to inspire musicians as successful as David Bowie, Robyn Hitchcock, and Robert Smith, each of whom at different times emulated Syd's attitudes, clothes, make-up, playfulness, and rock star magnetism. Lesser known artists remained fascinated with Syd, as well. Four years after Waters sang, "Nobody knows where you are," the Television Personalities released their song, "I know where Syd Barrett lives." In the 1980s, The Dukes of Stratosphear released two albums filled with Barrett-style songs and lyrics. Only the voice of Andy Partridge revealed that the Dukes were disguised former-punkers XTC wishing in their own way that Barrett were here.[10]

---

[10] After Syd's death in 2006, a minor pantheon of musicians—Chrissie Hynde, Damon Albarn, and Led Zeppelin's John Paul Jones—felt obliged to join Syd's former bandmates in a London concert-tribute to Syd's legendary spirit and creativity.

By the 1980s, Barrett himself was living quietly with family in Cambridge. With rare exceptions, he was not talking. But the larger conversation with him, and about him, continued as Pink Floyd's classic albums from the 1970s addressed Syd's departure, his breakdown, and the lingering anxieties and disappointments of the resulting estrangement. The albums remain a sustained examination—alternately sarcastic, bitter, and furiously angry—of the realities and dangers of modern life that seemed to deprive Pink Floyd of a once dear friend and propel them into realms of international stardom, wealth, and commercial obligation that, judging from what happened after the 1970s, the band may not have really wanted in the first place.

Wish You Weren't Here

After the enormous success of *Dark Side,* fault lines appeared and the band slowly began to disintegrate. Like the so-called White Album, which its cover art so resembles, *The Wall* arrived in the wake of escalating tensions and artistic differences. Mason played the part of Ringo, needed for his drum parts but little else, while keyboardist Wright was something of a George Harrison—a band member who, despite his talent, was never allowed to steer the ship for more than a moment or two. During *The Wall*'s recording sessions, Wright became increasingly distant from the band and eventually performed on the subsequent tour as a hired session player. And in the background were financial pressures stemming from the demands of the taxman and crises over financial advisers who decided to help themselves to Pink Floyd's (what else?) money.

At the center of the tornado, as Mason puts it, was Waters's "struggle to modify what had been an ostensibly democratic band into the reality of one with a single leader." By the time the aptly named album *The Final Cut* (1983) appeared, Wright was out of the band and Waters had become more than the dominant force he had been on the band's earlier albums. He controlled the album so tightly that it is widely seen as his first solo album. "After *The Final Cut* was finished," Mason writes, "there were no plans for the future . . ."[11]

---

[11] Mason, *Inside Out,* pp. 147, 273.

There were, however, more arguments. Waters commenced his official solo career with *The Pros and Cons of Hitchhiking* (1984) and reasonably assumed that Pink Floyd no longer existed as a band or commercial entity. Gilmour, and Mason, however, saw things differently. With Wright again hired as a session musician, they carried on as Pink Floyd without Waters. After legal wrangling and recriminations in the press, the two factions eventually agreed upon terms that allowed Pink Floyd without Waters to continue—with *A Momentary Lapse of Reason* (1987) and *The Division Bell* (1994)—while Waters continued his solo career—including *Radio K.A.O.S.* (1987), *Amused to Death* (1992), and his opera *Ca Ira* (2005).

Neither faction, even the most ardent fans are likely to agree, has managed to produce music that moves out of the shadow of the classic Pink Floyd albums or that covers new ground with the same originality. Pink Floyd (without Waters) continued to record sonically immaculate songs built largely around the warmth of Gilmour's voice and the graceful architecture of his guitar playing. But something—more than Roger Water's steady bass playing and occasional singing—was obviously missing. For Waters had taken with him both his sarcastic anger toward the tragedies and idiocies of modern life as well as his hopes that music might somehow illuminate, if not mitigate, these problems.

Once again, it turned out, Pink Floyd was faced with the prospect of making rock albums with buckets of talent and recording-studio know-how, but no overriding passion, vision, or axes to be careful with. The result pleased radio audiences and underwrote profitable tours. But the commercial success of post-1970s Pink Floyd seems unthinkable without the band's classic work from the 1970s that remains the core of its live shows. The band's newer material plainly recycles the riffs and sound effects, the saxophone and lilting female backup singers, that first debuted on *Dark Side*.

Waters's solo work has perhaps the opposite problem. It has no shortage of ideas and critical stances on modern culture. But it also tends to either recycle classic Floyd musical textures (without Gilmour's distinctive guitar and voice) or aims for new ones under the guidance of mainstream producers (like Madonna producer Patrick Leonard). Not unlike the post-breakup work of Lennon and McCartney, these separate musical projects seemed to lack the spark and creative tension that once pushed their collective work to places that no single leader or producer could have envisioned or planned.

In this regard, Pink Floyd's artwork and visual imagery—the most famous designed by Storm Thorgerson—continues to be as suggestive and compelling as ever. The cover of *The Division Bell* presents a frozen conversation between two enormous steel heads that face each other silently and motionlessly. Like the cow on the cover of *Atom Heart Mother,* they sit in a meadow. This is Pink Floyd and Syd Barrett circa 1975—separated and not speaking, yet staring intently, in confused wonder. This is Waters and Gilmour circa 1985 (or 1995), firm in their resolve and antipathy, speaking to each other only through lawyers, yet unable to pull themselves away from their shared musical past.

Looked at in the right way, the two heads are also halves of a whole—a single face peering directly at us from beneath a steel mask or helmet, or perhaps a human heart that is at war with itself and frozen in steel. "We're just two lost souls swimming in a fish bowl, year after year," Gilmour sang (and Waters wrote) in the song "Wish You Were Here." Decades later, the two halves remain locked in place, at least in the eyes (and ears) of ardent Pink Floyd fans who were tantalized by the momentary lapse of discord in the Summer of 2005, when the band reunited and performed in London. Other signs of life included Mason playing drums occasionally at Roger Waters concerts and the tribute concert for Syd Barrett in 2007. Though they did not perform together, both halves of the heart were present along with the many other musicians and fans for whom Syd remains a diamond helping to keep their hearts intact and their hopes alive.

Does Johnny Rotten Still Hate Pink Floyd?

Well, punk has come and gone, and so has his name, since he now goes by John Lydon. And he might still hate Pink Floyd.[12] But fans know that the standard complaints about the unthink-

---

[12] But probably not. Lydon's work with Public Image, Ltd. could be as dreamy and psychedelic as anything written by Syd Barrett ("Poptones" on *Second Edition* and *Metal Box*) and as verbally caustic as Roger Waters at his most biting ("Religion" on *First Issue*).

ing vacuity of corporate rock in the late 1970s has nothing to do with Pink Floyd. If punk music was all about rejecting authority, getting back to basics, paying attention to what you really feel and think and dream (and not what commercial interests tell you to feel and think and dream), then Pink Floyd was punk long before The Ramones and the Sex Pistols.

Pink Floyd never *sounded* punk because they embraced the sonic capabilities that EMI and other major labels offered them with state of the art studios and top-notch audio engineers. But that's not to say that they sounded like most other progressive rock bands, either. They may have played the same stadiums as Genesis or Yes, but they never aspired to be virtuoso instrumentalists or vocalists. Under Waters's leadership, they had an ax to grind, but they sharpened it methodically and carefully—with the well-turned phrase, a spine-chilling sound-effect, or just the right *thud* from Nick Mason's drums. They chopped away at the inauthenticity, alienation, and tragedy of modern life not with two-minute songs played at breakneck speed but words and music meticulously produced to reveal something, or at least share something with listeners, about the corrosive qualities of life and commerce that they saw first hand inside of the music industry. The pen may not always be mightier than the sword, but the music and lyrics of Pink Floyd—as the chapters in this book show—almost always turn out to be mightier and weightier than punk rock's power chords.

2

Life and Death on *The Dub Side of the Moon*

CARI CALLIS

Dark Side of the Moon's cover image of a beam of white light pass-ing through a prism and emerging as a full spectrum stands as a metaphor for life's complexity—though it may represent the mind of the listener after exposure to Pink Floyd's masterpiece as well. *Dub Side of the Moon*'s aim is to split that beam into reggae's red, gold and green without sacrificing the nuances that made the orig-inal so powerful.

— LEM OPPENHEIMER (*Dub Side of the Moon,* Easy Star Records September 2002, liner notes[1])

Side One

I was sixteen the first time I heard Pink Floyd's *Dark Side of the Moon,* and I was not impressed. My boyfriend had become obsessed with it and couldn't wait to play it for me. But it sounded dark, creepy and too symbolic for my taste. I was working as a lifeguard and all day long we listened to the Beach Boys and occasionally The Beatles. But "psychedelic" music was for stoners and dark rebels—which my first boyfriend was, and that's why I liked him. Eddy smoked a lot of pot, cigarettes, and he drank. He was only a year older but my parents were not thrilled about him, especially my father who caught us making out when he came to pick me up from the pool one day during a rain storm.

---

[1] All quotes by Lem Oppenheimer are from the liner notes.

The day he played *Dark Side* for me we were at his house. His parents worked, so we were alone and turned it up really loud. There was a fuzzy day-glo black light poster on the black walls of his basement bedroom of a woman metamorphosing from a wave. At sixteen I didn't want to think about death or madness, so I studied that poster and waited for it to be over. It was probably the last time we hung out, because we broke up shortly after that. I suspect my unwillingness to sleep with him was the reason, but we stayed friends over the years. Why is it that all of us who are familiar with *Dark Side* feel the necessity to recount when we first heard it and how it affected us?

He killed himself before he turned thirty. Just woke up one morning unable to face another day at the John Deere factory. He told his Dad (yes, he still lived at home) he was going to take a shower, went into that basement bedroom and shot himself with a shotgun his Dad had used to hunt with back in Tennessee where they'd grown up. I could never listen to *Dark Side of the Moon* again. Whenever I heard of it I thought of him. I could always feel his ghost in my eyes when I heard "The Great Gig in the Sky."

Side Two

Thirty-four years later, a friend who is aware of my reggae obsession gave me a copy of *Dub Side of the Moon* and I learned what so many of my Seventies peers had always known—including Eddy. Pink Floyd's music has universal appeal to anyone living in a "material world," enough to be adapted three decades later by a group of all-star reggae musicians. Initially, the idea of re-imagining Pink Floyd as roots reggae could not have been an easy sell. It seems ridiculous because reggae rhythms don't have guitar solos and David Gilmour's leads would have to be replaced. But Lem Oppenheimer, whose brainchild this was, must have been persistent, because he convinced the likes of well-known reggae stars Sluggy Ranks, Corey Harris and Ranking Joe, Kirsty Rock, Gary "Nesta" Pine, Dollarman, Frankie Paul, Dr. Israel and the Meditations to participate. Oppenheimer, executive producer and principle of Easy Star Records in New York, claims the notion came to him back in 1999 when he was walking around the New York streets listening to *Dark Side* on a walkman. It must have made sense to him that a group of Jamaican Rastas would find meaning in the words,

> Run rabbit run
> Dig that hole, forget the sun,
> And when at last the work is done
> Don't sit down it's time to start another one
> For long you live and high you fly
> But only if you ride the tide
> And balanced on the biggest wave
> You race towards an early grave.
> ("Breathe," *Dark Side of the Moon*, 1973)

Oppenheimer writes, "These universal matters suffer little in our translation; reggae has long tackled humanist themes, especially those that document daily suffering and endless hope. Many Jamaicans can understand where a lyric like "But if you ask for a rise it's no surprise that they're giving none away" is coming from (as shown in the lyrics of countless reggae songs, such as The Maytones' "Money Worries" and Junior Byles's "Fade Away")."

"The arranging of the material was a challenging task," he explains. "We were determined to get to the heart of the piece and turn it into something that might have been recorded this way in some parallel universe." They succeeded. It does become a sort of "gene splicing experiment" as Lem hoped. They explore what it means to be human through the processes of birth and death in a world of materialism, time, spiritual awareness and madness. Yet they make it uniquely "Rasta" and incorporate that philosophy.

Rasta Reasoning

Most people have misconceptions about what it means to be a true "Rasta" and know only what they've encountered from bad TV cop shows or a chance encounter with a Rent-A-Dread on the tourist beaches of the Caribbean. Rasta philosophy is based on the Old Testament and musical influences are often organized into the twelve tribes of Israel Rastafari. They follow a diet of no meat, no alcohol or drugs, other than ganja which is always smoked to connect to a higher power. Rastas live I-tal, or "vital life", and avoid all aspects of Babylon, defined as white imperialist power structures and lifestyles which have oppressed Blacks and other people of color. Though, curiously, every Rasta I know has a cell phone, the basic goal is to leave the planet the way we found it—to use plants and "natural" things, give praise and thanks for all living things and treat all people of all nations with respect and compassion. Pink Floyd's audience of millions could now connect to the music in a totally new way.

Dub music evolved out of early Jamaican 1960s reggae and usually takes a song and eliminates the vocals and emphasizes the drums and especially the bass. The tracks are heavily mixed with effects such as echo and reverb with the vocals dropping in and out of the mix. Sometimes sound effects are added, much like the cash register in "Money" or the clocks in "Time."

Dub Side of the Moon opens with the nyabinghi drums beating the heartbeat of man, mixed with the bubbles of the chalice or bong being fired and coughing. There's strange laughter and jungle sounds, echoing the original, and we instantly know we're being initiated into a sacred ceremony. Nyabinghi drumming is uniquely Rasta and carries the oral and musical traditions of Rastafarian. It is featured at island-wide religious gatherings of Rasta brethren and sistren at which communicants "praise Jah" and "chant down Babylon," to the three-part drum ensemble on which chants are composed, to the African-derived dance-drumming style performed at these events, and to the corpus of chants themselves" (Smithsonian).[2] The use of nyabinghi drums remains true to *Dark Side* as it is meant to evoke a "grounation" environment, as the Rasta gatherings are called, and to evoke the same frenetic meditative state of mind as the original.

Great care is taken to "combine the original melodies and chord structures with reggae rhythms, though it was never that simple" (Oppenheimer). But the only reason to pay tribute to a musical narrative such as *Dark Side* is to adapt it in a new way that is relevant to an audience today. Somehow, *Dub Side* finds the same sense of experimental "reasoning" that Gilmour, Mason, Waters, and Wright must have experienced in the studio. "David Gilmour's leads are replaced by horns ("Any Color you

---

[2] "The African Diaspora, Ethiopianism and Rastafari," at http://www .smithsonianeducation.org/migrations/rasta/terms.html.

Like"), melodica ("Time Version") and some improvised "toast-ing" ("Time and Money") which is chanting, singing, or a com-bination of the two called "singjaying."

There are also some other notable changes. The climax of "Speak to Me" features the coughing from "Money" and the drums are overlaid with the water bubbling of a bong. This occurs again in "Money" when the bubbling of the bong con-nects the narrative a bit more literally here and replaces the cash register with the sound of a lighter firing the chalice. Syd Barrett used to play his Fender guitar by sliding a Zippo lighter up and down the fret-board through an old echo box to create the "mysterious, otherworldly sounds" that first made the band famous in psychedelic London.[3] Perhaps this is a tribute, possi-bly even accidental, to the genius who got Pink Floyd started.

"Eclipse" has been changed to a standard 4/4 beat instead of triple meter which is not used in reggae. A cuckoo clock, a rooster and Reveille played on a trumpet is added to "Time." The cuckoo clock reiterates the madness and descent into men-tal illness in an ironic humorous way. Reveille clearly references the US military. But the rooster resonates most personally for me, having lived for brief periods in Jamaica where many fami-lies still keep chickens and roosters. This is the most likely way that a Rasta would be awakened at the crack of dawn.

On Rasta Time

Rasta belief is, for the most part, anti-capitalistic. Most Rastas live outside of society, often in the bush or the mountains, and reject traditional ideas of societal behavior. Rastas often sell wood carvings, handcrafted jewelry and art crafts, juices and bottled roots drinks on the street to survive, or trade goods among themselves. This allows them to exist outside of a tax system and to avoid rules they don't believe in. In Jamaican patois, the word for money is "coil." It's not surprising that they can iden-tify with the rebellious set of principles explored in *Dark Side*, especially those exploring time and money.

The tourist trade in Jamaica has been marketed with the phrase "soon come." This is well known to people who have

---

[3] *Wikipedia*, see article "Syd Barrett".

waited for anything in the Caribbean. It resonates with the
Buddhist principle that "things happen in their own time."
Patience, a virtue believed by some Rastas to be lost in the madness of Babylon, means waiting for that which is not instantly
accessible. For the Rasta, that means waiting for food to be
grown from seeds planted, or waiting for fruit to become ripe.
They often subsist on the gardens that they plant or by selling
ganja, the holy herb. For tourists waiting for Jamaican food to
be prepared properly—that is, without microwave or shortcuts—it's always a bit of a joke to see how rooted in Babylon
(and its fast food principles) they really are.

There are two tracks of "Time" on *Dub Side*, the first is performed by Corey Harris who sings Pink Floyd's lyrics in the original timing and phrasing while Ranking Joe "singjays" in the
breaks with repetitions like "Time is the master, and it can be a
disaster, ain't no time to play, it's serious time." What this adds
to the narrative is the sense of urgency Rastas feel about society's need to wake up and change the focus of modern life from
materialistic values to those of peace and brotherhood. The second version of "Time" is strictly an instrumental mix that uses a
melodica solo instead of vocal track. In reggae tradition, the four
bonus tracks are dub versions (or remixes) which go further into
the "uncharted territory suggested by the original." "Step it Pon
The Rastaman Scene" is probably the most interpretive and
explores racism and the call to see it from the Rasta point of
view (Oppenheimer).

"A New Broom Sweeps Clean, but an Old Broom Knows Every Corner"

This Jamaican saying sums up the state of today's music,[4] especially in regard to *Dub Side of the Moon*. It was released in 2003
and sold over 85,000 copies, though it remains relatively
unknown outside of reggae circles. *Vibe* magazine called it "a
magical groove." And that's exactly what it is—a set of tracks
that pay homage to Pink Floyd by reinventing and reviving the
messages of *Dark Side*.

---

[4] A useful Rasta-patois dictionary was compiled by Mike Pawka and is available at: http://niceup.com/patois.txt.

In different ways, those messages are everywhere. This week someone sent me an email with an anonymous quote that read, "In the 60s, people took acid to make the world weird. Now the world is weird and people take Prozac to make it normal." In the 1970s when Eddy first played me *Dark Side of the Moon*, I thought the world was friendly and that music like this was threatening and dangerous. Now, when I listen to the original, I still think of his pain that ultimately drove him to suicide. But I also think about how the members of Pink Floyd must have struggled to watch Syd Barrett dive head-first into madness. Sometimes both of their ghosts get into my eyes. *Dub Side of the Moon* takes all of this pain and madness and weaves it into Rasta reasoning, which—though it may sound simplistic, with its back-to-nature flight from materialism, poli-tricksters, and corporate greed—makes the music sound more optimistic than it ever has before.

3
Dark and Infinite

SUE MROZ

1981 (age 19)

I wrote this amazing poem the other day. I was in a really weird
mood. There was a full moon, and I put on Pink Floyd's
"Welcome to the Machine." I wrote this. I think I've discovered
my soul.

Welcome, my friend
I'll let you in
What do you see?
Can you see
The me that is me?
I breathe
I see
I live
I touch
I feel
I love
I'm melting, sinking
Reality dies
The darkness is me
Move with the music
The beats
Pulsate
My soul.

1982 (age 20)

Last night I saw *Pink Floyd: The Wall*. All I can say is WOW. After it, I couldn't speak for hours. Literally. I felt like I was inside the mind of a schizophrenic the whole time. It was so cool to see a film made out of music, I felt like it was made for us. There was one part where flowers turned sexual, then turned violent on each other. It really captured how frightening that really is. Oh, and the school! I get it! We don't need no education! It turns us into ZOMBIES!!!

1988 (age 26)

I love Alan Parker. I got to meet him yesterday. I love a lot of his films, but *The Wall* has really stuck with me. Only twice in my life was I left speechless by a film. *Pink Floyd: The Wall* and *Apocalypse Now*. I was nervous to tell him that, but I did. He said that was good company. I'm glad.

2007 (age 45)

Joe asked me to look at *The Wall* for an essay he's writing for a book about Pink Floyd and philosophy. I haven't seen the film since it first came out and I was in college. I remember it really affecting me then, but would it have the same impact now? Not only am I twenty-five years older, but I am now a filmmaker and film teacher. How would this perspective affect my viewing of the film?

Goodbye Blue Sky

My colleague Chap Freeman likes to say that everyone has a "dark and infinite" phase, where they write bad poetry using words like "dark" and "infinite." Pink Floyd was my ticket in to this stage of what he calls Teenage Romanticism. My older brother Mike played in a band in high school, and he turned me on to Yes, Emerson, Lake and Palmer, and, of course, Floyd. These bands had an air of danger about them that my Catholic school upbringing made me fear. But only at first. My brother's tutelage made it safe to sample Floyd, and the result is the poem above. I wonder how many mountains of bad poetry Pink Floyd alone is responsible for.

In the 1970s, I listened to music the way all of my friends did. We had a huge console stereo in our dining room, so we'd lie on the floor, turn out the lights, put our ears right next to the speaker, and close our eyes. Enter lucid dreaming, the phenomenon named by Swiss psychologist Carl Jung—a dream state where the dreamer is not only aware of dreaming, but has some control over what happens in the dream.[1] It's similar to guided meditation and feels like a conversation between one's conscious and unconscious mind. You can make decisions about what happens in your dream, knowing that with each choice made, the unconscious will respond in kind. Lying in front of that console stereo, every track seemed to create its own dream, and every night it could be different. I felt guided, but free.

As I tell my students, art is not an "object" or a "thing", but rather an emotional experience that is akin to a conversation. The same person can encounter the same artwork several times and have several different experiences, because each of us is constantly changing. Viewing a film, in that sense, is similar to lucid dreaming. As I will explore later in more detail, the viewer actively helps create the flow and structure of the images that are flashing on the screen. So, I expected that *The Wall* would be a very different experience as I watched it this time, being in a different time and place in my life. But it wasn't. Nothing had changed at all. It had me in the same death grip that it had me in all those years ago. Only this time I resisted.

But then a funny thing happened as I watched it a few times. Its layers began to reveal themselves and open up to me as we became re-acquainted with each other. *The Wall* is actually quite experimental and ambitious about what it expects from its audience. It doesn't intimidate me anymore. But it does feel like a dare.

Nobody Home

In *The Alphabet Versus the Goddess*, Leonard Shlain writes about the complementary functions of the two hemispheres of the

---

[1] David Fontana, *The Secret Language of Dreams: A Visual Key to Dreams and Their* Meanings (San Francisco: Chronicle Books, 1994), pp. 18–19.

brain and how they perceive the linearity of the written word versus the holistic nature of images. He writes:

> Images are primarily mental reproductions of the sensual world of vision. Nature and human artifacts both provide the raw material from the outside that the brain replicates in the inner sanctum of consciousness. . . . The brain simultaneously perceives all parts of the *whole* integrating the parts *synthetically* into a gestalt. The majority of images are perceived in an *all-at-once* manner. Reading words is a different process. When the eye scans distinctive individual letters arranged in a certain *linear sequence*, a word with meaning emerges.[2]

Later, Shlain goes on to describe each of these functions as being housed in a different hemisphere of the brain. "The right hemisphere integrates feelings, recognizes images, and appreciates music. . . .", he writes, while the left brain performs the complementary function of understanding speech, using logic and linearity as its processing tools (pp. 18–21).

Cinema can be described as an art form that is made up of other art forms, such as theater, photography, and music. It can also be described as an art form that unfolds in a sequence of *images* over *linear time*, so it engages both sides of the brain in a manner that resembles an inner conversation.

Reading the lyrics of the album *The Wall*, it becomes clear that the album is structured like a circle that closes back in on itself. The opening and closing lines are even written with ellipses: ". . . we came in?" at the beginning ("In the Flesh?"), followed by "Isn't this where . . ." at the end ("Outside the Wall"). This structure is reminiscent of the uroboros, the image of the serpent swallowing its own tail that is said to signify the eternal return, or eternity.[3] Watching the film *The Wall*, the experience feels anything but linear.

In attempting to translate the experience of the mosaic-like structure of the film into the linearity of sentences, it seems to me that the film centers around Pink, who sits in either a hotel room or insane asylum and thinks about his life, while the rest

---

[2] Leonard Shlain, *The Alphabet Versus the Goddess: The Conflict Between Word and Image* (New York: Penguin, 1998), p. 4.

[3] Hans Biedermann, *Dictionary of Symbolism: Cultural Icons and the Meanings behind Them* (New York: Penguin, 1989), p. 362.

of the film represents his memories clashing and colliding into one another. In a way, the film sits in an eternal moment of real time, while patterns of juxtaposition and association play out inside his mind. Here, the film resembles memory in that mother and wife become one and the same, for example. Psychologically, we do become, in a way, frozen in time at moments of trauma, and so the film feels like a representation of what that feels like. While this seems completely appropriate to filmed music and the inward, circular structure of the album, the effect of the film is startling.

Bricks in the Wall

When I was first learning to write for film, I learned all about Aristotle's Plot Curve and was expected to follow the same model for my films as well. Briefly, the Plot Curve charts the experience of the hero as she or he deals with the conflict supplied by the antagonist while in pursuit of a goal. Linda Cowgill describes it very neatly when she writes, "first, the setting and the hero are established. Next follows a development or the conflict which gives the hero his purpose and goal. Consequences and repercussions result, leading to a solution which answers the question the story has posed at the beginning."[4] The curve is represented on a graph as a line that rises

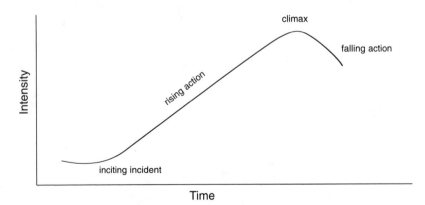

The Traditional Plot Curve of Western Drama (Aristotle)

---

[4] Linda J. Cowgill, *Secrets of Screenplay Structure* (Hollywood: Lone Eagle, 1999), pp. 3–4.

as it moves forward in linear time. The rise of the curve represents the "heightening of the conflict" as the film progresses. The "inciting incident" is the moment that propels the story forward, as it introduces the dramatic question that the film will answer. The conflict "rises" as the antagonist and hero encounter each other, leading to a climax, the life or death moment that everything has led up to. This usually happens near the end of the film and is followed by the falling action, which ties up all the loose ends in a meaningful way (Cowgill, pp. 2–3).

Another kind of plot structure is described by mythologist Joseph Campbell as the Hero's Journey, which is circular. While Campbell laid out more detailed steps in *The Hero with a Thousand Faces*, in his PBS interview with Bill Moyers he described it as simply "a cycle—it's a going, and a return. . . . leaving one condition, and finding the source of life to bring you forth in a richer condition. . . . departure, fulfillment, return."[5]

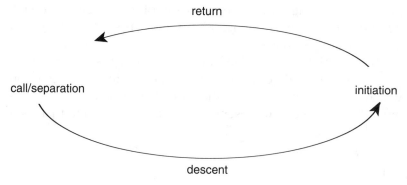

The Hero's Journey Cycle (Campbell)

My former colleague, mythologist Keith Cunningham, notes that Campbell's Hero's Journey outlines an initiation process into a new self for the hero. The "call to adventure" results in a separation from the tribe, the life that the hero had been living but which no longer fulfills his needs. During the descent phase, the old self "dies" as new skills and ways of being are tested and learned, leading to an initiation into a new way of being. Finally, the hero returns with this new self as a gift to

---

[5] *Joseph Campbell and the Power of Myth*, interview with Bill Moyers, originally broadcast on PBS (Apostrophe S Productions, 1988).

the tribe of origin.[6] And it was Cunningham who first opened my eyes to how these two structures can be placed on top of each other:

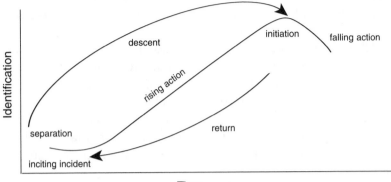

The Hero's Journey Cycle superimposed over the Traditional Plot Curve (Cunningham). Note the reversal of the cycle to better reflect the process of audience participation (projection) and the change on the vertical axis from intensity to identification.

In this way, the inciting incident of the Plot Curve corresponds with Campbell's call to adventure, but the climactic moment of Aristotle matches up with the revelation at the middle of the Hero's Journey. Though the climax of a film happens near its end, this combined diagram equates the (Aristotelian) climax with the (Hero's Journey) midpoint. What happens to the Return of the Hero when viewed this way?

Cunningham suggests that the experience described in each does not just happen onscreen, but, more importantly, in the mind and heart of the audience. These plot structures also represent how the audience participates in the drama unfolding onscreen. The rising line does not represent only a heightening of the conflict, but also a rising sense of the viewer's identification with the onscreen hero. We are pulled into a conversation with the film, and in this way, the climax represents the moment of highest identification. The Hero's Journey works much the same way, as we are "called" out of our seats and invited to participate in the onscreen journey, and eventually

6 Keith Cunningham, "Myths, Dreams, and Movies: Exploring the Archetypal Roots of Cinema," *The Quest* 5:2 (Spring 1992), pp. 30–40.

receive a revelation about our own lives as exemplified by the hero's exploits. Campbell's "return" seems to get short shrift in the narrative model, but Cunningham argues that it does not. Instead, the return happens in the moments, minutes or even days after the film is over, as we gradually return to ourselves, changed by this experience.

All of this assumes that the audience understands and increasingly empathizes with the character's motivations and dramatic problems, thereby becoming more and more invested in what will happen to the character. Traditional narrative feature films use images to build a logical and readily identifiable reality and sequence of story events taking place within that reality. But what happens if that doesn't occur, as in *The Wall?*

Roger Waters himself expressed disappointment in the final product, stating in an interview that ". . . at the end of the day I felt no sympathy at all with the lead character . . . and I found it was so unremitting in its onslaught on the senses, that . . . it didn't actually give me . . . as an audience, a chance to get involved with it."[7] I have to agree. If a narrative is driven by a character in search of a goal, I don't root for Pink because I don't feel him striving for anything, and he remains essentially a victim. I don't identify with him because he shuts us out. Oddly, in the sequences where Young Pink tries to find an adult to hold his hand on the playground, or is looking for his father at the train station, the camera is kept so far away that it, too, keeps me at arm's length. As for forward momentum, there seems to be none. It all feels so internal to Pink, as if nothing really happens in this story.

My sense of this film, therefore, has to go back to my devotion to Pink Floyd at age nineteen, to being internal in my own ways—so inward that all this bad poetry came out of me. Watching it now, I am still that bad poet, just as the rock star is still the crying baby boy emotionally abandoned by his mother. Maybe that's part of the point the *The Wall* makes best: in a sense, time does stand still for us at the point of emotional traumas.

---

[7] The quotation comes from an interview with Waters quoted on Wikipedia (Wikipedia.org) in the entry on "Pink Floyd The Wall" on July 9th, 2007.

We Don't Need No Interpretation

But more than ten years have got behind me, at least, and the movie no longer takes my voice away. This problem is one that stalks any effort to join music and film—the fact that looking at images created to accompany and enhance music can often limit the meanings those images can have. I'm too overwhelmed by many of the pictures in *The Wall* to really bring it back to my own life with any compelling meaning. In one of my screen-writing classes, I ask students to adapt a song into a screenplay. When I distribute the lyrics I also offer to show them the music video for inspiration, but most of them refuse. They fear it will limit them, and they're right.

Jung describes symbols as "terms, names, or even pictures that may be familiar in daily life, yet that possess specific connotations in addition to their conventional and obvious meanings. They imply something vague, hidden, and unknown to us."[8] My problem with a lot of the imagery in *The Wall* is that it feels like it's all right there. I don't have to put it together that The Judge who condemns Pink is an asshole, for example, because he's depicted in the animation as, precisely, a talking asshole. And the flowers that turn into sex, then into violence, and back again to sex are maybe, just maybe, saying that sex is a kind of violence. No interpretation of these symbols is required. There's nothing for me to do but sit there and take the interpretation offered. So it's hard for me to invest much in these symbols, to make them my own.

Feelings of an Almost Human Nature

There's one sequence in *The Wall* that affects me quite a bit, however, and it does so more and more each time I see it. Throughout the film, a simple, haunting image recurs and keeps getting cut off just as it seems to begin. It's a wide shot of a soccer field—the sky is amber, the goal sits on the horizon deep in the frame, and Young Pink runs from a far distance toward the camera. Finally, as "Comfortably Numb" begins to swell up, the image and sequence are allowed to play out into consciousness.

---

[8] David Fontana, *The Secret Language of Symbols: A Visual Key to Symbols and Their Meanings* (San Francisco: Chronicle Books, 1993), p. 8.

First, young Pink finds a sick rat in the field, and brings it home. He shows his mother, who rejects it, and then takes it to a shed and covers it with his sweater. But Pink himself soon gets sick, so he's not allowed to leave his bed or continue nursing the sick rat. When he's finally well enough to run back out to the shack, he finds that the rat has died. Here, finally, Pink becomes truly active and identifiable. It makes you care about whether anything he loves gets to live in this world.

I found myself caring again at the final turning point of the film, the final brick in the wall:

> Since, my friend
> You have revealed your deepest fear
> I sentence you to be exposed
> Before your peers.
> Tear down the wall.

These are the final words sung by "the judge" in the final animation sequence, "The Trial". With this, the giant wall comes tumbling down and all of those moments of victimization we so identify with at age nineteen and create who we think we are— each brick in the wall—are no longer there to isolate Pink. If *The Wall* is about the development and ultimate realization of your true self, the point at which you can finally tear down that wall and reveal who you really are, then that's why the final moments of the film feel so different from what came before. Amidst the ruins of the wall, children quietly fend for themselves, picking up the pieces left behind. The last child dumps out the contents of a Molotov cocktail, and with that, the frame freezes. They seem alone and vulnerable, but are they better off?

The final effect of *The Wall* feels lopsided to me. Rather than a conversation taking place between the two sides of my brain, or between me and the screen, it feels as if we remain separated, as if the film taking place in his head will forever be separate from the experience I am having in mine.

Which is where I came in—when I was nineteen and Pink Floyd's music drove me inward to discover parts of myself I didn't know were there. Inside the wall is something dark, infinite, and alone.[9]

---

[9] My thanks to Mary Dougherty for finding, with me, the door in the wall.

4

Pigs Training Dogs to Exploit Sheep: *Animals* as a Beast Fable Dystopia

PATRICK CROSKERY

Ever since I was introduced to it by my best friend in college, *Animals* has been one of my favorite albums. I first heard it in the fall of 1979. It had already been out for two years, and *The Wall* came out soon afterwards (my friend brought that album back from Christmas Break). I certainly appreciated the complexity of that far better-known work. For good reason, *The Wall* made Pink Floyd into superstars. But over the years I have found myself coming back to *Animals* and listening to it from beginning to end more often than any other album.

Animals is distinctive for combining the strongly evocative sonic elements of the early Pink Floyd—the sheer attention to sound—with the increasing lyrical directness of Roger Waters. While *Dark Side of the Moon* has powerful sounds and suggestive themes and *The Wall* tells an explicit story of artistic alienation, *Animals,* situated between the two, blends the two dimensions in a uniquely powerful way. I suspect that part of my appreciation for this album results from the more abstract nature of its political themes, which I attribute in part to the influence of George Orwell's *Animal Farm,* an allegorical account of the Russian Revolution.

Like many students before me (and after), I had first read *Animal Farm* in high school. In Orwell's story a group of farm animals, led by the pigs, overthrow the human owner of the farm, setting up a communist utopia. However, the pigs gradually abuse their power, and the animals' ideal society gradually collapses back into the original exploitative arrangement (with the pigs playing the role of the humans). As far as I have been able to determine, any direct influence of *Animal Farm* on *Animals* is very limited. Pink Floyd was already playing versions of "Dogs" and "Sheep," with somewhat different lyrics, and apparently Waters made a few adjustments to the lyrics and added the songs "Pigs" and "Pigs on the Wing (Parts 1 and 2)."

However, using Orwell's work as a loose model focused the band's attention in a particular way that makes *Animals* especially suitable for thinking about political philosophy. Orwell's work is a "beast fable"—a genre that includes works of Aesop and Chaucer's *Nun's Priest's Tale*. It uses anthropomorphized animals to bring certain features of human beings into sharp relief. *Animals,* of course, makes use of animal characters. It also has the form of a fable, one that starts with a thought experiment: "If you didn't care what happened to me / And I didn't care for you," what would life be like in this world?

The result is a sonic portrait of a world without empathy. Waters has suggested that empathy is the central theme of all the band's classic, mature works beginning with *Meddle.* Waters singles out the following lines from "Echoes":

Strangers passing in the street
By chance two separate glances meet
And I am you and what I see is me.

What's distinctive about *Animals* is that it builds on this idea by introducing various animal characters and using music to draw us into the particular frames of mind belonging to each. Once we're looking at the world through these animals' eyes, we can see just how much *Animals,* like *Animal Farm,* is a dystopia—the very opposite of a utopian, ideal world. In a dystopia, hope is futile. There is no empathy and sympathy, so we simply "zig zag our way through the boredom and pain."

We can therefore use *Animals* to explore what can go wrong with the basic institutions of society. In particular, we can illustrate the delicate balance that must be maintained among the three major institutions of society—the marketplace, the government, and the community. Each song in *Animals* can be connected to one of these institutions to explore the various ways they corrupt those who participate in them and the ways they can corrupt (or be corrupted by) the other institutions. As we move through *Animals*, drawing out general points in political philosophy, we can note a few critical points about *Animal Farm* as well.

The Dog-Eat-Dog Marketplace

Having set up the fable, or thought experiment, of a world where people do not care for one another, Waters explores the psychological and emotional experience of a hyper-capitalist market in the song "Dogs." The central experience is captured well by the opening lines: "you've got to be crazy, gotta have a real need." The sheer striving required to succeed in a hyper-capitalistic market seems irrational. Business books endlessly proclaim the need to be passionate about products, yet, in the end, the products involved seem rather mundane and unworthy of such passion. A classic example can be seen in the story of Steve Jobs recruiting John Scully away from Pepsi by asking "Do you want to sell sugar water for the rest of your life, or do you want to change the world?"

The standard justification for the role of self-interest in the market is to step back and appreciate the overall prosperity that it makes possible. This is the idea in Adam Smith's famous metaphor of the market as an invisible hand. Each participant, in pursuing his or her own self-interest and competing in the marketplace, indirectly contributes to overall well-being. Thus, one who is passionate about soda makes the soda a bit more cheaply or a bit more flavorful, and each person who drinks the soda saves a bit of money or finds the soda more enjoyable. Multiplied over millions of people, those small improvements add up to a substantial benefit.

However, if the competition is intense enough and regulation is inadequate, the market can create perverse incentives. This vision animates "Dogs" as a frenzied exploration of the unlimited pursuit of "success" at any cost. In a remarkably compressed line, Waters captures the spirit of a malfunctioning market: "You have to be trusted by the people that you lie to, / So that when they turn their backs on you, / You'll get the chance to put the knife in." In short, you lie to people, and need them to be deceived by you, knowing that in the end they will turn their backs and abandon you, at which point you will be in a position to betray them and stab them in the back. At this

point, the marketplace does not make much of a contribution to
the greater public good. Instead, it becomes a self-destructive
game requiring us to gain by deceiving and manipulating others. Greater effort is put into undermining the success of one's
competitors than producing valuable goods and services for the
consuming public.

In the end, a life like this is empty. If one believes that "no
one has a real friend" and that "everyone's a killer", one is left
to die alone, a "sad old man." The soundtrack of that death
would be Gilmour's guitar work and the haunting howls of distant dogs that convey the hopeless desolation of the hyper-mar-
ket. How do we end up in this awful position? The song
explains that the destruction of concern for others and the
development of ferocious competitive self-interest is a long and
steady process—one is "broken by trained personnel" and "told
what to do by the man."

Orwell's target in *Animal Farm* is totalitarianism, the domination of all aspects of society by an all-powerful state, but he
is also critical of the marketplace. Early in the story, he has the
boar named Old Major provide a powerful Marxist critique of
the exploitation involved in a capitalistic society. The reader
knows that the animals' efforts to form an ideal society has
failed when the pigs, having obtained the same power as capitalists, rejoin the global market economy. Now they even resem-
ble the humans they had overthrown, to the point of standing
on two legs and sleeping in beds.

Pigs in the Whitehouse

The market is not the only institution that can corrupt if it
extends its powers beyond its appropriate boundaries. In "Pigs
(3 Different Ones)" Waters sketches three characters who can be
used to illustrate the dangers of corruption in the state. The first
pig is dominated by greed, with his "head down in the pig bin."
He resembles the greedy record executive lapping up gravy in
Wish You Were Here, but he can just as easily represent special
interests feeding at the public trough. This connects to the classic problem within political science of special interests "captur-
ing" the agency that is supposed to regulate that particular
industry. The common practice of "revolving doors" (working
for the industry then the government and returning once again

to the industry) provides ample opportunities for corruption. The profits made by Halliburton, for example, when its former CEO Dick Cheney become Vice-President of the United States drew attention for this reason.

The state (as Dick Cheney could tell you) has the unique ability to wage war. This, too, is a tempting power to abuse. That is perhaps why the second pig (rumored to represent Margaret Thatcher, though the song was written before she was Prime Minister) likes "the feel of steel." This war-waging power is an appealing alternative to the difficult political work required of Presidents and Prime Minsters. In both the United States and Great Britain leaders have been accused of "wag the dog" wars—wars of choice that distract the public from difficult and controversial domestic issues and centralize power in the hands of the executive (though the exercise of this power requires the compliance of other branches of government).

Government can also corrupt by overextending its regulatory powers into cultural and personal issues. The third pig reflects this danger. Like many Americans, I assumed that "Hey you Whitehouse, charade you are" referred to the residence of the President of the United States (so I was always a bit puzzled by the next line, "House proud town mouse, charade you are"). English fans had no such difficulty; they well knew that Waters was attacking the notorious culture censor Mary Whitehouse, who led a crusade against obscenity. Pink Floyd was a particular target of her campaign (Monty Python also faced her wrath). Mary Whitehouse is just one individual in a long list of those who use the power of the state in an effort to impose particular values on the larger society.

Orwell, meanwhile, points out that the state cannot even be controlled by its own constitution. The rewriting of the animal's founding document on the side of the barn (finally leaving only "Some animals are more equal to others") reflects the uselessness of a constitution as a check on power in a totalitarian system. In such a system, the state's power is total, and it makes use of mechanisms like secret police to keep the public uncertain and afraid. The secret police are represented in *Animal Farm* by the dogs that Napoleon, the pig who represents Stalin, trains to viciously attack his opponents. Another means of control involves culture, as suggested by the sheep. Which takes us to . . .

Sheepish Exploitation

The market and the state can be corrupted and can corrupt those who participate in them. What about the community? Embedded as we are in our own community, we are easily led astray if the culture itself is in error. The state of delusion created by a misleading cultural ideology is a *false consciousness.* This is powerfully evoked in the early lines and music of "Sheep." The introduction to the song is reminiscent of the pastoral sound frequently found in earlier Pink Floyd works (I have always been particularly fond of the babbling brook in *Ummagumma*). A pastoral involves using the presumed idyllic life in the country to evoke a purer past (typically by disillusioned city dwellers). In "Sheep," we have the pastoral effect, with the contented bleating of the sheep and the gentle guitar. However, we soon learn that this contentment is false. In fact, we are "wasting away our time in the grassland" and the peaceful, pastoral existence is merely an illusion.

The reality that lies behind our false consciousness becomes clear in the "terminal shock" we feel as we turn a corner in the slaughterhouse and encounter the blades of steel. Our culture presents us with self-images as consumers, in control of the workings of the market, but our status as raw materials is hidden from view. False consciousness serves as a cover for exploitation. The Wal-Mart shopper who is happy to receive "everyday low prices" might also be a Wal-Mart worker, prevented from unionizing and tightly controlled for the purposes of management and stockholders.

Culture can do more than just hide the exploitation—it can even make us accept that exploitation as justified. This is the point of Waters's shocking parody of the Twenty-Third Psalm, in which the Shepherd "leadeth me the silent waters by" and then "converteth me to lamb cutlets." The American mythos that anyone can succeed can work in a similar fashion, leading those who are poor or powerless to believe that their situation is their own fault, due to limitations in talent or drive, and not due to any systematic exploitation.

Can community itself overcome exploitation? Can the animals rise up and overturn the existing order? The revolt at the end of "Sheep" is as frantic as it is short-lived. Culture is a source of energy and passion, but it does not possess enough ordering force in the short term to overcome the power of the market or the state. In the end, "you'd better stay home, do as you're told." We can get excited and upset about particular issues, but the storm passes and the powers that be retain their position.

Orwell, for his part, is interested in the ways that culture must be corrupted to maintain a totalitarian form of power. The pig named Squealer is said to represent *Pravda*, the Soviet newspaper that spun the party line and thereby controlled what the public thought. The Communist Chinese government's restrictions on Google to maintain control over the internet is a recent example of this kind of abuse. Religion, too, can be controlled, as suggested by Moses, the tamed Raven, who is said to represent the Russian Orthodox Church. After initially being chased out, Moses is allowed back on Animal Farm in a limited role. A tamed religion can serve the interests of a totalitarian government by counseling submission to the government as the representative of God's will.

Caring Dogs Watching Flying Pigs

If all three institutions can corrupt and be corrupted, how do we avoid the dystopias? Waters, at the end of the album, returns to empathy: "You know that I care what happens to you, / And I know that you care for me." But that, apparently, does not mean that empathy will create some kind of utopia. Waters himself is still a dog—as "any fool knows a dog needs a home." Nor does it mean that pigs are not a real threat. A home, after all, is "a shelter from pigs on the wing." Waters seems to recognize that some kind of balance must be struck among the three institutions of market, state, and community.

We must have empathy, and a community of mutual care. But we cannot escape the need for the tremendous productive power of the market—we must accept some role as "dogs" engaged in challenging competition. At the same time, those market forces must be regulated by the government and undergirded by a safety net motivated by mutual concern. Granting that role to government introduces a different set of threats, so we need to keep an eye out for the creeping abuses by governmental authorities (pigs on the wing) with checks and balances and a healthy suspicion of the use of political power.

Precisely how this balance is to be struck is a central topic of political philosophy. A typical error is to observe the flaws of two institutions and focus only on the strengths of the third, so that only one institution appears to be important or valuable. One error is committed by the overly zealous libertarian, who has excessive confidence in the market and fails to recognize the benefits of an effective government and the wisdom of cultural traditions. A quite different error is made by the radically statist liberal who has an inordinate belief in the power of government to do good and is unable to appreciate the productive power of the market and the insights of diverse communities. A third error is made by the fanatical traditional-values thinker, who sees only the good in tradition and resists the changes that a robust market demands and the toleration that government must support in a pluralistic society.

Our task, as thoughtful citizens, is to strike the correct balance. We can reasonably disagree, and should always be open to learning from those who have come to different conclusions. We can also learn from experience—which can temper excessive idealism or provide grounds for hope to the cynic. But we should also resist the temptations of simple answers, since the complexity of the real world and its sharp, spinning blades can quickly make cutlets of those who refuse to admit that this complexity is real.

5

Exploring the Dark Side of the Rainbow

ANDREW ZIMMERMAN JONES

No one is sure who discovered it or when. Wikipedia says the phenomenon was first discussed in 1994 on an online Usenet message board, alt.music.pink-floyd. I'm speaking of the synchronization of Pink Floyd's 1973 *The Dark Side of the Moon* album and the 1939 feature film, *The Wizard of Oz*. Together known as *The Dark Side of the Rainbow*, the two classics come together under the right circumstances to create a whole new experience—something like that other famous pop culture collision: "You got your chocolate in my peanut butter."

If you are uninitiated, place the *The Dark Side of the Moon* CD on pause immediately after pressing play. Then play the classic version of *The Wizard of Oz* and, on the third roar of the MGM lion, unpause the CD. Reports vary about which roar is actually the best, since the start speed of CD players can be different. For me, the third roar works fine.

Major Synchronizations

There are some subtle synchronizations early on. But for me, the first real indication that these two classics match up is the fact that the clock chimes from "Time" begin at exactly the moment when Almira Gulch appears on her bicycle. This is especially intriguing when you consider that the Wicked Witch, later in the film, will use an hourglass as the focus for her most climactic magical effect—the spell to kill Dorothy. Soon, Dorothy runs away from home to the lyrics, "No one told you when to run . . ." and the dramatic guitar solo begins just as we see the reveal of Professor Marvel's wagon bearing those time-like words, "Past, Present, and Future."

"The Great Gig in the Sky" synchs up well with the entire tornado sequence in the film. Clare Torry wails beautifully during the frantic race around the farm and ends precisely when Dorothy is struck in the head with the window.

As soon as Dorothy sets foot in colorful Munchkinland, we hear the first "cha-ching!" of "Money." She explores the village, not noticing the Munchkins peeking out from the bushes. In time with the lyric "Get back," they duck back into their hiding places to avoid being noticed. Glinda's bubble appears along with "Don't give me that do-goody-good bullshit." And when the Munchkins finally appear, Dorothy is handed flowers just as Pink Floyd tells us to "Share it, fairly."

The beginning of "Us and Them" sounds something like a funeral dirge and it coincides with the Munchkin coroner's pronouncment that the Wicked Witch of the East is dead—"really most sincerely dead." The words "black and blue" echo throughout the scene where the Witch first appears, the camera switching between the Witch (in black) and Dorothy (in blue). We hear the words "And who knows which is which?" as the Witch of the West explores her sister's body and Glinda explains which Witch is which. Glinda appears to whisper to Dorothy "Haven't you heard? It's a battle of words . . ." before resuming her heated conversation with the Witch.

The transition to "Any Colour You Like" precisely matches the scene transition from Munchkinland to the Scarecrow's intersection. The heartbeat that ends the CD matches Dorothy and the Scarecrow listening to the Tin Woodsman's chest. At this point, if the CD player is on repeat, the synchronization continues. The heartbeat that now begins the album once again coincides with the Woodman's rendition of "If I Only Had a Heart."

In the second cycle, the most dramatic synchronization is the song "Money" playing throughout the scene of the Emerald City. This time, the "Cha-ching!" coincides with the message "Surrender, Dorothy" written in the sky. And if you continue through the third cycle of the album, Dorothy's trip to Oz comes to an end with the lyric, "The time is gone, the song is over . . ." Indeed, she's "home, home again" when she awakens in Kansas. As she repeats, "there's no place like home," *The Dark Side of the Moon* refers to "the softly spoken magic spell."

Finally, the closing credits set against the Kansas sky roll out to "The Great Gig in the Sky."

There are other, less specific synchronizations throughout *The Dark Side of the Rainbow*. The Munchkins, for example, certainly look as if they're dancing to the guitar solo in "Money." Both the Lullaby League and the Lollipop Guild also appear to move in time with the music. And although the Scarecrow may not be "the lunatic [who] is on the grass" he's made of grass, and certainly looks a bit insane dancing around to the song titled (of course) "Brain Damage." Some commentators have listed over a hundred individual synchronizations.[1] But debate rages about whether, and in what ways, *The Dark Side of the Rainbow* really means anything. There are extremely dramatic visual cues in the movie, after all, which have no apparent synchronized connection to *The Dark Side of the Moon* at all.

Design or Chance?

Some people claim that *The Dark Side of the Rainbow* "really doesn't synch" at all.[2] Maybe they've put the wrong CD in the tray. Lots of people have observed the synchronizations I've described (and more), so the question is not whether they exist objectively. The question is what, if anything, they mean and how they are best understood.

The first reaction of most people is to assume that these remarkable synchronizations were deliberately created by Pink Floyd. But for over a decade the band members and the album's technicians have denied that it was intentional (except for Roger Waters, who refuses to comment at all). It's unlikely, however, that Waters would have been the man behind the curtain, effectively manipulating the entire album, his bandmates, and the studio technicians to achieve the desired result at the required level of precision. The prismatic rainbow on the album cover, an indication as obvious as any of the others, was created by Storm Thorgerson and Aubrey Powell, the design team Hipgnosis, and inspired by Rick Wright's (not Waters's) recommendation to keep the cover design graphic, and not photo-

---

[1] http://members.cox.net/stegokitty/dsotr_pages/secret_deflist.htm.
[2] http://www.straightdope.com/mailbag/mdarkside.html.

graphic. It seems likely that neither Waters nor anyone else planned to bring *The Dark Side of the Rainbow* into existence.

But it exists. It is said that if an infinite number of monkeys bang on typewriters long enough, one of them would eventually write the complete works of Shakespeare. Is this the origin of Dark Side of the Rainbow? It seems to be. But if you think about it, perhaps it's not so unlikely after all that a rock album from 1973 should mesh so well (at least in parts) with a 1939 cult classic film.

Synchronizations and Synchronicity

We've all experienced strange coincidences. You think of someone that you haven't spoken to in a while, perhaps even in a dream. Then, you soon run into them or get a phone call. Or, you might be a world famous rock band recording an album about loss, absence, and alienation only to find your old bandleader, out of the picture for years, suddenly turn up unannounced (and unrecognizable) in the recording studio. It's hard in these circumstances not to think that there is some connection between the two.

Swiss psychologist Carl Jung introduced a name for this concept in his article "Synchronicity: An Acausal Connecting Principle" (1952). Synchronicity is, in short, a pseudoscientific attempt to define "meaningful coincidences" apart from those that are meaningless, run-of-the-mill happenstance. But they don't get their meaning from causal connections—as would be the case if the long-lost friend called you *because* you dreamed about him the night before. According to Jung, the meaning exists in virtue of acausal principles (like the "collective unconscious") that link events and meaningfully relate them by symbolic meanings and their proximity in time.

During the research for this article I ran into two other intriguing examples of how synchronicity can seem to sneak up out of nowhere—in relations between the very concept of synchronicity and *The Wizard of Oz* itself. One of Jung's favorite quotes about synchronicity was from Lewis Carroll's *Through the Looking Glass*, where the White Queen says to Alice, "It's a poor sort of memory that only works backwards." *Through the Looking Glass* and *The Wizard of Oz* have much in common, for each has a girl transported to a magical realm where she encounters many strange things. In fact, in my DVD collection, *Alice in Wonderland* and *The Wizard of Oz* sit right next to each other. Another is the coat, purchased second-hand for Professor Marvel's costume, which was later discovered to have been previously owned by L. Frank Baum, the author of the *Oz* novels.[3] Most modern psychologists discount synchronicity, noting that Jung had a wide variety of paranormal and quasi-mystical beliefs that are not scientifically testable. It's generally acknowledged in modern science that, however meaningful we may believe a coincidence to be, if there is no causal link between the apparently related items then any meaning or significance they seem to have is created by ourselves. The events in question are *merely* a coincidence.

Apophenia and Paradigms

Even without Jung's synchronicity, however, there is a psychological concept useful for explaining the *Dark Side of the Rainbow*. In 1958, psychologist Klaus Conrad coined the term "apophenia" to describe the spontaneous perception of connections and meaningfulness of unrelated phenomena. Originally, the term was intended for those who found abnormal meaning in things, but it has since come into use for the general human tendency to find meaning in unrelated events.

Though in its most extreme form the phenomenon is central to schizophrenia and paranoia, finding connections is crucial to discovery and creativity of all kinds. Neurologist Peter Brugger goes so far as to suggest that apophenia links so closely to creativity that "apophenia and creativity may even be seen as two sides of the same coin." Thomas Kuhn's famous theory of science, holding that scientists learn to see the world according to the reigning "paradigm" of their day, also makes the ability to see patterns and similarities (even *suspected* patterns and similarities that others don't see) the lifeblood of scientific progress.[4] It would miss the point, therefore, to chalk up *The Dark Side of the Rainbow* to our silly, overactive imaginations—as if these things had no importance or role to play in the life of culture.

---

[3] See the Wikepedia article on synchronicity.

[4] See http://skepdic.com/apophenia.html; Kuhn, *The Structure of Scientific Revolutions* (Chicago University Press, 1962).

Thematic Synchronicity

That is perhaps where we should finally look for a satisfying explanation. Instead of seeking some causal connection (the Waters conspiracy model) or some kind of meaningful-but-acausal psychological connection (Jung's synchronicity model), we can attribute *The Dark Side of the Rainbow* to the very thematic elements of the two works and the *cultural* significance they have for most of us.

At its core, *The Wizard of Oz* is about trying to get out of a mundane existence and go somewhere more interesting, as signified by the song "Over the Rainbow" from the film, only to discover that home is the most important thing. *Dark Side of the Moon* says something similar—not that home is the most important thing, but that it's the only thing: "all you touch and all you see," after all, "is all your life will ever be." From here, however, *The Dark Side of the Moon* goes to a place that Hollywood would consider commercially suicidal: it asks whether or not we can accept that circumstance or whether we may be driven to madness by it. Despite their many differences, both works wrestle with conflicting desires for security and transcendence of the ordinary and familiar.

If we all wrestle with these desires, then perhaps that is why these coincidences and parallels between *The Dark Side of the Moon* and *The Wizard of Oz* seem so clear, objective, and real to those who are so struck by them. In the context of these larger themes, it is easier to see that the perceived synchronization is subjective and personal, but not less real because of it. The fact that the synchronization seems to work *even though we know* it wasn't planned or designed is perhaps the best proof we will get that it rests on something real in all of us. Oz is meaningful, even though it is a figment of Dorothy's imagination. And the wizard himself knows that reality is in many ways less important than perception. The same may be true of *The Dark Side of the Rainbow.*

6
Mashups and Mixups: Pink Floyd as Cinema

JOSEF STEIFF

The first cracks appeared in my world when I was fifteen. I was living on a farm in the foothills of the Appalachian Mountains, and I had recently graduated from AM radio to 8-track tapes. Still, my musical taste was firmly rooted in Top 40. Much to my mother's relief I had yet to discover "druggy music." At our house we listened to Henry Mancini and country bluegrass. My world was small. But it was expanding. My cousin had just moved from Missouri, bringing with him music unlike anything I had heard before. When he took me to the roadside Tape Barn, I bought my first Pink Floyd album, *The Dark Side of the Moon*. It was on 8-track tape and—in hindsight—I'm sure it was pirated.

After I went to college and traded up to the vinyl LP version, I had a nightly ritual: turning off all the lights in my dorm room and lying on the floor with my head precisely spaced between the stereo speakers. The needle would make its soft landing with the crackling and occasional pop of vinyl and diamond. From the dark, another heartbeat would merge with my own before fading into the sounds of man-made machines—ticking clocks, cash registers, engines—that were gradually overtaken by human voices, laughter and screams. In those brief moments I experienced the entire album in a flash. The lush slide into "Breathe" was like dropping out of warp speed, and for the next forty-three minutes I would simultaneously exist in both the human and the inhuman, an intimate interior world and a cold outer space.

Defining Cinematic Music

No big surprise, then, that Pink Floyd's music came to be considered cinematic. Heard from the floor of my darkened dorm room, *Dark Side of the Moon* evoked a progression of images and emotions that I couldn't always identify but which seemed full and dreamlike in the way that the best movies are.

Describing music as *cinematic* became common in the 1990s. The usage was introduced by music journalists and artists, and it is often applied retroactively to Pink Floyd. Pinpointing exactly what we mean when we say music is cinematic, though, is difficult since the term has been employed to describe many different things, including:

- music scores composed for specific films,
- generic music ready for incorporation into any film,
- recordings of predominantly instrumental music,
- ambient music,
- popular music that uses snippets of dialogue and/or sound effects.

Perhaps the simplest definition is the best: cinematic means possessing the qualities or characteristics of cinema. What, then, do we mean by *cinema*?

Kinesis, the Greek root of *cinema*, means "movement." Filmmakers think of this movement as the result of a series of still photographs recorded and projected at twenty-four frames (or images) per second, creating the illusion that elements within the frame are moving or exist within a specific space and time. Though most audience members don't register individual images or frames, they do experience movies as an overwhelmingly visual medium. Cinema is so closely linked with its photographic aspects that calling a piece of music cinematic implies first and foremost that the music produces images in the listener's mind. But if that's all we mean by cinematic, why not say, "painterly" or "photographic"?

If we accept the idea that cinema is a constructed illusion, ignoring for a moment our assumption that this illusion is accomplished by images, we open the door for other ways to think about *kinesis*.

First, like cinema, we experience music in time. We can't take it all in at once like a photograph or painting. I'm not suggesting that an image can be completely understood or appreciated in a single instant, but in many cases one look will allow us to see a photograph in its entirety. Then it becomes a question of *study*.[1] Music and cinema, however, move through time, and require the observer or audience member to do the same. There's a defined duration, a beginning, middle and end to both the work and the process of experiencing the work.

On this basis, cinema constructs a progression or journey—a *trip*, to borrow from the psychedelic slang that grew up around early Pink Floyd—for the audience to take through a variety of assimilations and juxtapositions of images. The links holding it together can be linear and logical or non-linear and, perhaps, dreamlike. Either way, the cinematic journey provides a sense of discovery, revealing not an entire world, but rather a series of glimpses that imply a larger context. By engaging our imaginations and emotions, we actively assemble this larger and more complex world through which we travel.

Unlike pop songs that typically focus on one emotion or idea for three minutes, cinematic music can feel epic as its emotions shift and change alongside the tones and textures. "Speak to Me" is a complete story, a movement, that lasts only a few moments. It is a mini-narrative that illustrates the cinematic technique of foreshadowing—hinting at what's to come—the experiences that lay ahead on the album. *Dark Side of the Moon* more fully develops those elements introduced in "Speak to Me" and creates a moving landscape mapped out by contrasts and juxtapositions—the soulful warmth of vocalizations, piano, and saxophone playing against the cold mechanics of electronic synthesizers. The many snippets of conversation, the melodic motifs (such as the reprise of "Breathe") and sound effects contribute to a sense of movement through that landscape as well as through time. The music is also cinematic in its dynamic range, the differences between quiet, almost imperceptible elements and the loudest explosions and crescendos.

---

[1] The photographs associated with Pink Floyd—their album covers—invite if not outright demand study because of the way that they imply larger stories than can be contained within a single image. I still remember my initial queasiness at seeing the cover for *Wish You Were Here*. Like their music, their album covers inspire (or haunt?) filmmakers like Alfonso Cuarón whose *Children of Men* (2006) includes a visual reference to *Animals'* floating pig amidst the smokestacks.

Music Videos and Music Films

If for these reasons, Pink Floyd's music can be considered truly cinematic, we can reasonably ask whether it even needs accompanying visual imagery. Is it cinematic enough on its own? Or do its cinematic qualities just lend it to being paired with films or cinematic images?

Options for pairing music with image were fewer when Pink Floyd started than now. I know. It's hard to imagine a time without music videos. I lived through those dark ages, and I have trouble remembering what it was like myself. But at the time, music was music, and one of the few pairings of music with film (besides creatively-starved concert films) was either what was lovingly called *rock opera* (talk about juxtaposition!), promotional films that would "stand in" for a live performance by the band on television, or feature films with soundtracks written by rock bands.

Like several music groups in the mid-1960s and 1970s, Pink Floyd made promotional films to some of their songs, including "Arnold Layne" (with its masks foreshadowing one of the creepier visual elements of Alan Parker's 1982 film *Pink Floyd: The Wall*), "Scarecrow" (which eerily resonates with the popular linking of *Dark Side of the Moon* with *The Wizard of Oz* discussed in the next section) and a psychedelic performance of "Jugband Blues." Though MTV was still almost twenty years in the future, a small corner of popular culture was preparing for it.

In film circles, the marriage of film and music only came about in one of two ways. Either a music score was composed specifically for, and in relationship to, a particular film, or a soundtrack was compiled by appropriating pre-existing (often pop) music that would serve the same function. The object in these approaches was to enhance the images by creating an emotional reflection of the inner world of the characters or the subtext of the scene—a cue or clue for how the audience was supposed to feel as they watched the story unfold visually. Pink Floyd wrote songs in this manner for Barbet Schroeder and Michelangelo Antonioni in the late 1960s and released these soundtracks as stand-alone albums (*More* and *Obscured by Clouds*). *Pink Floyd: The Wall* and *Pink Floyd: Live at Pompeii*, on the other hand, began with Pink Floyd's music and added images and visual stories to go along with it.

Mashups and Sync Ups

With digital technology, it's become easier to pursue yet another path to pairing film and music. Instead of writing one to match the other, they can simply be paired—ready made—to achieve remarkable results. Perhaps in a nod to the Jamaican Creole definition "to destroy," *mashups* combine two or more pre-existing works in various ways to form a new work. Certainly some artists have created and released official mashups that include their own material, but many mashups are the result of third parties who, sometimes without copyright permission, take separate works and put them together, such as Danger Mouse's "Grey Album," a mashup of Jay Z's "The Black Album" with The Beatles' so-called White Album. Mashups can be accomplished by overlaying one song upon another or by building a website out of elements from other websites or by editing a coherent film from the parts of other films. The pleasure of the new work lies in the tension created by the juxtaposition and the unexpected ways in which the pieces work together to create a unified and surprising experience.

This tension is something that all filmmakers work with because juxtaposition is a foundation of cinema. Through editing, two different shots or scenes are put next to each other in a way that creates larger and different meanings than either of the two shots or scenes have on their own. Film students are usually introduced to this by way of the early twentieth-century "Kuleshov Experiment" in which Russian filmmaker Lev Kuleshov juxtaposed images that had been shot at completely different times and places. When they were edited together, the viewer would assume that the images were part of a seamless, connected time and space. They would even assign emotional meaning based on the juxtaposition of the images, which included identical close-ups of a man's face edited with shots of a bowl of soup (hunger), a girl at play (delight) or a woman lying in a coffin (sadness). A similar effect happens when you watch *The Wizard of Oz* with *Dark Side of the Moon* or, for that matter, any film you might pair with random music. You begin to make sense of it, to see connections, some more satisfying than others.

Having done my own *Dark Side of the Rainbow* experiment,[2] I find that the lyrics from *Dark Side of the Moon* do not provide

---

[2] When I sync to the third black and white lion roar as is commonly suggested,

a meaningful resonance with the story on the screen. The lyrics and the film do not form a coherent whole, despite several single word or single line correspondences. In terms of emotional continuity, Pink Floyd's music only sporadically matches or enhances the emotional tone of the movie. When Dorothy sings "Somewhere Over the Rainbow," the movie scene is wistful and melancholic. The corresponding section of *Dark Side of the Moon* ("On the Run") is frenetic and in direct contradiction to the film's goals. The exceptions are "The Great Gig in the Sky," "Time" and "Us and Them" which feel like they could have been created just for this movie. And when I step completely back and ignore the story and emotional tenor of the film, I can find a few moments when there's a certain pleasure in how the music mirrors the purely graphic qualities of the movement within the frame, such as "Brain Damage" and the jerky movements of the Scarecrow.

For me, the *Dark Side of the Rainbow* mashup is interesting to watch once, maybe twice. It's not evocative or expansive enough to bear repeated viewings. Maybe getting high would help, and maybe that's part of the point. In an unaltered state, both the movie and the album seem constricted by the other, limiting the scope of each. From a filmmaker's perspective, *The Wizard of Oz* mashed up with *The Dark Side of the Moon* creates several interesting juxtapositions, but Pink Floyd's music does not really serve as an alternative score. It's a novelty.

A lesser-known mashup is the syncing of "Echoes" (from *Meddle*) with the final twenty minutes of Stanley Kubrick's 1968 film *2001: A Space Odyssey* (beginning with the title card, "Jupiter and Beyond the Infinite").[3] In this case, the mashup is coherent and cohesive. The emotional tone of the music and images work in near-perfect harmony, resulting in a mashup that stands up to repeated viewings. Juxtapositions that at first

---

the music seems to lag just behind the image, so I actually find the mashup more evocative if I shift the music just a second or so earlier.

[3] As with *Dark Side of the Rainbow*, you can find a number of sites on the web that will help you sync up your very own mashup. In general, pause Pink Floyd's *Meddle* CD right at the beginning of "Echoes" and pause the movie *2001: A Space Odyssey* just before the film's inner title "Jupiter and Beyond the Infinite" appears; the inner title should fade in as you hear the first "ping." Like any sync up, you may find more interesting results by adjusting the sync point slightly in either direction.

seem contradictory build over repeated viewings to reveal deeper connections, such as the musical "ping" (reminiscent of an underwater sonar) matched with the floating planets. Both the movie and the music feed into and expand the sense of mystery and unknowability that each explores independently. "Echoes" may actually be a better music score for this portion of *2001* than the music Kubrick chose, which is perhaps why, when Adrian Maben re-edited (remixed?) his 1972 film *Pink Floyd: Live at Pompeii* (Director's Cut, 2003), he added images of our solar system.[4]

In the End, It's Only Round and Round (and Round)

As effective as these mashups and soundtracks can be, there's at least one way to argue that Pink Floyd's music is self-sufficiently cinematic, that it doesn't really need any external film to be paired or mashed with. I say that in part because the cinematic qualities inherent in *Dark Side*, at least, remain as powerful and clear today as they did when I was in my late teens, lying on the floor and utterly unable to imagine breaking through the isolation I felt. I couldn't even imagine anyone else feeling the way I did. One thing that spoke to me then goes directly to the cinema in Pink Floyd's music—namely the circularity of the journey.

After the finale of "Eclipse," the album leaves us with the heartbeat that it begins with. This bookending of the narrative gives the story a sense of completeness and serves as either an optimistic reassurance that we are able to relocate and return to our inner world or a pessimistic warning that we are doomed to

---

[4] Some have suggested that Pink Floyd deliberately created "Echoes" in reference to *2001: A Space Odyssey* or even possibly that Stanley Kubrick, who often edited his films to music, might have originally tailored the sequence to "Echoes"—but the first seems unlikely in terms of logistics and the second is impossible since "Echoes" was written and recorded three years after the release of Kubrick's film. According to one urban legend, film director Stanley Kubrick asked Pink Floyd if he could use *Atom Heart Mother* for *A Clockwork Orange*, but Roger Waters said "No," and then later regretted it; a variation says Waters's regret was about not contributing music to *2001*. And if you haven't had your daily dose of irony, there are some reports that Kubrick later turned down Waters's request to sample some of the dialogue and breathing sounds from *2001: A Space Odyssey* for *Amused to Death*.

relive the cycle over and over. For many—and almost certainly for Roger Waters—the message was pessimistic. This image of the circle would become part of the logic of *The Wall*, the self-constructed fortress that Pink uses to protect himself from the world outside. While Pink was literally stuck in a circular prison, Waters embedded the circular idea more obliquely in the lyrics with the interlocking phrases "isn't this where" and "we came in" inviting the listener to think of the whole work as a seamless loop trapping us inside. This imagery is central to "Wish You Were Here," as well, where we see "two lost souls swimming in a fish bowl year after year." Like being in a maze that defies your escape, that viciously returns you only to where you started (or, into a slaughterhouse, if you're a sheep in the world of *Animals*), these two are imprisoned on "the same old ground" and "the same old fears" without a clue how to escape or transcend their situation.

What the cinematic qualities of the music convey most effectively is the sense of doom, of metaphysical necessity, that there is *no other outcome possible* than simply repeating and reliving the awful present. It's one thing to *say* that the world is an excruciatingly painful and lonely place. But something very different to lie on the floor in the dark and *see*—in your imagination and your mind's eye, for a good twenty or more minutes—the loops, the mazes, and the cruel, interlocking logic that makes everything "in tune" in just the way it seems to be.

At their best, Pink Floyd embrace the filmmaking maxim, "Show, don't tell"—cinema that allows us to experience the world of the artist, not simply be told about it. Like a well-made film, *Dark Side of the Moon* forges an emotional connection with its audience by creating a shared context through the juxtaposition of various motifs, sound effects, instrumentation and arrangements. This allows—in fact, requires—us to use our imaginations to interpret and discover for ourselves their meanings and relevance in ways that many pop songs and lyrics do not.

Consider, for example, what Roger Waters said about death and the brevity of life in 1972 when Pink Floyd's music was designed to function as a film score, in this case for Barbet Schroeder's film *La Vallée*:

Life is a short, warm moment
And death is a long cold rest.
You get your chance to try
In the twinkling of an eye:
Eighty years, with luck, or even less.
("Free-Four" on *Obscured by Clouds*)

Yes, Waters is trying to tell us something meaningful. But despite being written specifically for Schroeder's film, the song has all the depth (and rhyme structure) of a limerick. It has none of the cinematic qualities that make *Dark Side,* which says pretty much the same thing, so compelling and difficult to ignore. Once the needle dropped on my album and the heartbeat began, the forty-three minutes of the album *was* "a short, warm moment" in which the realities of time, insanity, death and war seemed to be *right there,* in front of you, as if you were watching a film. And when the heartbeat at the end looped around, you could feel as if you had just lived an entire, microcosmic life.

The cinematography, the "writing in movement," within the music gave it its sense of doom, of tragedy, and its metaphysical bite. But it also gave it a kind of a silver lining. Because I was being *shown* something about life—and not just listening to someone talk about something or other—it became clearer that I was not, in fact, the only one who felt the way I did. I was a lonely kid lying on his floor in the dark. But something in Pink Floyd spoke to me, giving me hope. Sure, it was a kind of dark, depressing hope. But others—Pink Floyd—had seen it too, so I knew that I was not the only one in life's theatre.[5]

---

[5] An Open Court Production . . . Written and Directed by Josef Steiff . . . Sound Designer: Jared Regan . . . Music Supervisor: Steve Hamann . . . Script Supervisor: George A. Reisch . . .

Alienation
(Several Different
Ones)

7

Dragged Down by the Stone: Pink Floyd, Alienation, and the Pressures of Life

DAVID DETMER

Few rock albums communicate a coherent message. It's even rarer for a band's entire body of work, stretching over several years, to maintain thematic consistency. Judged solely by their first seven albums—from 1967's *The Piper at the Gates of Dawn* to 1972's *Obscured by Clouds*—Pink Floyd's work might appear as incoherent as the next band's. But beginning with their 1973 breakthrough album, *The Dark Side of the Moon,* and continuing through *Wish You Were Here* (1975), *Animals* (1977), and *The Wall* (1979), Pink Floyd focused intensely on one issue. Despite their many differences, all these albums address alienation.

Wish You Were . . . Connected

To be alienated is to be cut off, or estranged, from something or someone with which one should be connected. One can be alienated from other people, as when one fails to relate intimately to one's family or friends, or when one cannot deal cordially and co-operatively with colleagues, or interact civilly with, or respond empathetically toward, other people in general. It can be a harmful failure to make contact, a troublesome inability to achieve closeness, a frustrating breakdown in communication. Since art is an attempt to communicate one's ideas and feelings deeply and intensely, artists are often especially sensitive to this problem. Artists of all kinds must confront the danger that this special communication might at any point be thwarted by their alienation from their audience.

But not all alienation is social. Workers can become alienated from their work if they must perform boring, uncreative tasks at the direction of others. They can become alienated from the products of their work, as might assembly-line workers who install one tiny part of a car, in accordance with someone else's design and production plans. Such workers are unlikely to see the finished product as having resulted from *their* personal creative effort. They may feel disconnected from the fruits of their labors (which they also, incidentally, do not own).

It's plausible that modern life leads increasingly to our alienation from nature, as well. We spend more and more of our time in artificial environments (for example, in the car, at the office, on city streets, or locked up in our homes); and we are likely, wherever we are, to remain glued to television or computer screens, iPods, or to other electronic media or devices. If the rhythms of nature are drowned out by these distractions, it's not a stretch to see that we can also become alienated from *ourselves*.

One who is alienated in this way may passively defer to others (such as parents, religious leaders, one's peers, or society at large) on the fundamental questions of life that each of us, if we are to be autonomous, must decide for ourselves: What do I stand for? What are my values? How should I treat other people? What do I think is important? What are my priorities? What do I want to accomplish with my life? Confronting these questions allows one to emerge as a *person*, an individual with distinct talents, interests, and sensibilities—and not just an anonymous and interchangeable member of the public. Insofar as one submerges or never develops these distinctive traits, one loses sight of oneself, and becomes alienated from it.

Indeed, in a broader sense all forms of alienation might be thought of as forms of self-estrangement. The reason is that I can only be truly "alienated" from something that is (or should be) *part* of me. I am not alienated from the cobwebs in the corner of my basement, even though I feel no connection to them, for I can only be alienated from that to which I *want* to be connected, or *should* be connected. That's why alienation involves disequilibrium, disturbance, and anxiety. It makes the world *feel* strange in ways that can sometimes be effectively expressed in music.

When the World You're in Starts Playing Different Tunes

While Pink Floyd's ideas on alienation are most clearly and precisely expressed through Roger Waters's lyrics,[1] the band's *music* also contributes greatly to the communication of those ideas. For one thing, rock music rarely attracts attention solely because of its lyrics.[2] One reason why ideas on alienation have reached such a wide audience is that millions of listeners have found the music on Pink Floyd's albums so compelling. They seem to *require* repeated listening, partly because they so effectively create and sustain a mood.[3] That's probably one reason why early Pink Floyd music was often used in the soundtracks for films, including *More* [1969], *Zabriskie Point* [1970], and *The Valley* [1972]. Such textural, atmospheric music tends to point away from itself, and to invite the listener to contemplate the images, feelings, and ideas it evokes. This evocative power intensifies when the emotive content of the lyrics matches, or harmonizes with, the music, making the ideas in the lyrics harder to ignore.

Another feature of Pink Floyd's songs relevant here is their sheer length. Two to three minutes, the standard length of popular rock songs in 1967, may be enough time for catchy musical "hooks," but the moods and ideas within Pink Floyd's music

---

[1] Pink Floyd's first album, *The Piper at the Gates of Dawn*, features the quirky, eccentric, whimsical lyrics of the band's original lead vocalist, guitarist, and songwriter, Syd Barrett. Shortly after its release, however, Barrett suffered a mental breakdown of such severity that he was unable to continue in the band, and was replaced by David Gilmour. On the next half-dozen Pink Floyd albums, songwriting chores were divided among all four band members (Waters, Gilmour, Rick Wright, and Nick Mason). But starting with *The Dark Side of the Moon*, and continuing throughout the remainder of Waters's tenure with the band (he left in 1983), Waters wrote all of the band's lyrics (though the other band members joined him, through *The Wall*, in composing music).

[2] "Empirical research demonstrates that virtually everyone likes or dislikes a particular song for its music before understanding the lyrics. Most popular music has lyrics, yet the music is designed to reward listening . . . apart from our grasp of the song's subject matter" (Theodore Gracyk, "A Different Plea for Disinterest," in David Goldblatt and Lee B. Brown, *Aesthetics*, second edition [Upper Saddle River: Prentice Hall, 2005], p. 506).

[3] Their music never lost this moody, evocative quality, even as they underwent a gradual transition from a free, wild, spacey, improvisational style to, by the time of *The Dark Side of the Moon*, one based on highly precise and structured (and often quite hummable) musical compositions.

require much more time. Indeed, Pink Floyd's very first album includes a nine-and-a-half minute instrumental, "Interstellar Overdrive." Eventually, the band worked on even larger musical canvases, with the title track from *Atom Heart Mother* (1970) and "Echoes" from *Meddle* (1971), for example, each clocking in at over twenty-three minutes and occupying an entire LP side. "Shine On You Crazy Diamond" from *Wish You Were Here* (1975) has a combined length of over twenty-five minutes.

Even when the band's songs are shorter, they're intended to be heard as part of a long, continuous listening experience in which the songs are segued one into another or broken into parts that repeat in the course of the album. "Breathe," for example, from *Dark Side of the Moon*, is reprised at the end of "Time," following a seamless segue. "Shine on You Crazy Diamond" is also divided into different parts on *Wish You Were Here*, as are "Pigs on the Wing" on *Animals* and "Another Brick in the Wall" in *The Wall*.

Pink Floyd's use of sound effects, such as bird calls, industrial noises, heartbeats, footsteps, chiming clocks, and spoken words are also essential to the kind of listening experience they create. These devices help to set the mood for the music—the use of the heartbeat at the beginning and the end of *The Dark Side of the Moon* being perhaps the most famous example. Gilmour explains that "the heartbeat alludes to the human condition and sets the mood for the music, which describes the emotions experienced during a lifetime."[4]

The sound effects also connect to the ideas and emotions in the band's music—sometimes fairly obviously (like the clanging of coins in "Money") yet sometimes in ways that expand the meaning and interpretation of the music. "On the Run," for instance, features airport announcements for a departing flight and frantic footsteps, all of which communicate a particular kind of panic that the synthesizers alone would not convey. Similarly, Claire Torry's wordless vocalizing on "The Great Gig in the Sky" overflows with musical feeling. But the spoken passages audible in the background—"I am not frightened of dying" and "If you can hear this whispering you are dying"—attach a specific

---

[4] Nicholas Schaffner, *Saucerful of Secrets: The Pink Floyd Odyssey* (New York: Dell, 1991), p. 176.

meaning to her emotionally-charged singing, and thus help us to understand and to share in the feeling it expresses.

One of the major challenges that creative artists face is that of balancing diversity and unity in their works. Just as novelists try to make one story out of hundreds of different incidents, and painters attempt to make a painting out of thousands of different brushstrokes (and, perhaps, out of an arrangement of many different objects that are each represented in paint), the great Pink Floyd albums bring all their sounds, ideas, and emotions together in a way that is unified, but not monotonous; varied and dynamic, but not incoherent. The songs sound as if they belong together, and would be out of place on some other album (even another Pink Floyd album). The band's secret weapon for creating this artistic unity is a final, distinctive feature of their music— its leisurely pacing. The band usually plays slowly, and avoids the aggressive, hectic, up-tempo sound favored by most rock bands. This does more than lengthen the songs, however, for it also adds to the musical atmosphere in which listeners can really think and pay attention to the music, without feeling the kind of rush or excitement that Led Zeppelin or The Sex Pistols would put in play. The slow pacing also underscores the clear, clean, uncluttered sound of Pink Floyd's great albums. Even with all the sonic "extras," such as sound effects and spoken narration, those recordings sound open and spacious, leaving ample room for the listener's thoughtful response.

Don't Be Afraid to Care

Waters tells us that his concerns while writing the lyrics for *The Dark Side of the Moon* were "political and philosophical."[5] He conceived the entire album as a meditation on "the pressures and preoccupations that divert us from our potential for positive action . . ."[6] the pressure of earning a lot of money; the time thing, time flying by very fast; organized power structures like the church or politics; violence; aggression."[7] That's why so

---

[5] Roger Waters as quoted in John Harris, *The Dark Side of the Moon: The Making of the Pink Floyd Masterpiece* (Cambridge, Massachusetts: Da Capo, 200), p. 89.

[6] Waters as quoted in Harris, p. 80.

[7] Waters as quoted in Schaffner, p. 171.

much of the album is negative and pessimistic. It deals with
political, social, and psychological maladies, and with the various stresses that contribute to alienation and stand as obstacles
to overcoming it.

But Waters also intended the album to convey a positive
message. Indeed, he calls it "an exhortation . . . to embrace the
positive and reject the negative."[8] Life, he says,

> is not a rehearsal. As far as we know, you only get one shot, and
> you've got to make choices based on whatever moral, philosophi-
> cal, or political position you may adopt . . . You make choices dur-
> ing your life, and those choices are influenced by political
> considerations and by money and by the dark side of all our
> natures. You get the chance to make the world a lighter or darker
> place in some small way. We all get the opportunity to transcend
> our tendencies to be self-involved and mean and greedy. We all
> make a small mark on the painting of life.

Jean-Paul Sartre and Simone de Beauvoir had a similar view of
life. Like these twentieth-century existentialists, Waters emphasizes

1. our "thrown" condition, that is, the fact that we find ourselves already immersed in a world full of economic,
   political, and cultural structures that we have not chosen;
2. the inescapability of our responsibility for how we
   respond to those structures, and,
3. the gravity of this responsibility.

The gravity—the weight of this stone—is only made greater by

4. the violence and cruelty of so many of those structures
   (this is the "dark" side of Pink Floyd's message) and
5. the fact that, "as far as we know," this life is not a prepa-
   ration for something else. It's our one chance to get things
   more or less right and to avoid the frighteningly many
   ways in which they can go horribly wrong. This responsibility is both prudential (we must avoid making a mess
   of our own lives, and instead take full advantage of the

---

[8] Waters as quoted in Harris, pp. 80–81

limited time, resources, and opportunities available to us) and ethical (we should try to "make the world a little lighter" for the benefit of our contemporaries and for others who will follow us).

The bright side, according to Waters, is "the potential that human beings have for recognizing each other's humanity and responding to it, with empathy rather than antipathy."[9] Accordingly, the very first words sung on *The Dark Side of the Moon* are "Breathe, breathe in the air / Don't be afraid to care."[10] But why should anyone need to be encouraged to care? What are the pressures of life that might make a person afraid (or otherwise unable or unwilling) to care about life and its existential responsibilities?

Don't Sit Down

Work could be one way for people to pursue interests, to exercise and expand their unique talents, and to leave their mark on the world. But it's usually something more like what Pink Floyd describes in "Breathe":

> Run, rabbit run.
> Dig that hole, forget the sun,
> And when at last the work is done
> Don't sit down it's time to dig another one.

The song points to a British wartime song "Run Rabbit Run," sung by the duo Flanagan and Allen, and to Karl Marx, who argues that when others control and direct my work—when, that is, it is not my spontaneous, self-directed action—I

---

[9] Waters as quoted in Harris, p. 9.

[10] These lines are from the song "Breathe." Waters tells us that he wanted these lyrics to be clear, direct, and open to comprehension: "I made a conscious effort when I was writing the lyrics for *Dark Side of the Moon* to take the enormous risk of being truly banal about a lot of it, in order that the ideas should be expressed as simply and plainly as possible." In this connection he notes that "If you write, 'Breathe, breathe in the air / Don't be afraid to care,' you leave yourself open to howling derision . . . It's very adolescent in its intensity, but I'm very happy now that I took that risk" (Waters as quoted in Harris, p. 89).

become alienated. This is alienation not only from both my labor and its products, but also from my very humanity. At work I lose control over my distinctively human capacities, such as my autonomy and my creativity. Indeed, in a sense, someone else *owns* my work activity. Consequently, I cannot feel that I am myself, or even human, when I am working. Marx concludes that, as a result, the worker "only feels himself freely active in his animal functions—eating, drinking, procreating . . . ; and in his human functions he no longer feels himself to be anything but an animal. What is animal becomes human and what is human becomes animal."[11] Kind of like a rabbit, perhaps.

Pink Floyd was not the first to wonder if, as a result of alienation from nature, the difference between a "green field" and "cold steel rail" was becoming irrelevant to an alienated British society. In 1921, the philosopher Bertrand Russell, argued that industrialism

> forces men, women, and children to live a life against instinct, unnatural, unspontaneous, artificial. Where industry is thoroughly developed, men are deprived of the sight of green fields and the smell of earth after rain; they are cooped together in irksome proximity, surrounded by noise and dirt, compelled to spend many hours a day performing some utterly uninteresting and monotonous mechanical task . . . The result of this life against instinct is that industrial populations tend to be listless and trivial, in constant search of excitement, delighted by a murder, and still more delighted by a war.[12]

This kind of alienation is especially corrosive because there is no break from the boredom, repetition, and alienation of the work routine. As Albert Camus put it, the modern workday for many goes like this: "Rising, streetcar, four hours in the office or the factory, meal, streetcar, four hours of work, meal, sleep, and Monday Tuesday Wednesday Thursday Friday and Saturday according to the same rhythm . . . But one day the 'why' arises

---

[11] Karl Marx, "Estranged Labor," in his *The Economic and Philosophic Manuscripts of 1844* (New York: International, 1964), p. 111.

[12] Bertrand Russell as quoted in Howard Kahane and Nancy Cavender, *Logic and Contemporary Rhetoric*, eighth edition (Belmont: Wadsworth, 1998), p. 30.

and everything begins in that weariness tinged with amazement."[13] ("And when at last the work is done / Don't sit down it's time to dig another one.")

Time, Finitude, and Death

Time" on *The Dark Side of the Moon* begins quietly. But we suddenly hear the very loud chiming of clocks. The effect is startling and jarring, much like the first point that "Time" makes. Young people, especially, have no clue about how precious and scarce time is. They "fritter and waste the hours in an offhand way," reasoning that they "are young and life is long and there is time to kill today." Then life's alarm clock sounds: "then one day you find ten years have got behind you / No one told you when to run, you missed the starting gun." It also underscores the existentialists' ideas about our "thrown" condition. We simply find ourselves already right up to our necks in the midst of a world that we did not create. Everyone, in that sense, has "missed the starting gun."

Waters says that, following his mother's advice, he spent his youth preparing for a life that he regarded as having not yet started—a life that was to start at some unspecified time in the future. The point was to get a good education so that he might be prepared, later, to have a family and a career, at which time his life would begin. He reports: "It came as a great shock to discover that I wasn't preparing for anything—I was right in the middle of it, and always had been."[14]

Both lyrics and recollection suggest that part of the problem is our overly passive reliance on others, our refusal to think and act for ourselves. Just because "no one told [us] when to run," that's not a valid excuse for not embracing life authentically. Everyone, especially those that are "kicking around on a piece of ground in [their] home town" and "waiting for someone or something to show [them] the way," should take a deep breath and "choose [their] own ground." Waters confirms that a fundamental message of *The Dark Side of the Moon* is that "[i]t's OK to

---

[13] Albert Camus, "The Myth of Sisyphus," in his *The Myth of Sisyphus and Other Essays* (New York: Vintage, 1955), p. 10.
[14] Waters as quoted in Harris, page 82.

engage in the difficult task of discovering your own identity[, a]nd it's OK to think things out for yourself'."[15]

The point is underscored in a familiar way for Pink Floyd—immediately after a provocative lyric, David Gilmour's guitar soloing takes over. It gives listeners time, literally, to think about the ideas just presented and joins those ideas to richly emotive music. Gilmour begins this solo by sustaining its first note for seven beats, as if he were saying "listen to me; I have something important to say; I won't be changing notes until I have your attention." Once he does, the listener is likely to hear in Gilmour's dark, moody, minor-key playing a restatement and intensification of the ideas conveyed by Waters's lyrics. He gradually increases his speed and moves to the upper register of his instrument until the mood suddenly relaxes into the major seventh chords of the chorus. Now, Gilmour's solo sounds no longer dark and menacing, but open, hopeful, even consoling (as if he were saying, "don't feel bad; I missed the starting gun, too; everybody did"), an effect that is underscored by the soothing female voices that accompany it in the background.

One likely reason for why this and other of Gilmour's solos work this way is that they are usually improvised, on the spot, in the studio. (This is true, for example, of all of his solos from *The Dark Side of the Moon*, including the one from "Time.") One can *hear* this. These solos don't sound canned or calculated, but rather strike the listener as free, spontaneous creations. He plays them "in the moment," and allows his emotional response to the music over which he is soloing to come through.[16]

---

[15] Waters as quoted in Harris, page 9.

[16] Of course, there are drawbacks, as well as advantages, to improvisational soloing. The main problem is simply that when one makes something up on the fly, there is always the possibility that some parts will not come out well. But this problem can easily be fixed in the studio. For example, consider Gilmour's explanation of how he created his famous solo on "Comfortably Numb" from *The Wall*:

> I just went into the studio and banged out five or six solos. From there I just followed my usual procedure, which is to listen back to each solo and mark out bar lines, saying which bits are good. In other words, I make a chart, putting ticks and crosses on different bars as I count through: two ticks if it's really good, one tick if it's good and cross if it's no go. Then I just follow the chart, whipping one fader up, then another fader, jumping from phrase to phrase and trying to make a really nice solo all the way through . . . It wasn't that difficult. (David Gilmour, interviewed by

"Time" ends with the frightening line, "the time is gone, the song is over / Thought I'd something more to say." You might think the song is speaking about itself as it winds down, but it's speaking about you and all of us who, when we reach old age and recognize that we have little time left, will be disappointed at our meager accomplishments. We will recall with dismay and disappointment all of the things that we had hoped and dreamed and planned to do, but had never done, perhaps because we had foolishly assumed that "life is long and there is time to kill today." We might instead recognize and confront our finitude, and take full advantage of the limited time available to us to make our lives meaningful and to ameliorate the hardships and the suffering that we share with others.

These thoughts harmonize with the famous argument of twentieth-century German existentialist philosopher Martin Heidegger that our refusal to face up to our own mortality—not just to acknowledge it in a vague, abstract, intellectual way, but rather to look it straight in the eye and feel it in one's bones—creates the inauthenticity and triviality of our lives. With Heidegger, the two problems raised in "Time"—relying on others to "show you the way" and failing to recognize mortality—have the same solution. For if we were to come to grips with our finitude, we would not willingly and uncritically go along with norms of thought and behavior simply because they are widely accepted by others. If I genuinely face the fact that I have but one short life to live, I will want to make sure that it is indeed *my life* that I live, and not that of the public at large. I will not simply do as "one" does, or think as "they" do, but rather I will think for myself, and do what *I* think (in the light of my best critical judgment, and on the basis of careful thought, and with full cognizance of my own unique interests and talents) is best. Nor will I squander my precious time, which could be spent in significant conversation with others, or in the development of significant personal projects or interpersonal relationships, on idle gossip or sensationalistic trivia. For I could only do so if I suffered from the delusion that "life is long and there is time to kill today."

Lenny Baker for *Guitar World* ["Careful with that Axe," February 1993; accessed online on April 15th, 2007 at http://www.pinkfloydonline.com/int79.html]).

Money

Taken literally, "Money" celebrates the acquisitive life. It says that the key to happiness is to accumulate a massive amount of money and then to use it to purchase expensive goodies—"new car, caviar, four-star daydream." Even better—"a football team."

But the song is satirical. It ridicules the simplistic notion that if you just "get a good job with good pay" you'll be "okay." Look at the song in the context of the others on *Dark Side*. Will acquiring money solve the problems of time, finitude, and death? Obviously not. Coming after "Breathe," "Time," and "The Great Gig in the Sky," its celebration of greed sounds shallow and puerile. The album then continues to dwell on the dark side of life—on war, racism, pointless divisions between people, insanity—in a way that makes the song, taken literally, a mere diversion and distraction from the basic problems that we face as human beings.

Perhaps because it is satirical, "Money" is the one song on *The Dark Side of the Moon* in which the music does not unambiguously support the real message behind the lyrics. Because the main riff first established by Waters's bass guitar is so catchy, and Gilmour's singing is so earnest and lacking irony, and his solo, like that of guest musician Dick Parry on saxophone, is so energized and joyful—it's easy to hear "Money" as thoroughly fun and jubilant. Little wonder, then, that it was a monster hit single in the United States (a rarity for Pink Floyd, a decidedly album-oriented band) and that it still receives steady radio play and makes cash registers go "ka-ching," even if not always in the song's distinctive 7/8 time signature.

For more of Pink Floyd's thoughts on the corrupting power of money and the alienating effects of greed (and for further evidence that "Money" is a satirical song), one need only turn to "Dogs," from *Animals*. This song attacks the ruthless, amoral social climbers who let no moral scruple or compassionate feeling get in the way of their relentless quest for wealth, power, and social advancement. "Dogs," and the entire *Animals* album, indicts capitalism for setting us against one another in a competitive system fueled by personal greed. To win this ugly game, you have to be a "dog," which is to say, "You gotta be crazy," and "when you're on the street / You gotta be able to pick out the easy meat / with your eyes closed." You cannot afford to have a conscience. Rather, "You gotta strike when the moment is right without thinking."

And, you have to dress well, like those working in the corporate business world, and in other "respectable" power sectors of society:

> And after a while, you can work on points for style.
> Like the club tie, and the firm handshake,
> A certain look in the eye and an easy smile.
> You have to be trusted by the people that you lie to,
> So that when they turn their backs on you,
> You'll get the chance to put the knife in.

These dogs are alienated from themselves in so far as they rationalize their conduct as necessary and defensible. They've persuaded themselves both that this is a cutthroat world with no room for empathy or moral principle ("you just keep on pretending / That everyone's expendable and no-one has a real friend"), and that everyone else is acting the same way ("everything's done under the sun / And you believe at heart, everyone's a killer").

But the clock is ticking on for these dogs, just as it is for the rest of us. The band even mocks their demise as they sing of an old dog who retires to "hide [his] head in the sand" of some warm, sunny locale.—"Just another sad old man / All alone and dying of cancer." At the moment of his death, it's especially ugly:

> And when you lose control, you'll reap the harvest you have
>   sown.
> And as the fear grows, the bad blood slows and turns to
>   stone.
> And it's too late to lose the weight you used to need to throw
>   around.
> So have a good drown, as you go down, all alone,
> Dragged down by the stone.

This disturbing image is reinforced by an electronically altered echo of the word "stone." It repeats and begins to sound neither human nor electronic—rather a disagreeable hybrid of the two. It sounds far away, but maybe not. One wants to keep an eye on it, lest it suddenly come back to attack. And this creepy atmosphere is enhanced by the faint, far off sound of barking and whining dogs.

Any Colour of Us and Them You Like

Another factor leading to our interacting with others in the hostile, violent ways described in "Dogs" is our tendency to draw artificial distinctions between people. We identify with some, but reject others as alien to us. This is the theme of "Us and Them" on *Dark Side*. The song does not deny that people differ from one another, but rather suggests that many of the commonly perceived differences are superficial, illusory, or contrived, and, in any case, are dwarfed by our commonalities. Certainly they are small enough as to pose no barrier to anyone seeking to empathize with others. But fear is a powerful human motivation, and those who profit from conflict can effectively invoke it to persuade "us" to distance ourselves from "them."

The first verse asserts that soldiers, being "only ordinary men," would not of their own accord choose to hate and attempt to kill each other. They have no genuine quarrel with one another, and do not differ in any significant way. So they have to be manipulated into their hateful attitudes and murderous conduct by those who stand to gain from the war, such as the military leaders who "sat" as "the lines on the map / moved from side to side."

The next addresses racism ("black and blue"), which is just as arbitrary and artificial ("who knows which is which and who is who"), and sometimes just as lethal. To empathize with the poor, the song concludes, one must see them as like oneself, and to believe that their lot might be changed for the better. But it's too often easier to see them as not like me, but rather as "them," the "down and out." After all, "it can't be helped," even though "there's a lot of it about."

The consequence of this indifference is revealed in the song's last four lines:

Out of the way, it's a busy day
I've got things on my mind.
For the want of the price of tea and a slice
The old man died.

In this case, "they" needed "us," desperately. In "Hey You" (on *The Wall*) the situation's turned around and we need them: "Can you feel me?," "Would you touch me?," and finally, "Can you help me?"

Artists and Crazy Diamonds

While *The Dark Side of the Moon* focuses on alienation in general, in a couple of places it does so by referring to the band's personal history and to the special challenges alienation poses to artists. For example, the reprise of "Breathe" might plausibly be interpreted both as a comment on the discontents of touring musicians, and as applying to anyone who works hard and travels extensively:

> Home, home again.
> I like to be here when I can.
> When I come home cold and tired
> It's good to warm my bones beside the fire.

Similarly, "Brain Damage" alludes both to mental illness in general and to Syd Barrett's descent into madness.

Both *Wish You Were Here* and *The Wall* adopt this approach more systematically and suggest that the plight of the artist is one we all face. The first album is widely known to reflect the band members' disengagement from one another and from their art in the wake of the stupefying success of *The Dark Side of the Moon*.[17] In a broader sense, the album is about the alienation of artists from each other, and about the dehumanizing aspects of the world of commerce (a world which artists must navigate in

---

[17] *The Dark Side of the Moon* is, by some measures, the most successful album ever released. It stayed on *Billboard's* Top 200 charts for 591 straight weeks, which is still a record. It also holds the record for longest total time on these charts (including non-consecutive appearances), at 724 weeks. It has sold thirty million copies worldwide, and continues, well over thirty years after its initial release, to sell over 250,000 copies a year in the United States alone. It's a staple of radio stations employing a "classic rock" format, and it even generally draws praise from mainstream rock critics, who usually disdain "concept albums" (or anything that might be called "progressive rock," or anything that anyone might consider to be pretentious.) It also frequently shows up on short lists of the greatest rock albums ever made.

order to reach their audience). And, in a still more general sense, it speaks to the phenomenon of estrangement between friends and colleagues, and to the general social alienation of modern individuals.

It seems to be extremely difficult for artists to work together co-operatively over an extended period of time. Few bands survive more than several years, because there are a huge number of pitfalls to be avoided—death, changing aspirations and goals, the ubiquitous "artistic differences," resented girlfriend-lyricists (à la *Spinal Tap*), money ("share it fairly, but . . .") and more. In the case of Pink Floyd, the band lost Syd Barrett, its original leader, songwriter, lead guitarist, and lead singer, to drug addiction and mental illness. In "Shine On You Crazy Diamond," they recall Syd with obvious affection ("Remember when you were young, you shone like the sun"), and lament the tragedy of his mental decline ("Now there's a look in your eyes, like black holes in the sky").

But they had been through a lot before they wrote these lyrics. *Wish You Were Here* was their seventh album after Barrett's departure and they had begun to grow apart. On the one hand, some may have felt robbed of their once-shared motivations and goals. Suddenly, with *Dark Side*, they had achieved everything they had been striving for. On the other hand, the success put pressure on them to produce a worthy follow-up album. *The Dark Side of the Moon* had put a spotlight on the band, and the whole world would take notice if they were to fail. No wonder they were feeling as lonely and vulnerable as the title track, "Wish You Were Here," suggests. It is usually heard as another tribute to the crazy diamond, but it is perhaps also a tribute to their former selves, to the members of Pink Floyd *before* they were mutually estranged and weighed down by their success.

"Welcome to the Machine" is like a report of the band's uglier experiences in the corporate music business at this time. It's about executives (in the parlance of *Animals*, they would be dogs) who deceive and manipulate musicians for profit. With its high-tech synthesizers and pulsating, industrial rhythms, the song evokes a place where human values are crushed by cold, impersonal, heartless forces ("Welcome my son, welcome to the machine"). "Have a Cigar" looks at this situation more cynically (and satirically) from the point of view of an executive high-fiv-

ing the band about the fabulous success of their last album—
"we're just knocked out!" and "We're so happy we can hardly
count." Counting, after all, is what it's all about. The executive
speaks as if he's part of "a team" with the band, but he's really
just "riding the gravy train." And he's not even sure which band
member is named "Pink."

This One's Pink

The Wall nods to this joke about the record company executive
and builds it up into an extended study of alienation—this time
between a rock musician named "Pink" and his audience. Again,
the band drew on their experiences playing in arenas to vast,
faceless crowds. Waters, in particular, began to resent the typically noisy, boorish, drunken behavior of fans at these shows
and took it as a sign that communication between the band and
its audience had broken down. Of Pink Floyd's 1975 tour,
Waters remarked: "I don't think there was any contact between
us and them."[18] During the subsequent *Animals* tour, his sense
of alienation only increased. "It's very difficult to perform in that
situation with people whistling and shouting and screaming and
throwing things and hitting each other and crashing about," he
said. But he also admitted that money had something to with
this problem about "us and them." "It was a situation that we
have created ourselves, out of our own greed."[19]

The phenomenon that Waters describes here is difficult to
understand. One would think that concert-goers, having
invested significant resources of time and money in order to
attend a concert, would want to listen to it attentively. Waters's
suggestion is that

> Audiences at those vast concerts are there for an excitement which,
> I think, has to do with the love of success. When a band or a per-
> son becomes an idol, it can have to do with the success that per-
> son manifests, not the quality of work he produces. You don't
> become a fanatic because somebody's work is good, you become

---

[18] Waters quoted in Toby Manning, *The Rough Guide to Pink Floyd* (New York:
Rough Guides, 2006), p. 95. Notice the reference to the song title from *The
Dark Side of the Moon*.
[19] Waters as quoted in Schaffner, page 219.

a fanatic to be touched vicariously by their glamour and fame. It somehow brightens up your life. Stars—film stars, rock 'n' roll stars—represent, in myth anyway, the life as we'd all like to live it. They seem at the very centre of life. And that's why audiences still spend large sums of money at concerts where they are a long, long way from the stage, where they are often very uncomfortable, and where the sound is often very bad.[20]

The problem, if Waters is right, is once again a kind of alienation—an alienation from artistic authenticity, another kind of "us and them." Rock musicians seem no longer "ordinary men" (or women) when record company hype takes over and they become mythical stars and idols that fans will pay large sums to see in person, even though the seats and the sound are pretty bad.

Waters put this disconnect between artists and their spaced-out audiences and placed it at the heart of *The Wall*. Once Pink's audience has gathered to see its idol "in the flesh," it turns out he's not really there at all—"Tell me is something eluding you, sunshine? /Is this not what you expected to see?" Pink is wearing a "disguise." And to face his audiences, he must be shot full of the drugs and become "comfortably numb."

We Don't Need No Indoctrination

The Wall also contains Pink Floyd's only #1 single, "Another Brick in the Wall (Part 2)," with its disturbing, but catchy refrain, sung by a children's chorus: "We don't need no education." It's not so much an attack on education *per se* as an attack (according to "The Happiest Days of Our Lives") on "certain teachers" who torment their students with "derision" and ridicule. And it is an attack on education when it becomes indistinguishable from "thought control." This occurs then students are simply told *what* to think, as opposed to being helped to learn *how* to think for themselves. (The fact that the children sing in unison, rather than in harmony, adds to the perception that they, as victims of thought control, all think alike.) Teachers whose main concern is simply to keep order, maintain a schedule, and get

---

[20] Waters as quoted in Jim Curtis, *Rock Eras* (Bowling Green: Bowling Green State University Popular Press, 1987), p. 291.

through the day, are well served by passive, docile students who, like the "Sheep" from *Animals* ("Meek and obedient you follow the leader") are content to take orders, let others think for them, and grow into modern, alienated citizens who over-pay for concert tickets because their local radio station tells them to.

Another reason why indoctrination is widespread in educa-tion is the fact, well-known by those who wield power, that independent, critical thought is dangerous to their interests. People who think for themselves can't be counted on to do your bidding, especially if your bidding is indefensible. Consider the difference between the teaching of arithmetic, on the one hand, and history or social studies, on the other. In arithmetic, it's not enough for students merely to memorize the correct answers; rather, they must understand the logic of arith-metic for themselves, so that they can calculate answers for themselves to problems that have never been posed to them by their teachers.

But in history and social studies, teachers face enormous pressure to produce students who hold the "right" opinions, to adopt "patriotic" positions which justify, if not celebrate, they very status quo that Pink Floyd indicts in these albums, in which the alienating powers, privileges, and wealth enjoyed by soci-ety's contemporary rulers (or chart-topping rock stars) are seen as important, legitimate and well-deserved.

The ugliness that results from this thwarting of independent critical thought and the substitution of indoctrination for it is well captured by Franz Kafka's memorable aphorism: "Probably all education is but two things: first, parrying of the ignorant child's impetuous assault on the truth; and second, gentle, imperceptible initiation of the humiliated children into the lie."[21]

That's why Pink Floyd's message is one of resistance—resis-tance to the forces of indoctrination and conformity, as well as resistance to the artificial barriers that separate "us" from "them." More specifically, the band urges us to resist those who would persuade us that money is more precious than time, that com-merce is more important than creativity, that spectacle is more

---

[21] Franz Kafka as quoted in Howard Kahane, *Logic and Contemporary Rhetoric*, fourth edition (Belmont: Wadsworth, 1984), p. 25.

valuable than communication, and that competition is more important than empathy. Indeed, according to Pink Floyd one of the keys to coping successfully with the alienating pressures of modern life is the reversing of these value judgments.

But the most important key is simply to think for oneself. Don't let others (even your favorite rock band!) decide for you what is true, valuable, and important. For if you think for yourself (and are not afraid to care), you have a chance to lead a richly meaningful life as an autonomous person. But if you don't, you run the risk of ending up, like so many others, as just another brick in the wall, dragged down by the stone.

8

Roger Waters: Artist of the Absurd

DEENA WEINSTEIN

"Mister Glum," the "gloomiest man in rock," a "ranting crank," a "mere misogynist"—these are but a few of the epithets hurled at Roger Waters by rock critics. For more than three decades, the author of Pink Floyd's massive best-selling concept albums (one of them, *Dark Side of the Moon,* spent fourteen consecutive years on *Billboard*'s top-200 album charts) has played rock's Rodney Dangerfield, getting no respect. Waters has consistently been described as holding "darkly cynical views of life and the human condition," projecting a "grim misanthropy," and writing "rock's most neurotic lyrics."

The critics' antipathy was sharpened by the contrast between Waters and his predecessor as leader and lyricist of Pink Floyd, Syd Barrett. Their styles could not have been more different, with Barrett specializing in trippy-dippy, whimsical, childlike dadaist songs. The fact that Barrett left as an acid casualty (or at least his descent into schizophrenia was interpreted in this Romantic mode) endeared him to the rock press and their readers who have always adored stars who sacrifice their mind or very life for their art.[1] This romantic reading of rock's casualties is largely responsible for misinterpreting Waters's lyrics as direct references to Barrett.

Critics see Waters as a depressive pessimist mainly because his view of existence and his understanding of the function of

---

[1] Physically, such as Buddy Holly, Jimi Hendrix and Janis Joplin, or mentally, like Roky Erickson, Brian Wilson and Syd Barrett.

rock run counter to theirs. Rock critics tend towards liberal progressivism, demanding hope from even the most critical lyricist
(which is why they could adore the "Give peace a chance" and
"Imagine" lyrics of John Lennon). Waters's words were not
hopeful at all, although they certainly were not understood by
the critics who dished out the slurs quoted above. Like that
fabled flock of ducks calling an abandoned baby swan an ugly
duckling, they don't get it. Waters is not some dyspeptic; he is
an existentialist. (Of course, writers for the mass media have
misunderstood existential philosophers too, labeling them
nihilists, when nothing could be further from the truth.)

(C)amused to Death

Waters's view of existence, and of what art should be, is
remarkably similar to that of French philosopher Albert Camus.
Camus's brand of existentialism became very popular with well-
educated youth of Waters's war-baby generation on both sides
of the Atlantic.[2] Waters was in high school when the British
critic and philosopher Colin Wilson wrote *The Outsider* in 1956.
It was hugely popular and a good introduction to French existentialists and their views of art. The same year, Camus, who
had published *The Stranger* and *The Myth of Sisyphus* in 1942,
released his well-received novel, *The Fall*, and won the Nobel
Prize for Literature a year later. When he died in a car crash in
France on January 4th, 1960, he was at the pinnacle of his
career.

Camus directly addressed art and artists in his two best-
known works: *The Myth of Sisyphus* and *The Rebel: An Essay on
Man in Revolt* (1951). Waters also focuses on the artist in several
of his best known efforts, the Pink Floyd albums, *Wish You
Were Here* (1975) and *The Wall* (1977). For both, art is reality-
based. "Creation is the great mime," Camus asserts in *The Myth
of Sisyphus*. "Real literary creation uses reality and only reality
with all its warmth and its blood, its passion and its outcries,"
he writes in *The Rebel*.[3]

---

[2] Camus was a central figure for members of the early SDS, and the group's
Port Huron Statement, which influenced the broader political youth movement
in the US in the 1960s, had several Camus-inspired passages.

[3] *The Rebel: An Essay on Man in Revolt* (New York: Vintage, 1956), p. 269.

Art is descriptive of life but it is not, Camus tells us, coincident with it. Art, by definition, requires some structure, some coherence, and that is precisely what is missing from life itself. This imposed structure is the artist's style or design. Like a painter who uses distinctive colors or specific subjects, Waters's art, its design, is of a piece. From his earliest songs through his post-Floyd albums, he has drawn on the same themes involved in Camus's understanding of existence, and has employed the same set of images such as the sun, the moon and darkness, stones and walls.

Art does not assuage the world's impact on us; it does not purvey pleasing illusions that provide us with escape or refuge from life. Nor is it, as Nietzsche would have it, in *The Birth of Tragedy,* nature's "metaphysical supplement, raised up beside it in order to overcome it"—a tonic to give us vitality, to enable us to endure the world. The art Camus and Waters created does not soothe us, does not provide solace; instead it intensifies our distress by evincing and heightening it. Why distress? Existence itself—and both authors see it this way—is absurd.

Waters's grasp of the absurd, of our desire for unity and the frustration of that desire, forms the thematic of all his songs. It appears from his earliest creations including "Julia Dream" and "Corporal Clegg" (both released in 1968), "Green is the Colour" and "Cymbaline" (both released in 1969), through his several post-Floyd albums. Of his major works—the four 1970s concept albums—two address the absurdity of the human condition in general (*Dark Side Of the Moon* and *Animals*), and two focus specifically on the absurd predicament of the artist, here the rock musician (*Wish You Were Here* and *The Wall*). In all his creations, Waters drew upon his own experiences to explore the variety of frustrated attempts at unity with others, the failed effort to connect, to communicate genuinely.

That Fat Old Sun

That desire to connect authentically, which is the basis of life itself for Waters and Camus, is frequently symbolized by them as the sun, Plato's metaphor for goodness itself in *The Republic.* Most of us take the role of prisoners in his allegory of the cave, ever allowed only to see mere shadows of the world flashed on the cave's walls, and thus having little chance of understanding the light that produces them, much less the sun that shines on the surface of the earth outside. Were the prisoners to escape and see the fire producing the shadows they had known all their life, they would be blinded and confused by the light.

When the corpse of Camus's absurd hero, Sisyphus, lay unburied, Sisyphus got Pluto's permission to return to earth from Hades so that he could chastise his wife for leaving his body in the public square, which he had asked her to do, rather than burying it. But Sisyphus so enjoyed the earth, especially the sun, that "he no longer wanted to go back to the infernal darkness." Pluto had to send one of the minor deities to retrieve him, and punished him with the eternal task of rolling a heavy stone up a hill. Of course, the stone would only roll back down, making Sisyphus look something like Waters's rabbit, forever running and digging holes ("When at last the work is done, don't sit down it's time to dig another one"). But this convergence of imagery is surrounded by another symbol—Waters's use of the sun throughout *Dark Side Of the Moon*. In "Time," we "run to catch up with the sun but it's sinking," and "Eclipse" is about all those things that Plato's prisoners in the cave could never even contemplate—what you do, people with whom you interact, all of it: "everything under the sun."

But life is absurd; it isn't all sunshine. Camus and Waters contrast life, symbolized by the sun, with its antithesis, death, which, as in *Sisyphus*, is symbolized by darkness—the eclipsed sun, and the side of the moon facing away from the sun. In *The Wall*, for example, we hear: "Hey you, don't help them to bury the light." The dualism of sun and darkness represent our existence—the desire, our striving, for unity; and its frustration, the gnawing absence of that unity.

When you recognize this basic antithesis of life and death, Hegel said, you are saddled with "unhappy consciousness"—the anguish derived from the fact that the world does not fulfill our wishes. Existence is rendered tragic, as one of the early existentialists, the Spanish thinker Miguel de Unamuno, wrote in his *Tragic Sense of Life*. There is no happy ending unless one can have some belief in the fiction of an afterlife, the happy synthesis that so many religions offer. Certainly Camus and Waters, both atheists, reject such fairy-tales. This judgment is most vividly expressed by Waters in "Sheep" from *Animals*: The stupid Orwellian bleaters, Nietzsche's herd men, recite the Twenty-third Psalm, "The Lord Is My Shepherd." But in this version the ovine herd is led by their shepherd to slaughter—with "bright knives" they are converted to "lamb cutlets." Camus also indicates his "unhappy consciousness," his understanding of the "universe . . . deprived of illusions [where] man feels himself a stranger," as he states in *The Myth of Sisyphus*. In his novel *The Stranger*, an official tells the absurd anti-hero Meursault that he may be saved if he repents and turns to Christianity. Refusing to lie, the prisoner remains truthful to his atheism. Later, when he has been sentenced to death, he is forced to meet with a chaplain and is enraged when the religious counselor insists that he turn to God.

For Waters, darkness is not merely death itself, that ultimate disconnect, but the living death of insanity, which is born of frustration. When we descend into madness, we can neither communicate with others nor with ourselves. At times Waters refers to this condition as lunacy, derived from the folk belief that the moon causes madness. Other frequent terms he uses in his lyrics include "crazy", "mad", being "on the run," "toys in the attic" and "insane." "The sun is eclipsed by the moon," Waters tells us in "Eclipse." Indeed *Dark Side of the Moon*'s original title was *Eclipse (A Piece for Assorted Lunatics)*.[4] Camus also deploys the binary relation: "There is no sun without shadow, and it is essential to know the night."[5]

Prisms and Diamonds

That the charismatic Syd Barrett did become a full-blown schizophrenic—so unable to connect with others that instead of singing on stage or on TV, he froze—led many to give Waters's songs a *roman-à-clef* reading. In interviews, Waters tried to set the record straight. "*Dark Side of the Moon* was an album about the universal condition of insanity," he said in one. In another, discussing *Wish You Were Here*, he insisted: "'Shine On' is not really about Syd; he's just a symbol for all the extremes of absence some people have to indulge in because it's the only

---

[4] The title was changed because a now long-forgotten band had just released an LP entitled *Eclipse,* so Pink Floyd changed their title to *The Dark Side of the Moon.*

[5] *The Myth of Sisyphus and Other Essays* (New York: Vintage, 1955), p. 167.

way they can cope with how fucking sad it is—modern life—to withdraw completely."[6] That many did not get Waters's point, that they confused his message with their Romantic fancy, is just another instance of frustrated attempts to connect, to have genuine communication.

Of course some people got it. Notable among them is Storm Thorgerson, mainstay of the well-named graphic art group, Hipgnosis, which createdPink Floyd's album covers. Thorgerson spoke about the songs on *Wish You Were Here*: "They seemed to be about unfulfilled presence in general rather than about Syd's particular version of it and he certainly had his own unique brand. The idea of presence withheld, of the ways that people pretend to be present whilst their minds are really elsewhere, and the devices and motivations employed psychologically by people to suppress the full force of their presence, eventually boiled down to a single theme absence: The absence of a person, the absence of a feeling."[7] His cover for that release—four sides including the inner jacket—represent four different absent presences. Each is related to the ancients' categories of substance, what they believed everything under the sun was composed of, the four basic elements: earth, air, fire, and water. (Camus's existentialism is also centered on absence: the absurd is defined by the absence of a response to the individual's demand for unity.) The cover created for *Dark Side of the Moon* is the best known and least understood of Thorgerson's Pink Floyd's graphics. A beam of white light passes through a prism and emerges in a rainbow of colors. White is the combination of all colors, and here it represents unity. The prism, which for Waters represents society, separates us, diffracting unity.

Society's basic structures, home, school and the military, erect the fundamental barriers that eliminate the possibilities for any unity. Each in its own way prohibits genuine communication. Home is represented as mother for both authors. In life, Camus's mother was "permanently melancholy" and Waters's was an ideologue—neither was there for her son. Camus begins

---

[6] Quoted in Nick Sedgwick, "A Rambling Conversation with Roger Waters concerning All This and That*"* in *The Pink Floyd Lyric Book* (London: Pink Floyd Music, 1982), p. 12.

[7] Hipgnosis, *Walk Away René: The Work of Hipgnosis* (London: Paper Tiger, 1978), p. 148.

The Stranger with Meursault's indifference to the news of his mother's death that day. In *The Wall*, Pink's mother never communicated with him, never let him relate his emotions to her; she was dead to him too. The songs "Mother" and "The Trial" show her desire to keep him safe, as an inarticulate baby. The wife too, representing the home of the adult, is not there for her husband. In "Nobody Home," Pink wails about his inability to communicate with her: "When I try to get through On the telephone to you There'll be nobody home."

Schools also block unity. Various songs in *The Wall* decry their negative impact on communication. In "The Happiest Days of Our Lives," teachers are seen as "pouring their derision Upon anything we did," stifling students' authentic expression. The school's "thought control" ("Another Brick in the Wall Part 2") replaces the individual child's beliefs with alien, standard-issue, views. This is partly why mass communication is an oxymoron for Waters. Radio and television do not genuinely communicate—the mass media's emanations are inanities. He first addressed this theme of meaningless communication in "One of these Days" (on *Meddle* 1971). And it's the main focus of two of his solo albums, *Radio Kaos* and *Amused to Death*.

War, the military, separates us from others in the most obvious way, by killing people, including the soldiers sent to kill others. Waters's father was killed in Italy during World War II when his son was an infant. Songs railing against warfare start with the shell-shocked "Corporal Clegg" (1968) and "Us and Them" (1973), where generals, safe in the rear, led the charge while "the front rank died," and proceed to the whole of the last Waters-penned Pink Floyd album, *The Final Cut* (1983).

Welcome to the Zoo

On *Animals,* some of these structures are in part personified, in part anthropomorphized, as pigs. They are the dictatorial moralists enforcing that British stiff-upper lip tradition of repressing expressions of emotion; those with "tight lips and cold feet," constantly "trying to keep our feelings off the street" ("Pigs (Three Different Ones)"). Camus agreed. In *The Rebel,* he shares Orwell's horror at the outcome of the Russian Revolution, seeing that attempts at improving society have failed and that people have been "delivered into the hands of bureaucrats and doctrinaires on the one hand (Waters's pigs on the wing), and to the enfeebled and bewildered masses on the other" (Waters's sheep).

Those pigs on the wing—society—harshly judge us when we defy them and attempt to communicate authentically. In both Camus's and Waters's narratives, this judgment is dramatized as a trial. And both the defendants, Meursault and Pink, are accused of the same crime: they are judged guilty of expressing improper emotions. Early in *The Stranger,* Meursault had gone to his mother's funeral and had no emotional reaction; he was, inwardly and outwardly, unaffected by her death. Later, when he is on trial for the murder of "an Arab," the prosecution does not focus on his murderous deed, but on his disinclination to cry at his mother's funeral. Pink, in contrast, but to the same effect, is tried for his acts of authentic communication of his emotions. The prosecution's case against him is based on the fact that he "Was caught red-handed showing feelings Showing feelings of an almost human nature" ("The Trial"). In expressing their emotions or lack thereof—being emotionally honest—both Meursault and Pink were seen to be alien to their societies, strangers to their norms. They have no home in the world.

Waters's discussion of the third animal, dogs, those self-interested exploiters, is best developed in his views of the music industry. Symbolized as the machine, the industry can so easily exploit the artist because it has told him to desire to be a big star—"we told you what to dream" ("Welcome to the Machine"). Music executives are seen as liars whose rhetorical flourishes— "I mean that most sincerely," "that is really what I think"—exude inauthenticity ("Have a Cigar"). The artist is lured with money to ride "the Gravy Train," but of course he will not be allowed to express himself on his lucrative album.

Depicting the antagonism between the artist and the industry, which is based on conflict between artists' desire to express their true feelings and the industry's demand to have them express anything that earns the most money, is of course not unique to Waters. The art schools that so many of the 1960s British rock stars attended (John Lennon, Eric Clapton, Keith Richards, among many others, including all the original members of Pink Floyd) emphasized the Romantic view of the artist in antagonistic relationship to commercial forces. This perspective was derived from the influential nineteenth century British philosopher of aesthetics, John Ruskin.

The Pros and Cons of Audiences

There is one thing that Waters, as an artist, could not exactly lament, as did Paul Klee: "Uns trägt kein Volk" ("The people do not support us"). Pink Floyd, starting with *Dark Side of The Moon*, had a huge fan base—one of the largest ever in music. But the majority of the band's millions of fans didn't quite "get it." Water's felt that they didn't understand his lyrics (and the critics, whom Waters mainly saw as hacks, didn't provide any help).

At Pink Floyd's gigs at the UFO Club in 1967, the audience was "living and feeling every note," according to an observer. But it was another story at their frequent forays to the hinterlands. At a concert in Dunstable, some people in the balcony poured beer over the band; at another, in East Dereham, broken beer mugs were smashed into the drums. Years later touring *Dark Side of The Moon* in the U.S., it became obvious that the song "Money" was wildly misunderstood. Instead of grasping Waters's message about the way money corrupts us, and thus prevents us from being honest with one another, Waters realized that that his fans thought the song was a celebration of super-rich, football team buying jet-setters. Pink Floyd's record label edited and released the song as a single that became a radio hit, which meant that it was heard out of the context of the other songs on the album—something which might partially account for the miscommunication. A single from *The Wall*, "Another Brick in the Wall, Part 2," was widely misinterpreted as a slam against education itself, as opposed to the *kinds* of educational practices Waters actually criticized. All in all, fans behaved like the stupid bleating sheep of *Animals*, and of Orwell's *Animal Farm*—Camus's "bewildered masses."

In Canada, during the 1977 In the Flesh tour, the disconnect between Waters and the fans became so intense that he spit at one of them. Waters's experience of his audience as an alien other with whom he could not connect, could not authentically communicate, gave him the idea of building a wall separating it from the band to signify this disconnect.

The artist unable to communicate, to unite with those for whom he creates, epitomizes frustration. Adding to that stress, an artist in a rock band does not create alone. Band members need to communicate with one another—to create the music, to make plans for its presentation, to reach agreement on a host of business matters, and to perform music on stage and in the recording studio. But after the success of *Dark Side Of The Moon*, whether it was due to their new found wealth or merely the fact that each of the members now had families pulling them away from their primary commitment to the band, Pink Floyd's unity was gone. The rest of the decade, through the ultimate break up of the band in the first half of the 1980s when Waters left, was perhaps foretold by *Dark Side Of The Moon*'s nod to Barrett's descent into madness—"and if the band you're in starts playing different tunes . . ."

Wish You Were Here, like all of Waters's works, obeys Camus's dictum to use reality "with all its warmth and its blood, its passion and its outcries."[8] The album's general view of the human condition was a reflection of relationships in the band. Waters has said "it's about none of us really being there," adding that it "should have been called WISH WE WERE HERE . . ."[9] Recalling the state of Pink Floyd while creating *Wish You Were Here*, Waters said that "no one was really looking each other in the eye, and that it was all very mechanical." (Here too, as with the music industry itself, Waters uses the word machine as the antithesis of life.) "Syd's state," he adds, "could be seen as being symbolic of the general state of the group . . . very fragmented" (p. 108). Things went from bad to worse. Their 1977 tour saw the members traveling separately. Waters would fly to the venue in a chartered helicopter while the others traveled there in a stretch limousine (p. 120). A couple of years later, touring *The Wall*, each had a separate trailer, parked in a circle at the venue, with the doors tellingly facing the outside of the circle.[10]

Alienation inside the Wall

To alienation from those with whom one creates, those for whom one creates, and those whom one loves, Waters adds the ultimate disunity—self-estrangement. "This very heart which is

---

[8] Camus, *The Rebel*, p. 269.

[9] Cliff Jones, *Another Brick in the Wall: The Stories behind Every Pink Floyd Song* (New York: Broadway, 1996), p. 104.

[10] Austin Scaggs, 'Q&A: Roger Waters," *Rolling Stone* (August 11th, 2005), p. 36.

mine will forever remain indefinable to me," writes Camus.[11] In Sartre's terms, we are not "coincident with ourselves." Waters recognized this vividly when he recoiled in horror after spitting at that fan in Canada. Camus captured that experience—"Men also secrete the inhuman" (p. 29). Disunity of the self is a central theme for Camus: "Forever I shall be a stranger to myself" (p. 15). And Waters's sense of horror is not merely the recognition of this disunity, but his action in response to it. In *The Rebel*, Camus says, "We all carry within us our places of exile, our crimes, and our ravages. But our task is not to unleash them on the world; it is to fight them in ourselves and in others."

Each time we are frustrated in attempts to connect, when our desire for unity fails to be realized, the negative feelings become something hard within us, the secretion of the inhuman. The metaphor both Camus and Waters use to characterize these secretions that are in us, yet not ourselves, is the stone. Stones weigh us down, and eventually lead to our unending disunity. In *The Wall*, Pink cries out: "Hey you, would you help me to carry the stone?" For the selfish, cunning dogs (*Animals*) "the bad blood slows and turns to stone." They drown "go down, all alone, Dragged down by the stone."

Camus's most famous allegory of existence is Sisyphus's eternal punishment of pushing a very heavy stone up a mountain; ". . . when the call of happiness becomes too insistent, it happens that melancholy rises in man's heart: this is the rock's victory, this is the rock itself. The boundless grief is too heavy to bear."

The absurd creates stones with which we build walls around ourselves that do not permit contact with others and block out the sun, shut out life, and preclude genuine communication. Each author has his protagonist imprisoned—and the prison walls are made of stone. The would-be architect (both Waters and his aptly named rhythm section partner Nick Mason were in architecture school together) built his symbolic wall with manmade stones—bricks. Each hindrance, each foiling of attempts at communication, produces "Another Brick in the Wall." The different parts of that song all express significant frustration at

---

[11] Albert Camus, "An Absurd Reasoning," pp. 3–48 in *The Myth of Sisyphus and Other Essays*, p. 14.

the absence of unity. The first is about the desire to connect with his father, which was rendered impossible because he had been killed in World War II when Pink was an infant. The second refers to the nasty, thought-controlling education system. Finally the perks of rock stardom, sex and drugs, are recognized as useless defenses against the inexorable brick by brick wall-building.

Walls don't permit contact with others, who are outside ourselves, outside the wall. And, of course, walls separate us from ourselves as well—we become "Brain Damaged," "Comfortably Numb" to any attempts to reach us; we are driven mad. For Pink, "The wall was too high" and so "the worms ate into his brain" ("Hey You"). Walls shut out the sun, symbolizing the absence of unity and vitality.

Would You Help Me to Carry the Stone?

Unlike Waters's dogs or Pink, Camus's Sisyphus is heroic. Rather than being weighed down by the stone, walled in by the bricks of frustrated efforts to achieve unity, he is able to push the stone up the mountain. And when he reaches the top and then must walk down and start all over again, he has the consciousness of absurdity. "But crushing truths perish from being acknowledged," Camus asserts. "One always finds one's burden again. But Sisyphus teaches the higher fidelity that negates the gods and raises rocks." Camus sees Sisyphus as one of his absurd heroes, persevering despite the consciousness of this absurdity. Sisyphus "is superior to his fate. He is stronger than his rock." Despite their contrasting subjective responses to a common vision of existence, Waters converges with Camus in his practice. His choice to be an artist, or at least to continue to create— knowing that he will mainly fail to communicate—is absurd in Camus's sense. Waters wishes for unity, to connect authentically with others through his creations, but does not make that connection. He is like Sisyphus who rolls the stone up the mountain knowing that it will roll down again and that his task will be infinite; yet he is not weighed down by the stone. Each new Waters creation, recording or live show, is an absurd act.

It is telling that Sisyphus does not experience delight in scaling the heights with his burden; rather, he gains relief as he walks down the mountain after his stone has rolled back to the valley. Camus is not a failed idealist who still cherishes the goal of perfection and completeness; he is an absurdist whose heroes are aware that their trials and tribulations are simply their fate, and they acknowledge and affirm that destiny. They have rejected suicide not because they find the goal that they pursue to be worthy, but because they have assented to necessary failure and still want to live that failure over and over again—as Camus insists, it is not the quality of experience that is important, but its sheer quantity.

Neither Camus nor Waters is an optimist or a pessimist. The absurd lies beyond that dualism, which is based on a judgment that world and self should be other than they are. For both of them, there are moments of release and satisfaction within the inevitable cycle of frustration.

At the end Camus concludes: "The struggle itself towards the heights is enough to fill a man's heart. One must imagine Sisyphus happy." I have seen Waters in concert on several occasions. At one, after his performance was so well received by a perceptive and enthusiastic audience, he smiled and I imagine Waters happy too.

9

Theodor Adorno, Pink Floyd, and the Psychedelics of Alienation

EDWARD MACAN

Part I: Interstellar Overdrive

It's hard to think of a major rock band whose output has confronted alienation in modern society as consistently and conscientiously as Pink Floyd. The subject is a red thread running from their first album, *The Piper at the Gates of Dawn* (1967), through their final studio album, *The Division Bell* (1994). Nonetheless, both the band's conception of alienation and their means of addressing it underwent a fundamental shift across the course of their career.

In Floyd's early output—up to and including *Meddle* (1971)—alienation is seen from an existentialist perspective as a metaphysical loneliness that is largely a private, individual experience. Beginning with their mid-period albums *Dark Side of the Moon* (1973) and *Wish You Were Here* (1975), however, this conception of alienation begins to fuse with a more explicitly sociopolitical, even Marxist, vision of alienation. Here, alienation becomes a social phenomenon, resulting from the atomization and commodification of modern society under the constraints of capitalism's political, social, and economic structures. This kind of alienation dominates the two final albums of the band's "classic" lineup, *Animals* (1977) and *The Wall* (1979).[1]

---

[1] For purposes of this investigation, I will not be considering the band's final three studio albums (*The Final Cut*, 1983, *Momentary Lapse of Reason*, 1987, and *The Division Bell*, 1994); not only do I feel they are musically and lyrically inferior to the band's output of 1967–1980, I also believe they were created at

Not only does the band's conception of alienation change across the course of their output; their means of conveying it changes, as well. On their early albums, Pink Floyd evoke alienation primarily through the music itself—specifically, through unfamiliar, even disorienting uses of timbre, texture, and structure. By the time of *Dark Side of the Moon*, their musical syntax has become more conventional, and the increasingly prosaic, unambiguous lyrics of Roger Waters bear an ever-growing burden in conveying the band's (increasingly, Waters's personal) conception of alienation. With *The Wall*, the music becomes thoroughly conventional—at times even stereotypical of contemporary rock forms and conventions—and the lyrics bear nearly the entire burden in the task of addressing and conveying alienation.

Since it was a major goal of the Pink Floyd project between 1967 and 1980 to come to terms with alienation in modern life, it would be useful to have a theoretical or philosophical framework with which to analyze the band's approach to alienation and gauge the relative success of its efforts. I will therefore frame my discussion with two key texts by social theorist and musicologist Theodor Adorno (1903–1969): his short but influential monograph "On Popular Music" and his best known book, *Philosophy of Modern Music*. The first offers a very pessimistic view of popular music's potential for engaging in meaningful cultural critique; the second considers the two major "schools" of composition in Adorno's time—one led by Arnold Schoenberg, the other by Igor Stravinsky—and asks how well they are able to honestly address the contemporary cultural situation.

Adorno's take on Stravinsky is particularly relevant, because psychedelic rock of the late 1960s, such as Pink Floyd's, inadvertently resurrected certain elements of Stravinsky's primitivism; understanding Stravinsky's attitude toward alienation in a

---

a time when Pink Floyd was no longer a "project," a group of individuals committed to a common creative vision, but were simply a vehicle for one member (bassist/vocalist/lyricist Roger Waters on *The Final* Cut, guitarist/vocalist David Gilmour on the next two). It could be argued that even with *The Wall* the band were largely a vehicle for Waters, but the creative friction between Waters and Gilmour on this album gave it a depth and perspective it would have otherwise lacked.

key primitivist work like *Rite of Spring,* his controversial ballet score that caused a riot when it was premiered in 1913, makes it easier to understand the nature of Pink Floyd's achievement in their more ambitious early works. In turn, reference to Adorno will shed light on the band's approach to alienation in their classic albums, and show just how difficult it is for any composer or songwriter to effectively confront alienation without recourse to music that is itself alienating.

It's Alright, We Told You What to Dream

Adorno's dismissal of popular music is well known, but his reasons for this dismissal are not so widely understood. A relatively early monograph from 1941, "On Popular Music," offers a concise, easily grasped distillation of his thoughts.[2] Although Adorno specifically addresses the two types of American popular music that were ubiquitous in the 1930s and 1940s, Broadway songs and Big Band jazz, one could easily extend his observations to much post-1940s American popular music.

The fundamental characteristic of popular music, Adorno argues, is its standardized structure, namely 32-bar popular song form or twelve-bar blues—two schemes that emphasize stock chord progressions, which are unfolded at particular points in the structure. It is true that substitute chords may be used, but because the scheme is so ingrained, listeners will always hear the substitutions and other gestures of individuality—"dirty notes," for instance—in the context of the expected chords. Unlike the best European classical music, where each detail "virtually contains the whole and leads to the exposition of the whole, while, at the same time, it is produced out of the conception of the whole," in American popular music, "the detail has no bearing on a whole, which appears as an extraneous framework."[3]

---

[2] Theodor Adorno (with the assistance of George Simpson), "On Popular Music." Reprinted in *On Record: Rock, Pop, and the Written Word* (New York: Pantheon, 1990), pp, 301–314. Excerpted from *Studies in Philosophy and Social Science* 9 (Frankfurt: Suhrkamp, 1941).

[3] Adorno, "On Popular Music," p. 304. Adorno allows for the fact that in unsuccessful European classical music, the relationship between the whole and its details can be just as fortuitous as he believes it to be in American popular music.

This doesn't mean that the music in question is necessarily simple, for Adorno admits that the harmonies and rhythmic patterns of American popular song and jazz can be rather more complex than those of some European classical music (see p. 305). It does, however, mean that the act of "listening to popular music" involves manipulation by "a system of response mechanisms wholly antagonistic to the ideal of individuality in a free, liberal society."[4]

For Adorno, the problem is not merely aesthetic. It is symptomatic of a larger socio-political problem. Through structural standardization, Adorno argues, "The composition hears for the listener. This is how popular music divests the listener of his spontaneity and promotes conditioned reflexes" (p. 306). Structural standardization leads listeners to regard commercial music as "natural," and anything that deviates from it as "unnatural": since the music industry will not disseminate music that doesn't conform to commercial norms, the listener's horizons will not be expanded. Furthermore, commercial music promises to deliver two things people desire from their leisure time: novelty, and "relaxation which does not involve the effort of concentration at all" (p. 310). Popular music grants them both: the standardized structures reassure, while the individual features—the seemingly individualistic substitute chords, timbral colorings, and so forth, that appear to be the hallmark of a particular musician, singer, or band (but which Adorno would actually call 'pseudo-individual')—offer the promise of novelty.

But the promise is never kept. "To escape boredom and avoid effort are incompatible," Adorno points out. Because popular music's offerings are "ever identical," novelty disappears and the listener becomes bored again. "It is a circle which makes escape impossible" (pp. 310, 311). The result is a relationship between industry and consumer that is something like a vicious circle: consumers like what they know and the industry knows what they like, and delivers it without fail. "The people clamor for what they are going to get anyhow" (p. 310). Or, as Roger Waters put it in his own critique of the music industry, some thirty-four

---

[4] Adorno, "On Popular Music," pp. 302, 303, 305.

years after the publication of Adorno's article, "What did you dream? It's alright, we told you what to dream . . ."[5]

Can the Machine Be Fixed?

For Adorno, the only music up to the task of confronting and critiquing the dysfunction of contemporary society was contemporary classical music. As he made clear in his book *Philosophy of Modern Music* (1948), he believed that a musical style can only exert its full expressive and communicative power in its own time. "Nothing in art is successfully binding except that which can be totally filled by the historical state of consciousness which determines its own substance."[6] A conscientious composer does not have the option of continuing to compose in the manner of an earlier style, for a listener will hear the composer's music in the context of contemporary developments and it will sound false. For this reason, Adorno relentlessly assailed composers such as Jean Sibelius, who continued to write tonal music after the musical revolutions of the World War I era, and believed only two currents of music were capable of addressing the circumstances of the modern world: those represented by Arnold Schoenberg (1874–1951) and his followers, and Igor Stravinsky (1882–1971) and his followers.

Arnold Schoenberg had a Strraaaange . . . Method

Schoenberg, like Adorno, held an evolutionary, virtually Darwinian view of stylistic development, believing that stylistic change is inevitable and that simple music must inexorably become more complex. Specifically, Schoenberg believed that the introduction of chromatic harmony by Franz Liszt, Richard Wagner, and other major composers of the mid-nineteenth century presented a historical imperative: thereafter, it was the des-

---

[5] Roger Waters's famous lyric from "Welcome to the Machine," on the *Wish You Were Here* album.

[6] Theodor Adorno, *Philosophy of Modern Music* (New York: Continuum, 2004), p. 213.

tiny of music to become more and more chromatic, for chord progressions to become increasingly less anchored to a home key, and ultimately, for any sense of home key to disappear entirely. By 1908, Schoenberg had begun to compose atonal music, that is, music in which no sense of home key is easily discernible. However, even this music could at times momentarily suggest a key center, so it was not until the early 1920s, when Schoenberg pioneered the so-called twelve-tone technique, that he felt he had brought the "chromatic revolution" initiated by Wagner, Liszt, and others nearly seventy years before to its logical culmination.

In Schoenberg's twelve-tone music, the composer follows very rigid guidelines. He or she must establish and repeat a sequence of twelve tones. While this sequence of notes may be transposed (begun on different pitches), inverted (the direction of its melodic motion reversed), presented backwards (so-called retrograde motion), or given in retrograde inversion (the direction of melodic motion of the retrograde version being reversed), it may never be abandoned.

Few will argue that twelve tone music makes for easy or pleasant listening. Adorno admits that this music "enchains music by liberating it,"[7] that it's "infinitely static," (p. 65) seeming to go nowhere, and relies on crudely obvious contrasts of register, dynamics, and timbre to make any expressive impact. Nonetheless, Adorno defends twelve-tone music as the most truly modern form of music, inasmuch as it honestly reflects modern cultural conditions. The counterpoint of twelve-tone music itself models social alienation, since the simultaneous melodic lines, rather than blending, are "totally alien to each other and, in their accordance, actually hostile to each other" (p. 94). That, however, is exactly how this contemporary music achieves its critical bite—"it points out the ills of society, rather than sublimating those ills into a deceptive humanitarianism which would pretend that humanitarianism had already been achieved in the present. This music is no longer an ideology."[8] Twelve-tone music confronts con-

---

[7] Adorno, *Philosophy*, p. 68.
[8] Adorno, *Philosophy*, p. 131. Presumably it is no longer an ideology because it is no longer propaganda.

temporary alienation by musically modeling it and flinging it at the listener.

An Echo of a Distant Time: Stravinsky's Primitivism

If Schoenberg's answer to the problem of contemporary alienation is to mirror it in his music, Stravinsky's is to use music to model a primeval, pre-alienated state. In Stravinsky's music, short themes, often consisting of just a few pitches (Cocteau called them "little melodies out of the roots of centuries"[9]) are tied to specific rhythm patterns. These are repeated at a steady, unyielding tempo in a manner that anticipates both jazz and rock: accents kaleidoscopically shift to different parts of the patterns (which are often minutely but perpetually varied), generating considerable energy. Stravinsky often presents two or more short melodic-rhythmic patterns simultaneously, creating a dissonant chord that is sounded until a new network of rhythmic patterns suddenly appears, sounding a new chord. With this emphasis on rhythm, Stravinsky's music of 1911 through the early 1920s earned the label of "primitivism." His admirers believed, as Adorno described it, that in his music "he has excavated the buried origins of music; as, for example, the events of *The Rite of Spring* might well evoke the simultaneously complex and, at the same time, strictly disciplined rhythms of primitive rites" (p. 154).

For Adorno, "primitivism" describes not only the sound of Stravinsky's music, but its goal: these works, Adorno wrote, "imitate the gesture of regression, as it belongs to the dissolution of individual identity. Through this attitude, these works would appear to achieve collective authenticity." By dissolving individual identity through hypnotically-repetitive rhythms and slowly-shifting harmonies, Adorno took this music to present "an inner stage which . . . is the scene of pre-individual experiences which are common to all" (p. 162). But Adorno denied that any such return to a pre-alienated mode of experience was available through music or other art forms. "The belief that the archaic simply lies at the aesthetic disposal of the ego—in order

---

[9] Jean Cocteau quoted by Adorno in *Philosophy*, p. 150.

that the ego might regenerate itself through it—is superficial," he wrote. This is because history "has crystallized the firm contours of the ego" in ways that prevent listeners from truly taking leave of their ordinary modes of consciousness (p. 168). Pink Floyd might set up their equipment and play in the middle of an ancient Roman amphitheatre, for instance (as they did in the film *Pink Floyd Live at Pompeii*) but, Adorno would insist, no musical experience could possibly allow a modern listener to experience the world as it was experienced by the ancients.

Still, Adorno admitted one pathway by which the modern individual might regress to the primitive, collective identity—mental illness. In Stravinsky, Adorno sees an evocation of mental illness in the obsessive repetition of short rhythmic patterns with ever-shifting accents. It reminded him of a parallel "process observable in certain schizophrenics by which the motor apparatus becomes independent, leading to the infinite repletion of gestures or words, following the decay of the ego. Similar behavior is familiar in patients who have been overwhelmed by shock" (p. 178). Whether or not it is coincidence that Pink Floyd managed to inadvertently resurrect key aspects of Stravinsky's primitivist approach at the same time that it was led by Syd Barrett—the "crazy diamond" himself—is a question that may forever remain obscure and unanswered. But there is no doubt about another potential route to "the desired primeval world"[10] that was not widely recognized when Adorno wrote *Philosophy of Modern Music*: hallucinogenic drugs. Syd Barrett certainly knew a thing or two about hallucinogenic drugs. Indeed, in Barrett's case, the boundary between the psychedelic experience on the one hand, and mental illness on the other, eventually became blurred. It is perhaps not surprising, then, that the goals of Stravinsky's primitivist music, and even some of its techniques, converge with Pink Floyd's psychedelic rock of the late 1960s.

The LSD Factor

Tonite Let's All Make Love in London is a documentary film from 1967 featuring a classic performance by Pink Floyd of "Interstellar Overdrive." It was filmed at the UFO Club, one of

---

[10] To quote Adorno, *Philosophy*, p. 146.

swinging London's original hipster clubs where Pink Floyd, Soft Machine and other bands first honed their performances. Not only is the dancing and general mayhem captured in this film evidence that London's pop music fans had discovered (and embraced) LSD; the camera itself (and, obviously, the cameraman) seem to float and twist around the hall as it moves through an orgy of light and sound.

Michael Hicks has identified three fundamental effects of the LSD experience, namely *dechronization* (the breaking down of conventional perceptions of time), *depersonalization* (the breaking down of the ego's ordinary barriers and resulting awareness of undifferentiated unity), and *dynamization* (whereby static physical forms appear to dissolve into molten, dripping objects).[11]

According to Hicks, various elements of psychedelic rock music are shaped by one or more of these factors. *Dechronization* results in songs being lengthened and their tempos being slowed down, with open-ended forms becoming the rule; the quasi-hypnotic repetition of an ostinato (a short melodic pattern) by the bass guitarist, over which the guitarist or keyboard player weaves long, non-directional solos, contribute to a sense of stasis. *Depersonalization* affects both dynamics and texture: extremely loud amplification in live settings results in a diminishing of individual consciousness, as listeners feel the music as much as hear it (the "space cadet glow," as Roger Waters put it in *The Wall*). Among the band itself, the distinction between lead and accompaniment players is dissolved, resulting in a kind of democratic counterpoint that is denser and more complex than the texture of any earlier rock music.

Dynamization leads to a number of techniques that are especially closely associated with psychedelic rock—the use of artificial reverberation, echo units, and stereo panning to suggests enormous interior spaces, unusual, "sliding" or "floating" chord progressions, and the use of wah-wah pedals, feedback, and pitch-bending to dynamize and render "molten" otherwise

---

[11] Michael Hicks, *Sixties Rock: Garage, Psychedelic, and Other Satisfactions* (Urbana: University of Illinois Press, 1999), Chapter 5, "Getting Psyched," pp. 58–74.

stable timbres. In the most characteristic structural approach of psychedelic rock, dechronization and dynamization converge in the multi-movement "song" in which the meter, tempo, texture, instrumentation, and sometimes key of each section or movement contrasts with that of the others. As Hicks points out, eventually a band could "psychedelicize" a song at the macro level by simply juxtaposing disparate sonic blocks (p. 66). As we'll see, nearly all of these approaches are evident in the music of early Pink Floyd, and many continue to linger long after 1970, by which time they were no longer, strictly speaking, a psychedelic rock band.

Set the Controls for Maximum Creativity

In March 1967, the original lineup of Pink Floyd—guitarist-vocalist-songwriter Roger "Syd" Barrett, keyboardist Richard Wright, bassist Roger Waters, and drummer Nick Mason—recorded the nine-and-a half minute instrumental track, "Interstellar Overdrive." By the standards of the rock music of its time, the track was revolutionary. With the possible exception of "Saucerful of Secrets" (recorded a year later), it remains the band's most radical and utterly original musical statement. While its title and outside ambience tagged the band with the "space rock" moniker they bore for years, I will argue that the track's structural trajectory was its most important legacy to the band's future.

The structural outline of "Interstellar Overdrive" is simple enough: it consists of three sections, which we can represent as A-B-A. The A section opens with a chugging guitar and bass drone that soon gives way to the main "theme," Barrett's memorable E major guitar riff that descends chromatically from a B major to the tonic E major chord.[12] Although Barrett's trebly timbre and ringing power chords evoke Pete Townshend and the mid-sixties "Freakbeat" sound more generally, the asymmetrical six-bar construction of the riff, replacing the more usual four-bar

---

[12] This riff is similar to his main riff in "Astronomy Dominé," the other "space rock" blockbuster of Floyd's debut album, in which major triads descend chromatically a perfect fifth from A major to D major. I suspect that one of the main themes of Gustav Holst's "Mars, the Bringer of War," which involves chromatically ascending and descending major triads, may have been an unconscious influence; it certainly ties into the "outer space" imagery of Barrett's two songs.

length, adds some irregularity that hints of things to come. The riff is repeated four times.

The long B section begins at 0:52. During the first part of the B section (0:52 to 2:16), the drum's 4/4 rock backbeat and the bass guitar's throbbing ostinato patterns provide the rhythmic center of gravity that supports a kaleidoscopic web of fragmentary keyboard themes, ringing guitar power chords, and atomized lead guitar lines. As unusual as this passage was by the standards of its day, it is positively ordinary compared to what comes next. At 2:17, the drums drop out entirely and the center of rhythmic gravity shifts to bass: while the tempo remains constant, the meter shifts from 4/4 to 6/8 as a result of Waters's insistently repeated dotted half note G# that he plays behind the bridge of his Rickenbacker bass. This high, piercing single-note ostinato (one could easily imagine Adorno saying it models insanity) is accompanied by somber sustained organ chords and pointillist bursts of guitar notes. The drums seem to magically reappear out of a pulsating organ chord at 3:34, at first reinforcing the prevailing 6/8 meter, but at 4:01 Mason shifts back to 4/4 in response to Waters's fragmentary bass ostinato patterns. Over the next two minutes, the center of rhythmic gravity shifts unpredictably between the bass and drums parts, with slowly drifting organ chords, fragmentary guitar and organ lead lines, and eerie guitar glissandi swirling higher in the mix.[13]

It is at 6:15 that the track goes deepest into interstellar space. The drums again drop out, and the sense of pulse threatens to dissolve entirely into a maelstrom of pulsating organ chords and shimmering cymbal splashes. At 6:48, Waters's bass line makes a brief, cryptic reference to the chromatically-descending opening guitar riff; from this point on, the sense of pulse is slowly reestablished and, almost in the manner of waking up from a dream, elements of the opening guitar riff appear with increasing clarity. Barrett enters at 7:12 with a chromatically-descending arpeggio that makes a particularly obvious reference to his opening riff; the B section ends with a furious snare drum roll that returns us to the chugging drone that opened the track.

---

[13] A glissando is a gradual ascent or descent from one pitch to another through the entire pitch continuum, as for example is produced by a siren; on guitar, a glissando is produced by the use of a slide device on the strings.

Now, however, the main riff pans dizzyingly between right and left channels, after which Mason finally brings the interstellar space trip back to earth with a muttering bongo drum soliloquy.

Although the lengthy middle section of "Interstellar Overdrive" may not be immediately reminiscent of Stravinsky's *Rite of Spring*, the technical features of the two are surprisingly similar. Both consist of discrete sectional "blocks" defined by short melodic-rhythmic ostinati that are overlaid with a dense layer of flickering, unstable themes and fragmentary chord progressions; one "block" suddenly shifts to another that may be quite different in terms of meter, tone color, and texture.

Is the goal of Pink Floyd in "Interstellar Overdrive"—of psychedelic rock in general—similar to Stravinsky's primitivist regression to a time before, or place beyond, the corrosive effects of modern alienation? It would seem the answer is "yes." If anything, the structural dynamic of "Interstellar Overdrive" suggests the dissolution of the ego and its ultimate re-emergence and reintegration *more* definitely than Stravinsky, who in his primitivist phase tended to dislike the obvious recapitulation of important themes. "Interstellar Overdrive" begins with a clearly-sketched theme—representative of the ego, perhaps. The musical fabric is then subjected to varying levels of dissolution, until it reaches a "furthest out" point where it dissolves entirely— here, at 6:15, when the sense of pulse essentially disappears. Is this the final dissolution of the individual into the collective? And finally, the recap of the opening section—does this signal the reemergence of the ego, now deeper and wiser after its journey? The structural trajectory of "Interstellar Overdrive" depicts the hallucinogenic experience, the plunge into the depths of inner space, as both an alienating experience—purely individual, lonely, and often frightening—and as an antidote to alienation, since the moment of dissolution signals escape from the limits of the ego into the great collective, as depicted in *Tonite Let's All Make Love in London*. Paradoxically, the musical structure of "Interstellar Overdrive" both models alienation, and suggests an antidote to it.

Part II: From Axes to Echoes

Much has been made of the stylistic shift that took place in Pink Floyd's music when Syd Barrett was replaced by David Gilmour during the recording of their second album, *Saucerful of Secrets*, in 1968. Certainly there was a shift in sensibility after Barrett's departure; nevertheless, I don't think enough emphasis has been given to the essential continuity of approach between the more ambitious pieces of Barrett-era Floyd and post-Barrett Floyd. This is especially true in the realm of musical structure: the general structural process of "Interstellar Overdrive" (and the other "space rock" blockbuster from the debut album, "Astronomy Dominé") can be detected in the major works of Pink Floyd's post-Barrett psychedelic period. Some aspects of it linger well into the 1970s.

The term "structural process" is key to understanding this continuity. Until *Dark Side of the Moon*, few (if any) of the band's most ambitious and characteristic tracks use anything approaching a standard song form: to apply Adorno's standard, the details of each of these works contribute to the creation of a unique structural outline, and, conversely, the structural plan of each of these works is a reflection of their unique musical content. Nonetheless, a general structural process can be discerned across the band's most characteristic works of 1968–72. I will describe it here, and then briefly examine three of their finest works of this period—"Careful with that Axe, Eugene," "Set the Controls for the Heart of the Sun," and "Echoes"—to demonstrate how the general contours of the process unfold in specific contexts.

First, there's an instrumental introduction of a meditative or mystical nature. Always unusual, often somewhat forbidding, the purpose of the introduction is not just to set a mood (although it does), but to draw the listener out of the realm of ordinary experience. Next is the song proper, or, at least, the principal melody, since conventional song form is not always in evidence. This is followed by a lengthy instrumental section, which reaches a climax, after which the "song" is recapitulated more or less (at times decidedly less) literally. This was the general outline of "Interstellar Overdrive," which lacked only the fully-developed introductory section.

One important aspect of this four-part process is its commitment to organicism, meaning all the events of a song flow logically from the implications of its opening material. This commitment, shared by Pink Floyd's British progressive rock peers, is quite different from what one encounters in contemporaneous experimental American bands like the Mothers of Invention who insert glaringly "out of place" passages to generate satire and ironic displacement in their music. Judit Frigyesi has observed that, in reference to Stravinsky's contemporary Béla Bartók, organicism represents "the idealistic demand for coherence into the personality of the world."[14] That is, there is a utopian impulse behind organicism's demand for unity across diversity, its faith in an essential unity beneath apparently random surface events. Nonetheless, during the lengthy instrumental section, the third part of this four-part structural process, the band commit a breach of organicism by including a "breakthrough" passage, either shortly before, during, or shortly after the climax itself—a passage with "unmusical" content that is not obviously inherent in the song's basic musical material. Ordinarily, in British progressive rock the climax is a triumphant moment; but in Pink Floyd's structures, the climactic section often takes on a double-edged meaning. By introducing an "unmusical" and disruptive element where the listener expects affirmation, the band musically evoke alienation, and not until this "alienating" passage has played out can the process of reintegration, accomplished by recalling the main melody, be launched.

Careful with that Axe, Eugene

In November 1968, the band recorded a B-side for their upcoming single release, "Point Me at the Sky." Based on a short one-chord instrumental called "Murderistic Woman" the band had recorded for a BBC session the previous June, they rechristened their newly-recorded, more fully-developed creation "Careful with that Axe, Eugene." By the standards of its era the studio version of "Eugene" was already a highly unusual piece of work, but over the next several months they developed and elaborated it further in live performance. By April 1969, when they recorded the live version of the piece that would feature prominently on their upcoming *Ummagumma* album, they had crafted a masterpiece of instrumental rock expressionism.

---

[14] Judit Frigyesi, *Béla Bartók and Turn-of-the-Century Hungary* (Berkeley: University of California Press, 1998), p. 44.

Compared to the live version which I will be discussing below, the studio version is, as Nick Mason has remarked, "extremely mild, jig-along stuff."

"Eugene" falls into four distinct sections. The track opens with string orchestra-like Rick Wright organ chords, accompanied by Roger Waters's slowly treading quarter note bass drone in alternating octaves and Nick Mason's unobtrusive but highly effective swing-based ride cymbal groove. Barely rising above *pianissimo*, the introduction sets a mood at once mysterious and melancholy. At 0:44 Mason commences a soft rock backbeat while continuing the ride cymbal patterns, and the track opens into the second section, the song proper—perhaps "song" would be more accurate, as there is no ordinary vocal tune. The main melody is played by Wright on a Farfisa organ setting that suggests a Middle Eastern flute; Wright slowly unfolds the melody with phrases of different length—four bars, six bars, four, two, etc.—that weaken the sense of passing time. Just before 1:30, David Gilmour commences a similarly free falsetto vocalese (i.e., a wordless vocal melody) that intertwines with Wright's organ melody to create a shadowy counterpoint.[15] As Waters' bass line nearly dematerializes, Gilmour's vocalese seems to float in a mysterious dimension beyond time. At 2:33, however, Waters returns to the even quarter notes that opened the track and, just before he whispers "Careful with that Axe, Eugene," the band commences an ominous crescendo.

The climactic third section is heralded by Waters's blood-curdling screams—the "breakthrough" passage where the band abandons the established pitch and timbral parameters to create a sense of maximum alienation. Waters's screams are hugely effective in evoking stark terror; they continue to make a highly unsettling impact on many first time listeners nearly forty years later. Shortly after the first scream—at 3:14, to be exact—David Gilmour (whose guitar up to this point has contributed mainly spacey glissandos and flecks of reverberating

---

[15] As John Cotner notes, "The experienced listener might potentially hear these formulas as indirect references to medieval modal practices, and, at a residual symbolic level of meaning, suggestive of something ancient, sacred, or mystical." See Cotner, "Pink Floyd's 'Careful with that Axe, Eugene': Toward a Theory of Textural Rhythm in Early Progressive Rock," in Kevin Holm-Hudson, ed., *Progressive Rock Reconsidered* (New York: Routledge, 2002), p. 72.

chords that occupy the dark recesses of the track's texture) commences a blistering guitar solo that brings "Eugene" to its climax. There's a somewhat fractured aspect to Gilmour's solo—like many guitarists of the psychedelic rock era, Gilmour constructs his solo by linking one short idea to another to form a kaleidoscopically-shifting "chain" of short melodic figures. Nonetheless, his solo unfolds in symmetrical phrases, and reestablishes (with the help of Mason's heavy back beat) the presence of passing time.

By 6:43 the energy of Gilmour's solo has finally dissipated into sporadic reverberating chords. Wright inaugurates the track's fourth and final section by making a clear (albeit not exact) reference to his main melody that had opened the track's second section, and Gilmour soon resumes his vocalese from the second section as well. At 7:56, Gilmour's "brighter than major" Lydian guitar arpeggios give this extraordinarily shadowy track a momentarily luminous quality; soon afterwards the music dissipates, seemingly into the shadows out of which it appeared. What is perhaps most significant about this fourth section is that music that had sounded shadowy, mysterious, even vaguely sinister upon its first appearance now sounds almost peaceful (albeit still supremely lonely) in the context of the harrowing journey the track has taken. I don't want to press the drug analogy I used when discussing "Interstellar Overdrive" too hard: none of the other members shared Syd Barrett's enthusiasm for LSD, and no one would argue that Barrett successfully integrated his LSD experiences with his ordinary consciousness. On the other hand, it's not hard to hear the track as a musical psychobiography, a depiction of the ego shattering under enormous pressure, but ultimately reintegrating.

Set the Controls for the Heart of the Sun

In August 1967 the band recorded a new Roger Waters composition, "Set the Controls for the Heart of the Sun," which appeared on the band's second album, *Saucerful of Secrets*. Like "Eugene," the track continued to develop and expand in the band's live performances, and most Floyd fans judge the definitive version of the song to be the live version (again recorded in April 1969) from *Ummagumma*. This is the version I will discuss below.

Although the expressive character of "Set the Controls" is in some ways quite different from "Eugene," the two tracks have important similarities as well—above all, adherence to the same four-part structural process. "Set the Controls" begins with a long cymbal roll crescendo, out of which emerges the elemental bass riff based around just five notes and three pitches—E F E D E—that is to define the entire song. From 0:29, the two-bar bass riff is repeated six times, accompanied in unison by Wright with the Farfisa's "Middle Eastern" organ setting, and by Mason's "tribal" two-bar timpani pattern.

The song proper begins with a twenty-four-bar verse, repeated twice. The arrangement of the song is, to say the least, highly unusual. Waters's vocal melody simply doubles his bass line, which continues to be based around the opening E F E D E pattern. Wright doubles Waters's vocal on organ, playing the same basic melody but providing ornaments (mordants and other quick melodic turns) that are more idiomatic to keyboard than to voice or bass. Mason, for his part, continues his "tribal" timpani accompaniment. The overall effect is oracular, ritualistic, and austere, the austerity resulting both from the elemental, archaic nature of the melody, and from the empty registral spaces between the three simultaneous statements of the melody. The vague yet tantalizingly evocative lyrics are drawn from an unspecified ancient Chinese poem, except for "set the controls for the heart of the sun" itself, which comes from Michael Moorcock's sci-fi novel *Fireclown* (not, as has generally and mistakenly been believed, from William S. Burroughs).

The instrumental third section, which includes the climax and the "breakthrough" passage, begins at 2:31 with Rick Wright soloing with a particularly searing variant of the "Middle Eastern" Farfisa setting. As in "Eugene," Wright's solo here spills out in non-symmetrical phrases of irregular length, confusing the sense of ordinary time passage. Gilmour finally makes his presence felt with some ringing power chords based around the bass riff, and as he launches into strident ascending glissandi (3:43), Wright's melodic line becomes increasingly atonal, until he too abandons any sense of definite pitch content in favor of sliding clusters of notes. A final set of ascending glissandi over Mason's urgent "tribal" rhythm evokes a huge rocket's blastoff, bringing the song to an enormous climax at 4:47.

Unlike "Eugene," the climax and "breakthrough" passage of "Set the Controls" are not one and the same. The "rocket liftoff" climax blasts the music into oblivion, and the song begins to reassemble itself as Waters plays a trebly restatement of the main riff. The guitar and organ return, but their parts dissolve into a series of buzzes, wooshes, and Morse-code like signals that, for the Apollo 11 generation (and the *2001: A Space Odyssey* generation), would have evoked a lonely trip through the depths of outer space. *This* is the breakthrough passage, the moment of maximum alienation, the moment when the song's basic pitch and rhythm content dissolve into pulsating ribbons of sound.[16]

After the climactic "rocket blastoff," the song was obliged to re-establish its sense of definite pitch: now, after its "cosmic breakthrough," it is obliged to reestablish a sense of rhythmic pulse, as well. Waters begins the reassembly with a new one-bar bass riff based around the dominant note, B, that is followed soon by a tabla-like drum part played by Mason with his hands on the toms, and finally, Wright's "snake charmer" organ. Against Gilmour's cosmic wooshes (guitar slides), the fourth and final section is heralded by Waters's recap of the main riff at 7:37, followed by a third and final vocal verse. Afterwards, Wright weaves a closing organ solo over the bass riff and "tabla" pattern, and the song fades into nothingness. As with the recapitulation sections of "Interstellar Overdrive" and "Eugene," the recapitulation raises the issue of reintegration: specifically, the return of Waters's oracular vocal line after the deep space "melt down" that marks the end of the third section seems to illustrate Walter Benjamin's quip about James Joyce attempting to construct "the primitive history of the modern."[17] In "Set the Controls," as in so much of Stravinsky's primitivist music, the archaic and the modern inextricably intertwine, as the music seems to seek a psychic integration of the two.

---

[16] The "breakthrough" passage of "Set the Controls" happens at the precise golden mean of the piece's structure (61% of the way through); that of "Interstellar Overdrive," just past it (65% of the way through). Béla Bartók, who was, like Stravinsky, deeply invested in the primitivist movement, often used golden mean ratios to structure his compositions, believing these ratios could be identified in the structure of folk melodies from around the world, and of many living organisms.

[17] Walter Benjamin quoted by Adorno, *Philosophy*, p. 183.

Echoes

Pink Floyd's release of *Atom Heart Mother* in 1970 marked a new stage of their development. It is their first post-psychedelic album; the side-long title suite, co-composed by the band and Ron Geesin, features a full orchestra and choir. It also finds the band expanding and elaborating the quasi-independent sections into full-blown movements which seamlessly segue one into another, with the main theme (reminiscent of a Western movie theme) being recalled at key junctures. While some of the thematic material is of dubious quality, the lavish scoring often makes it sound better than it deserves, and the structural flow from one movement to the next is well conceived. It would probably go too far to call "Atom Heart Mother" an impressive achievement: indeed, the band consider it one of their least successful efforts. (Roger Waters has said he wouldn't mind if the suite were "thrown in the dustbin and never listened to by anyone ever again."[18]) Nevertheless, it provided an important blueprint for the band's future progress: it's almost impossible to imagine "Echoes" or the trilogy of mid-1970s concept albums that defined Pink Floyd's place in rock history without the example of this suite. And while the bland semi-acoustic ballads of the second side are not terribly memorable, either, they likewise provide the band with a model capable of further development and elaboration.

One might justifiably see the band's next release, *Meddle* (1971) as a more successful reworking of the main concerns of *Atom Heart Mother*. In particular, it's "Echoes," the side-long suite that occupies the second half of *Meddle*, which marks the biggest step forward for the band as they return to the multi-movement approach of "Atom Heart Mother," but now with far more substantive and personal material. On a purely musical level, "Echoes" is arguably Pink Floyd's masterpiece, magisterially bringing together their folk-like songwriting manner with atmospheric instrumental soundscapes, jazz-funk jamming, and frankly experimental passages. It's also an important transitional work, the last major statement of Pink Floyd as a band operating outside the popular music mainstream, yet simultaneously pointing forward to *Dark Side of the Moon*.

---

[18] Roger Waters quoted in Nicholas Schaffner, *Saucerful of Secrets: The Pink Floyd Odyssey* (New York: Harmony, 1991), p. 154.

"Echoes" is *leisurely*—there is a patient, unhurried pace to the track's unfolding that even for this band is rather unusual. This piece's instrumental introduction begins with Rick Wright striking the note b3 on a piano, the signal being run through a Binson echo unit to produce a sound not unlike a drop of water splashing into a pool in a cave, reverberating and echoing. The note is sporadically repeated, and eventually begins to be juxtaposed with a C# (similarly treated) in the bass register of the piano. The tonality is hazy for a moment, and only after about thirty seconds do we begin to unambiguously hear C# as the tonic, and B as its seventh; a tonic-dominant organ drone, and sparse, reverberating piano figuration that fills in the gap between C# and B with the notes of a C# minor pentatonic scale, clinches C# minor as home key. A little over a minute in, accompanied by extremely understated rhythm section backing, David Gilmour enters with a slow, mournful electric guitar lead. As with the other pieces discussed above, this introductory section creates an air of mystery, but the mood is quite different from the shadowy, somewhat forbidding openings of "Eugene" or "Set the Controls"; there's a new sense of warmth, an almost womb-like ambience, and a sense of steadily growing luminosity as the introduction unfolds.[19]

The song proper begins with Gilmour and Wright singing the airy vocal harmonies that were forever after linked to Pink Floyd, no matter who was singing. There is a real song here, with a twelve-bar verse followed by an eight-bar instrumental refrain. The style is reminiscent of the acoustic ballads they had been perfecting on both *Atom Heart Mother* and side one of *Meddle*, but the smoothly contoured vocal lines are their most memorable yet, and the warm orchestration (sustained organ chords, echo-treated piano filigrees, liquid electric guitar obbligato, languid 4/4 rhythm section accompaniment) ties the song securely to its introduction.

Roger Waters's lyrics to "Echoes" have unfortunately been tagged as a mere "seascape." This totally misses their point. The first verse opens with a vision of the ocean as the womb of all life, and renders a word painting of an archaic creature, in an

---

[19] This sense of luminosity and warmth results in part from the latter half of the introduction's recurring chord progression swinging the music into C# major.

unimaginably distant past, groping its way out of the ocean onto land. The lyric thus shows similarities to the creation mythos of Yes's "Revealing Science of God" and Emerson, Lake and Palmer's "Great Gate of Kiev." But for Waters the main point is the *loneliness* of this first attempt to ascend toward the light. Alienation here appears as a metaphysical, individual experience that is far older than humankind itself. The second verse suddenly snaps us into the present, with its word painting of two strangers momentarily locking eyes on a busy street and seeing themselves in the other person; here Waters beautifully expresses a monist vision of universal interconnectedness that instantly ties together alienation as a metaphysical and individual condition on the one hand and a social, communal phenomenon on the other. Just as "Echoes" marks the point of convergence between Floyd's past and future musical directions, it marks the point of convergence between their earlier and later conceptions of alienation.

The third part of the four-part process—the instrumental breakthrough and climax—takes in three distinct sections. First is a lengthy jazz-funk jam over a C# Dorian chord pattern, with Gilmour's lyrical, circular guitar lead defined by a much bigger, more searing timbre than anything he had ever recorded before; Wright comps on Hammond organ, occasionally supplying spare countermelodies, as Waters and Mason accompany. At about 10:35, the sound of howling wind begins to emerge in the sonic background, and grows until it has quite overwhelmed any other sound. This is the breakthrough section, where the piece's pitch/rhythm parameters are transcended, and it evokes a pantheistic vision of enormously powerful natural forces of which human life is but a tiny part, with its evocations of howling wind, synthesized whale cries, and plaintively screaming seagulls (Gilmour's wah-wah guitar run backwards).

Near the fifteen-minute mark, a drone note B furtively emerges, then begins to steadily grow in presence, even as the "wind" and other "natural" sounds begin to slowly fade, and soon the piece's opening piano b3 is recalled: out of the newly established B minor harmony emerges a descending bass line (B-F#-D-E, at 15:32), which soon is joined by a pulsing sextuplet drone played by guitar and bass (run through the Binson echo unit), that gives the piece a new sense of rhythmic energy. The track continues to build, until finally, at 18:14, Gilmour launches into a dramatic electric guitar fanfare that brings "Echoes" to its radiant climax. Thereafter, the bass line and its accompanying chords are transposed up a step to the "correct" key, C# minor, allowing for a recapitulation of the song in its original key. Unlike the other tracks discussed here, in "Echoes" there is a jockeying for supremacy between two pitch centers, B and C#, that takes on both structural and dramatic significance; "Echoes" is often called Pink Floyd's prog rock masterpiece, and certainly it is a relatively rare example of the band using tonality in a dialectical sense, like their prog rock peers Emerson, Lake and Palmer and Yes who were more explicitly inspired by European classical music.

The song returns at 19:12, adding to the earlier sun imagery and monist vision of interconnectedness a plea for mutual recognition that is at once metaphysical and social, individual and communal—"And so I throw the windows wide and call to you across the sky." Appropriately, the instrumental coda consists of a call-and-response between Gilmour's liquid guitar leads and Wright's reverberating, melancholy piano. Both are finally consumed by the "howling wind" that emerges again to take over the sonic soundscape, before retreating into the silence from whence it came.

The Eclipse of Musical Alienation

The rest, as they say, is history. On *Dark Side of the Moon,* the band transformed the multi-movement suite structure of "Atom Heart Mother" and "Echoes" into a cycle of interconnected songs, tied together with instrumental interludes and imaginative collages of sound effects and spoken dialogue that continue to transfix audiences around the world. Roger Waters's lyrics continue to explore alienation from both individual and social, metaphysical and socio-political perspectives. The famous final line of the album's closing song, "Eclipse" ("everything under the sun is in tune/but the sun is eclipsed by the moon") not only ties together the album's sun and moon symbology, but continues to pursue the humanist monism of "Echoes."

The historic success of *Dark Side* is due both to Waters's great lyrics and the band's now refined ability to cover the structural skeleton of their acoustic ballads with a sleek, futuristic sonic surface drawn from their psychedelic-era space rock epics.

But both factors began to change as the band ascended to mega-stardom in the mid 1970s.

On the one hand, Waters soon and forever abandoned that monism as his lyrics became increasingly pessimistic, cynical, and preoccupied with a peculiarly misanthropic socio-political alienation. On the other hand, as good as the music often was—not only on *Dark Side*, but on *Wish You Were Here*, *Animals*, and *The Wall*—it never again had the power of unfamiliarity that characterized the early Floyd classics. To put it another way, while one might argue that a track like "On the Run" played the same "breakthrough" function on *Dark Side* as the analogous sections of "Eugene" and "Set the Controls," it's unlikely that most listeners found it particularly disturbing or difficult, even if they did find it somewhat unusual. Early Pink Floyd fans did not conform to Adorno's stereotypical popular music listener who listens for reassurance and relaxation. They instead sought stimulation and challenge in the new and novel. Which is a good thing: it took genuine commitment to truly absorb and comprehend such music as "Interstellar Overdrive," "Careful with that Axe, Eugene," "Set the Controls for the Heart of the Sun," and "Echoes."

After *Dark Side*, listening to Pink Floyd did not take quite the same level of commitment, since the songs tend to follow standard song forms more closely—and, to quote Adorno again, "the composition hears for the listener." Even the surface novelties—the unusual electronic timbres, the unexpected juxtapositions in the sound collages—tend toward a generally smooth, sleek sonic sheen that can be appreciated or ignored with equal ease. Granted, there are a few exceptions—the suite-like structure of "Shine on You, Crazy Diamond" shows a continuing engagement with earlier, more adventurous structural approaches—but these are offset by the largely conventional musical syntax and smooth, unobtrusive sonic surfaces. And although the classic lineup's final two albums, *Animals* and *The Wall*, feature the band's most abrasive sonic surfaces since *Ummagumma*, they are much more conventional by the standards of their day.

Indeed, Roger Waters often seemed to *want* the music to function as a neutral canvas upon which he could sketch his lyrics and realize his conceptual ambitions—that is, he wanted the music to support his literary message, without vying with it for attention.[20] But here we encounter a paradox and, for a musician like Waters who aspires to social criticism, a problem. As Adorno would have probably advised him, at the point at which the composition is *hearing for the listener*, the listener is probably not paying much attention to the lyrics that are intended to challenge or stimulate, either. The point is not that listeners may not know the words; it's that even if they do, they may well not be inclined to puzzle through what they mean, or inquire about how individual songs fits into the album's conceptual framework as a whole. Waters's ever-growing contempt for Pink Floyd's enormous post-*Meddle* fan base is well-known. As the 1970s wore on, he became increasingly frustrated with what he perceived as the audience's indifference to the sophisticated analyses of alienation and the critiques of contemporary society he undertook on *Dark Side, Wish You Were Here,* and *Animals.* Adorno would likely say that this state of affairs was simply the result of the paradoxical effort—and, I suspect Adorno would say, mistaken effort—of addressing alienation through music that is not in itself alienating. Indeed, Waters may have moved in the wrong direction by insisting that the band's music be ever more conventional. When the band hired the successful producer Bob Ezrin to produce *The Wall* in 1979, Ezrin coached them, as he himself put it, "in things like what a good tempo would be for a single, and how to get an intro and an outro—I know all those things, and they were quite open to trying them."[21]

Some will say "yes, but this music rocked harder than their earlier music." Perhaps. But so did thousands of other rock songs released during the late Seventies. Others will say "yes, but the album's plainspoken, harrowing critique of modern capitalist society is far more straightforward than their obtuse, abstruse, airy-fairy early stuff." Perhaps. But if that's the case, why does the music from *The Wall* seem to be so much easier to listen to than—to name just one example—"Careful with that Axe, Eugene"? The point is that at this juncture in time, rocking

---

[20] Waters on "Shine on You, Crazy Diamond": "I think we made a basic error in not arranging it in a different way so that some of the ideas were expounded lyrically before they were developed musically." See Schaffner, p. 199.

[21] Schaffner, *Saucerful of Secrets,* p. 228.

hard was no longer transgressive, nor was "plainspoken" social critique; the fact that one in fifty persons in the U.K. purchased *The Wall* upon its release would seem to demonstrate this rather eloquently. I believe there is one more lesson to be drawn from this state of affairs: in our visually oriented postmodern society, it would appear that challenging music has a more alienating effect, and thus a more liberatory and transgressive potential, than seemingly shocking words or images. The fact that contemporary society seems so much less engaged with music than with visual imagery is probably the best evidence I can offer for this assertion.

In the end, though, a rock band does not operate in a perfect world: they operate in a capitalist system where an inability to capture and hold an audience and thereby "move product" will mean commercial ruin. Under these stark circumstances, the large majority of popular musicians of whatever genre give relatively little, if any, thought to crafting a serious ongoing critique of society. Furthermore, there is a very different temptation that faces successful bands: to indulge in a kind of aesthetic navel-gazing once they have "made it," to confuse solipsistic self-absorption with the genuine artistic growth that results from an attempt to maintain a continuous dialogue with one's audience as well as one's art.[22] Under the circumstances, it's impressive that Pink Floyd turned out substantive albums for as long as they did, and one can only admire them for creating such a genuinely substantive critique, and carrying it forward for so long.

---

[22] Although it seems to me that every major British rock band of the 1970s ended up erring on the side of over simplification and over accessibility rather than on the side of obscurantism.

10

I and Thou and "Us and Them": Existential Encounters on *The Dark Side of The Moon* (and Beyond)

DAVID MacGREGOR JOHNSTON

> When all 'directions' fail there arises in the darkness over the abyss the one true direction of man, towards the creative Spirit.
> —Martin Buber

> And everything under the sun is in tune
> But the sun is eclipsed by the moon.
> —Roger Waters

My introduction to Pink Floyd was a high school friend's TDK SA90 cassette tape with *The Final Cut* on Side A and *Wish You Were Here* on Side B. He told me to listen to Side A when I went to sleep and Side B when I woke up the next morning. I think I fell asleep somewhere in "The Fletcher Memorial Home" or on "Southampton Dock." At least that's where I usually fell asleep once I got into the habit he initiated. Of course I listened to all of *The Final Cut* later the next day. I was impressed by the lyrical aspect of each album, but my initial response was toward the more purely musical elements that I took to be the point of Tony's temporal instructions. He slowly introduced me to other albums. *Animals, Meddle,* and *Ummagumma,* figured prominently, but it was *The Dark Side of the Moon* that drew most of my attention. I was captivated by the rich musical texture, even if (because?) the individual elements might not traditionally be considered "music." In any case, I found that infectious sound as dynamic as the greatest jazz masterpieces and classical compositions. So, it's not surprising that my first CD purchase con-

sisted of three discs: selections from Richard Wagner's *Ring*
cycle, Mel Tormé with the Boss Brass, and Pink Floyd's *The
Dark Side of the Moon*.

I came to Martin Buber's classic *I and Thou* much later in my
life (and not on a cassette). I was teaching an Ethics class while
in graduate school, but Buber's ideas didn't grab me. I put them
on the shelf until my second job after graduate school. My introduction to the department members there came in part through
a course called "Living Philosophically," which was jointly
taught by the entire department. Each member of the department took two weeks of the semester to work through a particular philosophical author, work, or viewpoint that he or she
found especially important in shaping how they live their lives.
As this was the second time they offered the course, I was a bit
of a spectator, but it gave me a peculiar insight into each of my
new colleagues. It was an interesting mix, including Buddhism,
feminism, and Buber's *I and Thou*.

Very Hard to Explain Why You're Mad, Even if You're Not Mad

Following the stylistic cues of one of his philosophical inspira-
tions, the existentialist Friedrich Nietzsche, Martin Buber wrote
I and Thou as a series of aphorisms—relatively short statements
meant to convey a general sense of the truth—rather than as a
traditional philosophical argument working logically from stated
premises to a desired conclusion. This more poetic presentation
may appear as a haphazard collection of random ideas, but it
actually serves to reinforce Buber's central concern: that people
in modern society have lost touch with the genuine mode of
encountering others in favor of an analytical mode of experiencing the world. What he calls the mode of experience
engages the world by collecting data through our senses, ana-
lyzing and classifying that data, and then developing theories
about it. When we experience something or someone in this
mode, we treat that thing or person as a mere object. A traditional philosophical essay echoes the mode of experience. By
writing instead in a more poetic style, Buber hoped to awaken
a fundamental appreciation of what he calls the mode of
encounter, which is opposed to logic and reason. When we
encounter something or someone, we enter a reciprocal rela-

tionship with that other person or thing in its full being. This unpredictable, unanalyzable mode of encounter is generally ignored as a way of engaging the world, not only by philosophers in their academic pursuits, but also by the average person in his or her daily life.

It was a character called the madman who uttered Nietzsche's famous dictum, "God is dead." What is often forgotten is the addendum: "And we have killed him." The problem of Enlightenment theology, as Buber saw it, was that this part of Western philosophy tried to carve out a place for God within a new, rational understanding of the world. By doing so, these philosophers made God into an abstract principle whose function was to serve as a basis for rationality itself. God had lost any human-like features, and we had lost any way of personally relating to Him. If God exists as Enlightenment philosophers believed, He would be a mere thing, a tool for humans to use in their investigations of the world and of themselves, and we would engage God through the mode of experience. According to Buber, Nietzsche is correct that such a God is dead; in fact, He could not be alive in any meaningful way. But Buber does not follow Nietzsche's atheism, which takes religious belief as a sign of weakness. Instead, Buber shows that religious belief is achieved through the mode of encounter and serves as a model to develop an antidote to the alienation that modern society engenders in human beings.

The religious core of *I and Thou* came from Buber's interest in Hasidic Judaism. Developing about one hundred years before Buber's birth, Hasidism stressed a personal dialogue with God through prayer, ritual, and ecstatic song and dance, as opposed to the scholarly study of Jewish law that rabbis of the time advocated as the way to God. Since this more demanding intellectual pursuit required both the financial and intellectual resources to spend one's day immersed in learning, the new Hasidic teachings had wide appeal. For Buber, Hasidism showed that in a society where secular acts could become sacred, all people and all activities could be equally holy. "Man's will to profit and will to power are natural and legitimate as long as they are tied to the will to human relations and carried by it."[1] When we

---

[1] Martin Buber. *I and Thou* (New York: Simon and Schuster, 1970), p. 97.

approach our daily activities through the mode of encounter, in other words, we can build communities that meld our existential endeavors and our spiritual inclinations.

So, it is not surprising that mundane activities such as making or listening to rock 'n' roll records could have a spiritual connection if they take us out of our ordinary mode of experience and direct us to the mode of encounter. At least as far back as *Meddle,* Pink Floyd's songs have addressed this alienation that comes from engaging the world through the mode of experience and the search for a more fulfilling mode of being in the world. Discussing the lyrics of "Us and Them," Roger Waters said they were about "those fundamental issues of whether or not the human race is capable of being humane."[2] When we live in a cruel world full of unconcerned caregivers, backstabbing businessmen, and self-absorbed politicians, we add bricks to the walls that simultaneously protect and isolate us from them. In other words, in the modern world of commerce, war, and manufactured existence, we find people unconnected with each other who look out only for themselves instead of seeking relationships that stress the full dialogue of two beings engaged in the mode of encounter. As Waters said, "The fundamental question that's facing us all is whether or not we're capable of dealing with the whole question of us and them."

Live for Today, Gone Tomorrow, That's Me

These two modes of experience and of encounter correspond to what Buber calls the basic words I-It and I-You. When I engage things and people in the mode of experience they become 'Its'. I understand objects and people as instrumental for achieving some purpose, as what Martin Heidegger later calls a "standing-reserve."[3] The cashier at the record store or the server at Amazon.com is useful for obtaining compact discs. The teacher at school is useful for obtaining information and receiving a grade. My car is useful for getting me from place to place. In any

---

[2] Unless otherwise noted, all quotations within this chapter from Waters and people other than Martin Buber come from the DVD *Classic Albums: The Dark Side of the Moon* (EV-30042-9).

[3] Martin Heidegger. "The Question Concerning Technology," in *Basic Writings* (San Francisco: HarperCollins, 1993).

case, I don't get beyond the surface of Its. I understand them as members of a class, as belonging to a particular intellectual category. So there's a necessary distance between the experiencing I and the experienced It. As well, I do not experience the It in the present because I experience it through my understanding of its particular temporal and spatial place in the world, an understanding that is fundamentally tied up with the categories and judgments I previously made. Thus, the I-It is understood as a relation with oneself, as a monologue.

On the other hand, the I-You encounter is understood as a dialogue between the two participants fully engaged in the present moment. When I engage things and people in an I-You encounter, I know the You with my whole being through an unmediated relation, not with my senses, my intellectual categories, or my judgments. In other words, there are no conceptual constraints or expectations separating the I from the You:

> When I confront a human being as my You, and speak the basic word I-You to him, then he is no thing among things nor does he consist of things.
>
> He is no longer He or She, limited by other Hes or Shes, a dot in the world grid of space and time, nor a condition that can be experienced or described, a loose bundle of named qualities. Neighborless and seamless, he is You and fills the firmament. Not as if there were nothing but he; but everything else lives in *his* light. (*I and Thou*, p. 59)

The I-You relation stresses the mutual, holistic, and dialogical existence of two beings. Perhaps the clearest expression in Pink Floyd's lyrics of this dialogue comes in "Echoes" on *Meddle*. "It was the beginning of all the writing about other people," said Roger Waters. "It was the beginning of empathy, if you like. You know, 'Two strangers passing in the street / By chance two separate glances meet / And I am you and what I see is me' is a sort of thread that's gone through everything ever since then and had a big eruption in *Dark Side*."

Of course, my mode of engaging the world not only alters the nature of the thing. In each case the nature of the I is determined by the attitude with which the I understands the other person or thing. When I treat you as an It, I degrade myself: I, too, become a mere thing:

To be sure, he views the beings around him as so many machines capable of different achievements that have to be calculated and used for the cause. But that is how he views himself . . . He treats himself, too, as an It. (*I and Thou*, p. 118)

The experiencing I is an objective observer rather than an active participant in this mode of engaging the world. But when I treat you as a You, I am enriched in my own being. It is only in the mode of encounter that I am transformed and become fully human. "Relation is reciprocity. My You acts on me as I act on it" (*I and Thou*, p. 67). Buber uses the example of an artist in the act of creation to explain this mutual transformation. Put simply, the raw material is made into an artwork, while the artist simultaneously evolves through a variety of psychological, emotional, and intellectual processes. "The world is twofold for man in accordance with his twofold attitude . . . the I of man is also twofold. / For the I of the basic word I-You is different from that of the basic word I-It" (p. 53).

I Never Said I Was Frightened of Dying

In terms of our relations with other people, Buber says that the I-You encounter is best explained as love. But not love as most people understand the concept. For Buber, love is not an internal feeling. Rather, love is a situation in which we live, and which transforms our entire perception of the world. "Love does not cling to an I, as if the You were merely its 'content' or object; it is between I and You" (*I and Thou*, p. 66). When I love someone, I see that person as completely unique and irreplaceable, and I see that love bridging any distance between us and somehow completing myself. "So I don't feel alone / Or the weight of the stone," to borrow from *Animals*. When deeply in love, I would be lost without my beloved. There's a sense in which the lover views the entire world through him or her. That song becomes our song. That place is where we first met. This food is his or her favorite. And with that love comes a sense of responsibility for the loved-one. I would do anything for him or her.

Buber shows that the desire for encounter is basic to human beings. When we look at languages of some pre-technological cultures, we see that they focus on relations between humans, rather than on categorical distinctions and isolated objects as we see in modern society.

> We say 'far away'; the Zulu has a sentence-word instead that means: 'where one cries, "mother, I am lost."' And the Fuegian surpasses our analytical wisdom with a sentence-word of seven syllables that literally means: 'they look at each other, each wanting for the other to offer to do that which both desire but neither wishes to do'." (*I and Thou*, pp. 69–70)

In regard to child development, Buber traces our need for encounter back to the perfect reciprocity of the womb, where there is no separation between the mother and the child, and the womb is the entire universe for the fetus. From the moment of birth we long for some such similar immediate and all-encompassing encounter, a desire that Buber calls the innate You. We witness this desire in infants when they reach out even without wanting something or make noises even when they do not wish to communicate, and we hear this desire on *The Wall* in the pleadings of "Hey You." Languages and child development show that encounter is actually the primary human state, and our need to relate is a result of how we enter the world.

These examples are the best Buber can do to explain the nature of encounter, since any attempt to analyze or to describe it necessarily returns us to the mode of experience. Similarly, the mode of encounter itself is always fleeting: any You will inevitable degenerate into an It as soon as I become aware of the encounter and begin to reflect on it. Any loved-one will become an It as soon as he or she is seen, for example, as beautiful, energetic, or green-eyed. Buber does not want to suggest that love cannot endure. Rather, what we call love is a continual oscillation between encounter and experience. "This, however, is the sublime melancholy of our lot that every You must become an It in our world" (p. 68). Of course, the encounter can occur again, but I cannot constantly dwell there. Still, my transformation has a kind of permanence, for it allows me to enter the I-You relation more often and more easily, and to feel that loving responsibility for the particular You and ultimately toward the entirety of existence. "What counts is not with these products of analysis and reflection but the genuine original unity, the lived relationship" (p. 70).

I Don't Know, I Was Really Drunk at the Time

Modern society is structured to direct us away from encounter and toward experience. The project of human culture has been steadily to improve our experience of the world. Modern science and technology, not to mention philosophy, direct us to see everyone and everything as an object to be understood intellectually and to be used for practical purposes to support our own well-being and happiness. Governments, economic systems, schools, and sometimes even the institution of marriage are built up out of I-It relations with the great cost that, "the improvement of the capacity for experience and use generally involve a decrease in man's power to relate" (p. 92). Thus, in what Buber calls the It-world, we "zig zag our way through the boredom and pain" and become comfortably numb.

Philosophers of the Frankfurt School, particularly Max Horkheimer in *Eclipse of Reason*, had concerns similar to Buber's (and Waters's).[4] Horkheimer claims that since the Enlightenment, thinking has degenerated into what he calls "instrumental reason," the subjective application of self-interest to all situations so as to promote technical efficiency. In the realm of politics, for example, candidates and elected officials treat their constituents and contributors as things to get them elected or keep them in office. Constituents, contributors, and lobbyists view elected officials as things to provide services or favors. In the work place, personnel have become human resources—understood not as genuine Yous to be honored and respected, but merely as replaceable Its waiting to be mined from the applicant pool. Of course, employers are just a means to obtaining a paycheck, itself only a means to obtaining both necessities and trivialities.

The It-world of education is undoubtedly the institution Pink Floyd fans most often recognize. In its most ideal circumstance, the relation between student and teacher can approximate the I-You encounter, but Buber claims that it can never unfold into complete mutuality:

---

[4] Horkheimer, *The Eclipse of Reason* (Seabury Press, 1974). Other Frankfurt School philosophers (Adorno and Benjamin) are treated in Chapters 9 and 17 in this volume.

The teacher who wants to help the pupil to realize his best potentialities must intend him as this particular person, both in his potentiality and in his actuality. More precisely, he must know him not as a mere sum of qualities, aspirations, and inhibitions; he must apprehend him, and affirm him, as a whole. . . It is essential that he should awaken the I-You relationship in the pupil, too, who should intend and affirm his educator as this particular person; and yet the educational relationship could not endure if the pupil also practiced the art of embracing by living through the shared situation from the educator's point of view. Whether the I-You relationship comes to an end or assumes the altogether different character of a friendship, it becomes clear that the specifically educational relationship is incompatible with complete mutuality. (*I and Thou*, p. 178)

Overworked and unconcerned educators may treat their students as mere objects filling the seats, which will be filled by an entirely new batch of Its next year. Administrators facing community pressure are often concerned merely with the graduation and placement of the school's degree products. The lessons themselves are often designed not to liberate students' minds, but to prepare them to be cogs in the societal machine. When faced with thought control and dark sarcasm, it's no surprise that students shout, "Hey, teacher, leave us kids alone!" Buber reminds us that, "There are better ways to learn than to have a teacher hold a weapon over the students' heads."[5]

In the It-world, the I and the It become separated from each other into "two neatly defined districts: institutions and feelings." We make a distinction between what is out there and what is in us. We feel trapped by the external institutions that we understand as forces beyond our control. Buber compares these incapacitating forces to an Incubus, a mythical demon believed to lie upon sleepers, especially women, keeping them pinned down and draining them of their energy. Taken together, the forces of modern society function as an uncaring and inescapable apparatus. Without a doubt, Buber would find "Welcome to The Machine" an apt salutation in the It-world. For relief from these overpowering forces, modern humans seek

---

[5] Quoted in Brad Art's *Ethics and the Good Life* (Belmont: Wadsworth, 1994), p. 324.

refuge in the I-district of feelings. "Here one is at home and relaxes in one's rocking chair" (p. 93). The lyrics of *Dark Side's* "Breathe (reprise)" echo this sentiment. "Home, home again / I like to be here when I can / When I come home cold and tired / It's good to warm my bones beside the fire." Unfortunately, our inner feelings are just as impotent as our external institutions. "Institutions yield no public life; feelings, no personal life" (p. 94). Feelings are not between an I and a You. Feelings are had by and I toward an It.

> Whoever is overpowered by the It-world must consider the dogma of an ineluctable running down as a truth that creates a clearing in the jungle. In truth, this dogma only leads him deeper into the slavery of the It-world. (*I and Thou*, p. 107)

"Hanging on in quiet desperation" is not just "the English way;" it's a symptom of the modern It-world.

Give 'Em a Quick, Short, Sharp Shock

For Buber, the only way to keep the thin ice of modern life from cracking under our feet is to focus on I-You relations. But the mode of encounter is risky. It should not surprise us that the punishment for "Showing feelings of an almost human nature" is to tear down the wall and "to be exposed before your peers." In the comfortable world of experience, very little is more frightening than to open oneself to the full reciprocity of encountering each other.

When I love, I make myself vulnerable to rejection and loss. Often, the pain and happiness of my beloved become more important than my own. In any case, I must drop all pretense, lower my defenses, and remove my masks in order to be fully open to the genuine dialogue of the I-You relation. I must bare my naked feelings and tear down the walls I have built in the It-world. Although those walls keep me safe and secure in the predictable I-It mode of experience, they simultaneously block my access to an encounter with the You. More importantly for Buber, they block my access to an encounter with God, what he calls the eternal You.

Buber claims that a relation with God is important because the eternal You will not degenerate into an It, since God cannot be intellectually comprehended or qualified. My relation with the eternal You goes beyond the typical I-You encounter in that it is fully inclusive.

> For entering into the pure relationship does not involve ignoring everything but seeing everything in the You, not renouncing the world but placing it upon its proper ground. (*I and Thou*, p. 127)

It's not just God but also His entire creation with whom I relate.

Buber claims that the encounter with the eternal You is the only way to transform modern society from an It-world into an ideal community that functions in the mode of encounter. As Roger Waters put it, "not just individuals, but hierarchies, authorities are capable of rehabilitation." Of course, before you can encounter God, you must decide that you want to do so in what Buber calls "man's decisive moment." Although this decision is not an easy one, Buber believes that once it is made, the encounter with God inevitably will occur if you want it with all of your being. Still, this decision to leave behind the world of experience is frightening because the world of encounter is intellectually incomprehensible and utterly beyond my control. "What has to be given up is not the I but that false drive for self-affirmation which impels man to flee from the unreliable, unsolid, unlasting, unpredictable, dangerous world of relation into the having of things" (p. 126). With all its risks and sacrifices, the I-You encounter is essential. While it is true that we can live entirely immersed in the safe, secure, and predictable I-It mode of experience, experience alone keeps us separated from what makes us fully human.

Again, the encounter with the eternal You is not an end in itself. We know that we have been met by God because we have been transformed and find ourselves filled with a loving responsibility for the whole of creation, a responsibility that arises not out of obligation but from a genuine desire not unlike the desire for my beloved's well-being and happiness. It promises a new society based on the I-You mode of encounter.

> The encounter with God does not come to man in order that he may henceforth attend to God but in order that he may prove its meaning in action in the world. All revelation is a calling and a mission. (*I and Thou*, p. 164)

The truly religious person does not only contemplate his or her own personal relation with God. Instead, the religious person turns toward the world and builds a community, "Where you can speak out loud / About your doubts and fears . . .You can relax on both sides of the tracks . . . And no-one kills the children anymore." This new, religious drive provides a different sense in which I wish You were here, in which we might build a community in which we all can flourish.

Although Buber's personal religious beliefs tie the building of such a community to a relation with the Judeo-Christian God, it may be possible to engage the eternal You without such a specifically religious transformation. Consider that Buber rejects Buddhism as a full encounter because it aims to free people from the suffering that comes from the cycle of re-birth. From Buber's perspective, if reincarnation were true, we should embrace the opportunity to encounter the eternal You in every existence. Furthermore, the Buddha's way turns the human spirit back into itself as a monologue instead of turning to the world in a dialogue. "His inmost decision seems to aim at the annulment of the ability to say You" (p. 140) As the Buddhists say, change comes from within:

> But whoever merely has a living "experience" of his attitude and retains it in his soul may be as thoughtful as he can be, he is world-less—and all the games, arts, intoxications, enthusiasms, and mysteries that happen within him do not touch the world's skin. As long as one attains redemption only in his self, he cannot do any good or harm to the world; he does not concern it. Only he that believes in the world achieves contact with it; and if he commits himself he also cannot remain godless. Let us love the actual world that never wishes to be annulled, but love it in all its terror, but dare to embrace it with our spirit's arms—and our hands encounter the hands that hold it. (*I and Thou*, pp. 142–43)

But Buber's rejection of Buddhism is circular. It cannot provide a completely reciprocal encounter only because of how he defines such a relationship and how he characterizes Buddhism.

Buber forgets that Buddhist enlightenment is not merely ending the cycle of re-birth. This cycle ends because the enlightened practitioner becomes one with everything. In fact, the Buddhist model more closely parallels the innate You of the child in a womb that Buber characterizes as a state of perfect reciprocity. The Buddha, the enlightened one, does not "touch the world's skin" because he becomes one with the world itself. Thus, there is no separation between him and the world. Furthermore, Buddhism is essentially an atheistic system. The Buddha is not worshipped as a god, but revered as an enlightened human. As a system of practices, Buddhism provides a path to enlightenment, to perfect reciprocity with the whole of creation, without recourse to an omnipotent creator. The eternal You of Buddhism is the world itself, a world that is ultimately mysterious and unanalyzable, but that is loved and embraced "in all its terror" and "with our spirit's arms."

I Can't Think of Anything to Say Except. . . I Think It's Marvelous!

Whether Nietzsche's and Buddhism's atheism is true, we still need to explain the fact that atheists and agnostics like Horkheimer and Waters feel called to build the sort of community that Buber's encounter with the eternal You inspires. It could be that atheists and agnostics encounter God but do not recognize it as such. It could also be that the world itself provides enough of an eternal You, since the true nature of the world remains fundamentally incomprehensible. Or, it could be sufficient just to recognize the alienation of the It-world and our own responsibility for sustaining it. For Horkheimer, the solution to modern society's ills is to develop our capacity of reason so as to provide a critical inquiry into the possibilities and limitations of thought itself. If we can identify the problems of society, we can begin to solve them.

What Horkheimer's critical theory of society demonstrates is that true democratic co-existence and the free exchange of ideas provide a way out of "instrumental reason," even if they can never be fully realized by any existing culture. What we can do is critique the ideology of a society by comparing it with the social reality of that society. For example, given the ideal of equality as opposed to the real social inequality in our democratic system, we may be drawn to empathize with the oppressed members of society so as to bring practice in line with theory. Buber writes, "There are not two kinds of human beings, but there are two poles of humanity" (p. 114).

As I come to empathize with the situation of other people, I enter the mode of encounter. As I better understand the inconsistency between theory and practice, my empathy increases, and so does my ability to encounter the You. It may be true that the sun is eclipsed by the moon, "But that's not to say that the potential for the sun to shine doesn't exist, you know. Walk down the path towards the light rather than walk into darkness." urged Roger Waters. "If through your own internal efforts you can give the empathetic side of your nature a better chance in its battle against the devil within you, well then, so be it. And that is a struggle we can all engage in every day of our lives."

Buber and Horkheimer both uphold art as a way for us to get beyond ourselves and our ordinary mode of experience, as a way to reclaim our fundamental humanity. Our engaging a work of art, either as creator or perceiver, can approximate the full reciprocity of the mode of encounter. The inspiration for the work of art is often a mystery even for the artist, reason enough for Plato to criticized the poets. Michelangelo's claim that when carving a statue he was merely releasing the forms already present in the blocks of marble parallels Buber's notion that a work of art emerges when

> a human being confronts a form that wants to become a work through him . . . What is required is a deed that a man does with his whole being: if he commits it and speaks with his being the basic word to the form that appears, then the creative power is released and the work comes into being. (*I and Thou*, p. 60)

Waters acknowledged a similar impulse when he described *Dark Side* as "an expression of political, philosophical, humanitarian empathy that was desperate to get out."

Once it's out, of course, an artwork is a thing in the world, capable of being experienced and analyzed as an It. I can follow the notes on a musical score or analyze the shapes and colors in a painting. But I can also encounter the work of art as a You. The work can "speak to me" or move me emotionally. In fact, our initial engagement with a work of art is usually in the mode of encounter. We relate to it first as a whole, not as a collection of analyzable qualities, and get lost in the song or image.

Only later do we engage it in the mode of experience. "Even a melody is not composed of tones, nor a verse of words, nor a statue of lines—one must pull and tear to turn a unity into a multiplicity . . ." (*I and Thou*, p. 59).

Still, some artworks resist degenerating into Its. The Modern art movement was generally more concerned with artistic processes and art marketing than with creating representational works that most perceivers would be comfortable viewing. Jackson Pollock's drips of paint and Mark Rothko's monochromatic canvases can be analyzed in terms of their shapes and colors, but they remain fundamentally mysterious and unanalyzable in terms of our usual artistic categories. Marcel Duchamp's found objects can easily be described in relation to their ordinary functions, but they approach incomprehensibility as works of art.

In music, John Cage and Karlheinz Stockhausen departed from traditional composition and notation techniques in order to emphasize the element of chance in performance. Stockhausen's *Spiral* is written for soloist and shortwave radio, where the soloist improvises in response to the radio reception using one or more instruments to imitate the radio's output. Cage's *Imaginary Landscape No. 4* involves twelve radio receivers, each with two players who control either the frequency the radio is tuned to or its volume. Both pieces have scores with instructions about how the performers should set their radios and control them over time, but the sound coming out of them is dependent on whatever happens to be tuned in at the time of the particular performance. Cage is perhaps best known for *4' 33"*, a composition he refers to as his "silent piece" in which three movements are performed without playing a single note. Although there is no music in the traditional sense, there is a performance that emphasizes the fact that sound is everywhere. The seminal sound collage band Negativland explored this notion explicitly on the album *Escape From Noise* in the song of the same name by assaulting the listener with a barrage of dissonant voices, piercing instrumentation, and a variety of dissected and reassembled found sounds. Such compositions challenge the very definition of music and as such approach the incomprehensibility of the eternal You.

There is No Dark Side of the Moon Really.
Matter of Fact It's All Dark

In its own way, Pink Floyd's *The Dark Side of the Moon* also challenges the very definition of music. As early champions of synthesizers and tape loops, Pink Floyd was derided by critics as talentless button-pushers. But it was precisely this unconventional use of musical technology that made *The Dark Side of the Moon* the masterpiece that it is. By technologically altering the recorded music and lyrics and by adding decidedly non-musical elements such as ringing clocks, station announcements, and interview responses, *Dark Side* moves away from our usual categories of musical analysis. Similar techniques are found throughout Pink Floyd's catalog, but the addition of a musical "heartbeat" underneath the main elements of *The Dark Side of the Moon* gives the album a sort of life of its own. Although we can transcribe the notes corresponding to the primal screams of "The Great Gig in the Sky," the tonal qualities and performance of the actual vocals in many respects defy description. According to journalist and broadcaster Robert Sandall:

> There's no question in my mind that *Dark Side of The Moon* was one of the most important artistic statements of the last fifty years probably. It touched very many people all over the world in ways that could not simply be put down to the fact that "Oh, they're nice tunes," and "Oh, I like that bit at the end." I mean, this was a complete experience.

Certainly, it is a complete "experience" in terms of Buber's ideal of a reciprocal relationship. We encounter *The Dark Side of the Moon* as a You that resists degenerating into an It. "It's driven by emotion; there's nothing plastic about it. You know, there's nothing contrived about it, and I think that may be one of the things that's given it its longevity," Roger Waters said.

Longevity, indeed. Having spent seven hundred forty-one weeks (over fourteen years) on the Billboard 200 album chart and being one of the top five selling albums globally of all time, it is clear that *The Dark Side of the Moon* engages listeners in a way that goes beyond experiencing the album as an It. Even my mother, who was too conservative to be interested in Elvis or The Beatles, found *Dark Side* compelling. It seems to engage the listener in an I-You relation, not only in terms of its nontraditional musical elements, but also in terms of its lyrical content. "He created a story; he created, basically, a theater piece about what it was like to live in the modern world," said David Fricke, Senior Editor of *Rolling Stone* magazine. "What he was feeling as an individual mirrored almost exactly what a lot of other people were feeling at the time in their own lives."

Right from the start, with "Speak to Me," we are instructed to engage the world in the mode of encounter, even if the lyrics quickly move us to the mode of experience. "Breathe, breathe in the air / Don't be afraid to care / Leave but don't leave me / Look around and choose your own ground." "Yahweh," the name given to the God of Israel in the original consonantal *Hebrew Bible*, when pronounced as you inhale and exhale each syllable respectively, mimics the act of breathing itself. In both Hebrew and Greek, the word for "spirit" and "breath" is the same, and the Spirit that breathes life into His creation does so in the very speaking of His name. So, we may interpret Psalm 150:6, "Let everything that has breath praise the Lord," not so much as a command, but as a description of a fundamental act of living. According to Buber, "The purpose of relation is the relation itself—touching the You. For as soon as we touch a You, we are touched by a breath of eternal life" (*I and Thou*, pp. 112–13). Similarly, on *The Dark Side of the Moon*, as soon as we hear the opening "heartbeat" and initial lyrics, we are directed to the eternal You. As Roger Waters said, "In fact I think within the context of the music and within the context of the piece as a whole, people are prepared to accept that simple exaltation to be prepared to stand your own ground and attempt to live in an authentic way."

The album's final lyric also captures the essence of Buber's ideas, directing us away from the It-world and toward the eternal You. When Roger Waters writes that "everything under the sun is in tune / but the sun is eclipsed by the moon," we can take solace in the fact that our current darkness is temporary and that the world subsists in its proper mode even if we do not currently encounter it. And even if the moon is all dark, the light of the sun can illuminate it for us. We can turn toward the creative Spirit, toward the eternal You, and find our full humanity. Of course, we generally continue to inhabit the It-world of experience and ignore the mode of encounter. So, as David Gilmour commented, "The ideas that Roger was exploring apply to every new generation. They still have very much the same relevance as they had." Perhaps that fact explains why even in 2006 *The Dark Side of the Moon* continued to sell over nine thousand copies in the United States every week. We still face the alienation from society that Buber outlined, and we still seek the antidote in an encounter with a You. *The Dark Side of the Moon* can be that antidote.

Apples and Oranges?
Or Just Apples?

11

Pulling Together as a Team: Collective Action and Pink Floyd's Intentions

TED GRACYK

> For if the identity of soul alone makes the same man; and there be nothing in the nature of matter why the same individual spirit may not be united to different bodies, it will be possible that those men, living in distant ages, and of different tempers, may have been the same man.
>
> —JOHN LOCKE

> We spent eighteen years touring with people shouting "Where's Syd Barrett?" But so far we haven't had one person shout, "Where's Roger?"
>
> —NICK MASON

Overwhelmed by the amount of music that's readily available, students sometimes ask me to recommend music. Suppose a student asked me to recommend some Pink Floyd. What would I say? *Dark Side of the Moon* is the obvious starting point for any exploration of their music, and then I'd probably recommend my personal favorite, *Wish You Were Here*. I'd steer a novice away from *Atom Heart Mother*.

But then what? I see the group's music as dividing into four very distinct eras—the Syd Barrett years, the "classic" lineup of David Gilmour, Roger Waters, Nick Mason, and Rick Wright, and then two final phases, the first where keyboardist Wright was absent (for much of *The Wall* and *The Final Cut*) and the second after Waters's departure (and Wright's return). The problem is, there's not much common ground between the Barrett years and the grim concept albums *Animals*, *The Wall*, and *The Final*

Cut. Pressed to recommend something, I'd point to the two-disc collection *Echoes*, whose generous track list was decided by shared agreement of four individuals who have been members of Pink Floyd. It represents each phase of the band and emphasizes the classic quartet. No member of the band actually appears on every track.

But recommending *Echoes* presents a moral dilemma. As every Pink Floyd fan knows, to endorse *Echoes* is to endorse a particular history of the band. More urgently, it is to endorse a particular vision of Pink Floyd. According to Waters, the music recorded and performed by the "so-called Pink Floyd" after 1985 is a fraud, a fake, and a ruse.[1] To endorse *Echoes*, I must treat Waters as mistaken. As I'll argue in this chapter, he is mistaken to claim that Pink Floyd ended when he quit the band on December 12th, 1985. Waters is wrong, and I'll explain why and, more importantly, why *it matters*. It isn't just a trivial matter of semantics. This issue bears directly on any assessment of Pink Floyd's musical accomplishments.

Waters's Position: Raving and Drooling, or Serious Argument?

Waters presented his position in a media campaign that followed his 1986 lawsuit to dissolve Pink Floyd. Waters and the other members of the band eventually reached an out-of-court settlement, and I have nothing to say about the legal issues. What interests me, instead, is the series of moral arguments that Waters offered which are independent of—but seem to have motivated—his lawsuit. His arguments revolve around long-standing philosophical debates on two topics: the nature of identity over time and the possibility of collective responsibility. These issues, in turn, interest me especially because they are a foundation for interpreting and evaluating a body of music made collectively, by a group.

Suppose that someone claims that Beethoven's musical genius is of a different kind than Handel's musical genius.[2]

---

[1] Timothy White, "Pink Floyd," in *Rock Lives: Profiles and Interviews* (New York: Holt, 1990), pp. 510, 520–21. The essay, which draws heavily on interviews with Roger Waters, originally appeared in *Penthouse* (September 1988).
[2] Peter Kivy argues that the achievement displayed by Beethoven and Handel

There might be factual questions of whether certain pieces of music were composed by Beethoven, and whether others were composed by Handel. ("Did Beethoven compose the *Water Music*," someone might ask, "or is that Handel?") Having sorted the Beethoven from the Handel, we can get on with the business of deciding what these patterns of activity reveal about each composer. However, there's no obvious philosophical problem here, because there are no arguments about what kinds of things Beethoven and Handel were. They were individual people.[3]

Now suppose, in contrast, that I want to compare Pink Floyd with the Sex Pistols, as so many in England seemed to want to do back in 1977. At the time, the Pistols seemed fresh and relevant and the Floyd seemed worn out and decadent. While there's not a lot of controversy about how many albums the Sex Pistols recorded (exactly one studio album), there is dispute about whether two studio albums and two live albums are actually the work of Pink Floyd. The studio albums are the two made after Waters left the band: *A Momentary Lapse of Reason* and *The Division Bell*. The live albums are *Delicate Sound of Thunder* and *Pulse*. If we want to complicate things further, we might question whether *The Final Cut* is a Pink Floyd album— some regard it as Waters's first solo album with limited musical participation by Gilmour and Mason. If we decide that none of these five albums are really by Pink Floyd, then nearly a third of the *Echoes* compilation doesn't belong there.

Our first problem, then, is to decide what kind of thing or entity Pink Floyd is. At first, there might not seem to be any problem here. Some things, like flocks of birds and schools of fish, are essentially groups of individuals. Obviously, we want to say that Pink Floyd is a musical group, and the group's music is easily distinguished from music created outside the group. Those are solo projects. Barrett, Wright, Mason, Waters, and

---

were distinct kinds of genius; *The Possessor and the Possessed: Handel, Mozart, Beethoven, and the Idea of Musical Genius* (New Haven: Yale University Press, 2001).

[3] I am not denying that there are problems with authorship in the classical repertoire. Problems very similar to those I'm raising about Pink Floyd are generated by Mozart's *Requiem* and Mahler's Symphony No. 10, both of which were completed by others after their deaths.

Gilmour have all released solo albums and none of this music belongs on *Echoes*. But as any Pink Floyd fan knows, some Pink Floyd music was created by individuals in a more or less "solo" fashion—we have, for instance, the four distinct parts of the studio disc of *Ummagumma*. The problem is to determine when these various individuals—acting independently or together in various combinations—constitute the group Pink Floyd.

Perhaps Waters is right that *Lapse of Reason* is a Gilmour solo project masquerading as Pink Floyd. Perhaps *The Final Cut* is a Waters solo album passed off as Pink Floyd. After all, each has the same number of participating Pink Floyd members as does Syd Barrett's *Barrett*. If one thinks that either *Lapse of Reason* or *The Final Cut* is weak—as many people do—then including them in the Pink Floyd catalogue suggests that the band went into a decline immediately after *The Wall*. If Waters is correct and Pink Floyd ended in 1985, then the band ended just after its creative peak of four consecutive masterpieces (*Dark Side, Wish You Were Here, Animals, The Wall*).

More urgently, this debate affects our interpretation of the kind of band that Pink Floyd really was. If *The Final Cut* is the last Pink Floyd album, then the group ends its career as the undisputed king of concept albums. Beginning in 1973, they made nothing else, and each album was conceptually unified by the ideas and concerns of Waters, the band's lyricist. It then makes sense to regard the entire second half of their career as having a unified philosophy or vision.[4] However, if *Lapse of Reason* is a Pink Floyd album, their later music is no longer so easily pigeonholed. It is not a concept album, Waters contributed nothing to it, and it is no longer true that Pink Floyd's final decade presents a unified vision of the world.

An Enduring Lapse of Identity?

Waters offered many reasons why *Lapse of Reason* and what follows is not the work of Pink Floyd. In the end, they boil down to one basic reason: In 1985, Waters notified the band that he had quit. Pink Floyd did not exist after that. But how does the

---

[4] This vision is articulated at length by Phil Rose, *Which One's Pink? An Analysis of the Concept Albums of Roger Waters and Pink Floyd* (Burlington: Collector's Guide: 1998).

one fact support the other? Does his argument hang together? Waters offers three slightly different reasons why his departure constitutes the end of the band.

First, Waters argues that an album created by only one member of Pink Floyd is a solo album by that musician, so it cannot be a Pink Floyd album. Waters contends that *Lapse of Reason* is almost solely the work of Gilmour, with Mason and Wright in supporting roles that do not constitute genuine membership. *Lapse of Reason* is just a Gilmour solo record relying heavily on hired studio help. Part of Waters's case is that Gilmour hired multiple session musicians and worked with many songwriters besides Mason and Wright, that Wright was on salary and not a co-equal member with Mason and Gilmour, and that Mason was not the primary drummer for any of the actual music. The subsequent tour (documented on *Delicate Sound of Thunder*) also used Mason and Wright as mere sidemen. According to Waters, there was no "functioning" band.[5] Therefore selling it as Pink Floyd is an intentional fraud. On this argument, Pink Floyd is essentially a group. Hence music that does not emerge from the group is not legitimate Pink Floyd music.

Second, Waters wrote the words and thus furnished the concepts for Pink Floyd's music after Barrett was booted from the band in 1968. In Timothy White's formulation of this argument, Pink Floyd depended on Waters "lyrically, musically, and conceptually" in their glory years.[6] Even if Mason and Wright had contributed more fully to *Lapse of Reason*, their reliance on multiple lyricists who never joined the group invalidates the music as a product of the *group* Pink Floyd.

Third, Waters argues that his leaving is not the end of the band, because "the group disintegrated long ago."[7] His 1986 departure was simply a public admission of what had already taken place—evidently during the recording of *The Final Cut*, if not *The Wall*. Therefore Gilmour's revival of the band for *Lapse of Reason* is dishonest. There is no group to revive.

---

[5] Waters, quoted in White, "Pink Floyd," p. 519. Note that if this argument is sound, it follows that *The Wall* may not be a Pink Floyd album either, since Wright became a salaried musician during the recording sessions.

[6] White, "Pink Floyd," p. 514.

[7] Waters quoted in White, "Pink Floyd," p. 508.

The third argument is the easiest to dismiss. Unless a group has very well formalized rules requiring regular periods of activity, as does, for instance, the United States Congress, then the group can very easily exist for long periods of time in a dormant state. In the absence of formal action taken to disband, a group can exist for years without being active, as indicated by recent reunions of The Pixies, Iggy and the Stooges, and others.

The second argument is also very weak. As every Pink Floyd fan knows, the group's existence cannot depend on Waters's "unifying" role as lyricist and primary idea man. Waters had no such role before *Dark Side of the Moon*. Originally, Barrett played that role. In fact, Waters's ability to *take over* a certain role demonstrates that the continuity of the band does not depend on any particular individual's continuity in that role.

Furthermore, I am personally in agreement with Mason's and Gilmour's independent assessments that the band was adrift after Barrett's firing and remained that way until *Meddle*. One interesting thing about *Meddle* is that only one of the album's six songs is primarily a Waters composition. George Gershwin's songs are primarily attributed to him—despite the fact that he wrote none of the lyrics—and the opera *The Marriage of Figaro* is primarily Mozart's—despite the fact that he hired a lyricist. Likewise, Waters's role as lyricist for the songs on *Meddle* (half the album) does not make him the unifying force in the band. Yet *Meddle* is their breakthrough to a recognizable "Pink Floyd" musical style.

This response to Waters's second argument might be seen as supporting his first. If Pink Floyd is a musical collective, then a musical project in which only one member plays a significant part is not the work of a musical *group*, which is what Pink Floyd essentially is. However, this argument could be used against *The Final Cut*. In fact, that very point might be what's behind Waters's claim that the group "disintegrated long ago" (back during the sessions for *The Wall*?). But if that's true, then Waters himself (just like Pink, perhaps) was perpetuating a fraud when the group performed the stage version of *The Wall*.

These points raise a huge philosophical problem. How can a group that changes its members be *the same group* at two different times? If different groups of individuals can be the same group at two different times, then why isn't it equally permissible for the group to operate by different sets of rules at different times? So we must deal with two closely related problems. First, how does anything remain the same thing if it keeps changing? Second, how does a group have any identity at all?

The Same in a Relative Way?

The problem of identity arises for every thing that exists over time. It's easiest to see it by thinking about things that keep changing over an extended period of time. Seventeenth-century English philosopher John Locke put it in terms of living organisms.

> In the state of living creatures, their identity depends not on a mass of the same particles, but on something else. For in them the variation of great parcels of matter alters not the identity: an oak growing from a plant to a great tree, and then lopped, is still the same oak; and a colt grown up to a horse, sometimes fat, sometimes lean, is all the while the same horse: though, in both these cases, there may be a manifest change of the parts; so that truly they are not either of them the same masses of matter, though they be truly one of them the same oak, and the other the same horse. The reason whereof is, that, in these two cases—a mass of matter and a living body—identity is not applied to the same thing.[8]

For many kinds of things, it is not the actual materials of an object that must remain the same in order to say that the same object exists both before and after a change. With a wide range of things, we must locate some principle of organization for the temporary arrangements of material that we observe.

We might think of the members of Pink Floyd as analogous to "matter" or material parts. The lesson from Locke is that having the material parts does not equal having the group. Putting Barrett in a room with Waters, Mason, and Wright in 1975—as actually happened when Syd wandered into the studio during the sessions for *Wish You Were Here*—does not automatically bring the Pink Floyd of *Piper* back into existence.

Locke is particularly useful for addressing this problem because he uses his insight about identity to distinguish between the continuing existence of the same man and the

---

[8] John Locke, *An Essay Concerning Human Understanding* (1690), Chapter XXVII.3.

continuation of the same person. The *man* is the animal. The *person* is the combination of consciousness and memory: "For it is by the consciousness [any intelligent being] has of its present thoughts and actions, that it is self to itself now, and so will be the same self, as far as the same consciousness can extend to actions past or to come."[9] Personal identity requires awareness of one's past and ability to think of oneself in future actions. The *man* Syd Barrett was in Abbey Road Studio Three on June 5th, 1975, but it was only by virtue of his remembering who Waters and Gilmour were that the *person* Syd Barrett was present. The fact that most band members didn't at first recognize Barrett when (as Waters later put it, quoted in Schaffner, p. 203) this "great, fat, bald, mad person" wandered in shows that Syd Barrett the person was not *immediately* present, for them.

So why do we want to agree with Locke that we should distinguish between Barrett the man and Barrett the person? Because the person, not the man, is the appropriate object of punishment and reward, or of our praise and blame. As it goes in "Brain Damage," we want to account for times when "there's someone in my head but it's not me." Locke's own example is the common case of admitting that someone is "not himself" any longer. If someone is temporarily insane and then reverts to sanity, we do not want to punish the sane person for what happened during the temporary insanity. So we must allow for the reality that two different persons can consecutively share the same "man" or body.

But a musical group isn't a living organism, nor is it a thing with persisting consciousness and memory. In so far as its members can be regarded as its parts, the parts of Pink Floyd have persisting memory and consciousness. However, that doesn't show that the organized combination of the parts has its own memory and consciousness. After all, a grain of sand is tiny, but the combination of millions of grains of sands into a beach does not ensure that the beach is tiny. So we need some independent criterion of identity. If we want to treat Pink Floyd as the kind of thing that merits praise and blame, then we need something like Locke's criterion of personal identity.

---

[9] Locke, *Essay*, Chapter XXVII.10.

The Echo of a Distant Time: Identity and Change

We've looked at three examples—an oak tree, a horse, and Syd Barrett—but haven't directly examined the general philosophical problem of identity over time. To do this, I'll take one of Waters's arguments, extract its underlying assumption about identity, and then identify the resulting problem.

Waters argues that earlier versions of Pink Floyd didn't need to hire outsiders to write lyrics. The Gilmour-era Floyd of *Lapse of Reason* relies on them, so the band did not really endure Waters's departure. This argument contains an unstated assumption that two things with different features or properties are different objects. We can prove that two things are genuinely different by showing some difference in their properties. As the principle of the identity of indiscernibles holds, two things can't be different if there's no way to tell them apart.

The principle says, specifically, that for any object a and any object b, if a is identical with b, then a has property X if and only if b has property X. It means that two things cannot turn out to be one and the same thing unless there are no differences between them. This concept of being one and the same thing is known as numerical identity. Suppose I see a small puppy dog in my friend's house and then two years later I see a larger dog of the same breed in my friend's yard. Remembering the puppy's name, I point to the dog and ask, "Is that Seamus?" I'm asking about numerical identity.

So, taking the identity of indiscernibles along with numerical identity, Waters is arguing that if we find a property that identifies an object, and then time passes and the object loses that property, then the subsequent object cannot be numerically identical with the earlier object. Pink Floyd that loses the property of having Waters as a member, in other words, cannot any longer be the same Pink Floyd.

Unfortunately for Waters, his argument has the same logic as another that employs the principle of the identity of indiscernibles in just the same way:[10]

---

[10] My reconstruction and discussion of this argument is based on a similar argument in Trenton Merricks, "Endurance and Indiscernibility," in Michael J. Loux, ed., *Metaphysics: Contemporary Readings* (London: Routledge, 2001), pp. 364–65.

1. Let *a* refer to Pink Floyd in 1967, when Barrett is sole lyricist.

2. Let *b* refer to Pink Floyd in 1975, when Waters is sole lyricist.

3. Assume that Pink Floyd endures from 1967 to 1975, so *a* is numerically identical with *b*.

4. Because of the identity of indiscernibles, what's true of *a* must be true of *b*. So Pink Floyd in 1967 has Barrett as sole lyricist if and only if Pink Floyd in 1975 has Barrett as sole lyricist.

5. Because our third step assumed the numerical identity of Pink Floyd in 1967 and 1975, we're entitled to conclude that Pink Floyd in 1975 has Barrett as sole lyricist.

6. However, we noticed in step 2 that Pink Floyd in 1975 has Waters as sole lyricist. So Pink Floyd had two sole lyricists in 1975.

Because a band can't have two different "sole" lyricists, the last step of the argument is absurd.

Something must have gone wrong. The primary candidate for the mistake is step 3, which says that the earlier and later groups are numerically identical. They might share a name, but that merely hides the fact that they're different bands. The same reasoning that "proves" that Pink Floyd no longer existed after Waters quit can be used to show that Pink Floyd no longer existed once Gilmour was added to the band, or after Barrett was fired, or after Wright was fired, or because Barrett changed the band's repertoire by teaching them the song "Lucifer Sam." According to the identity of indiscernibles, *any* change demonstrates a lack of numerical identity.

Some philosophers endorse the conclusion that nothing endures change.[11] I don't. More importantly, Waters doesn't—he wants to take credit for keeping the band going after Barrett. But if there's a mistake in the argument that "proves" Waters couldn't have kept the band going, then the same mistake must occur in Waters's own argument against the numerical identity of the group that recorded *Dark Side of the Moon* and the group that

---

[11] For an introduction to this doctrine, known as perdurantism, see Michael J. Loux, "Endurantism and Perdurantism," in Loux, *Metaphysics*, pp. 321–27.

created *Lapse of Reason*. There must be a problem, that is, in the very pattern of the argument.

Let's return to Locke's insight that "in these two cases—a mass of matter and a living body—identity is not applied to the same thing." Instead of endorsing the principle of the identity of indiscernibles as it was used in the argument, we should recognize that "*a* is identical with *b*" or "*a* is the same as *b*" make no sense until we ask, "Same what?" We need to specify what kind of thing is involved. Building on Locke's insight that the ongoing identity of the same man does not necessarily involve the ongoing identity of the same person, we can see that not every property of *a* is relevant to the issue of whether *a* is identical with *b*. We can only resolve our difficulties by getting a better handle on what kind of thing we are seeking when we posit the identity of Pink Floyd.

Actions Brings Good Fortune: Actions, Intentions, and Evaluation

Now I have to complicate things, because the task of distinguishing Pink Floyd from non-Pink Floyd is closely related to the relationship between responsibility and intentions. This relationship will provide the criterion for the identity of a musical group that we need in order to solve the overall problem. But not before we look at this relationship itself.

We engage in both aesthetic and moral evaluation of other people. However, not all human behaviors are equally subject to evaluation, at least not in the same way. If a baby cries because she is hungry, disrupting our activities, we do not evaluate the baby's behavior in the same way that we would judge, for example, a college student who suddenly disrupts a classroom by yelling irrelevant bits of information. Although the baby's crying and the student's yelling have the same practical effect of disrupting us, the baby's behavior is not intended to. Unless the student has an uncontrollable condition, such as Tourette syndrome, we judge the student's disruptive behavior as an action for which we can hold the student personally responsible. The individual's capacity for forming intentions and acting on those intentions is central to the practice of assigning moral responsibility.

Aesthetic evaluation is a bit more complicated. We aesthetically evaluate things that are intended, but we also aesthetically

evaluate things and arrangements of things that aren't. The
Grand Canyon did not result from an intended action, yet visitors find it aesthetically sublime. Similarly, no one intended
for David Gilmour to have great cheekbones, but he does, and
as a result he's better looking than many men. On the other
hand, when we know that something is intended to appear a
certain way, we look for a unifying purpose and we evaluate
it accordingly. (Famously, the philosopher Immanuel Kant
argues that we evaluate the same thing very differently
depending on whether we classify it as either a "free" or a
"dependent" beauty—a bird's song is a free beauty, but a
human imitation of a bird song is a dependent beauty.) If
we're hiking and see golden poppies growing wild, we admire
their beauty. If we then look closer and see that someone has
put plastic flowers all along the trail, we will revise our evaluation (and perhaps get angry). Waters is attributing a similar
deception to Gilmour when he argues that *Lapse of Reason* is
"fake" Pink Floyd.

The point is that an intended result is evaluated in terms of
someone's goals relative to her situation. Where we can identify
goals, we evaluate things differently than we do for unintended
or merely accidental consequences. With objects created intentionally, we try to identify the aims or intentions that account for
it being the way it is. Because songs are created and shared
intentionally, we can evaluate them in two ways relative to
intentions. We can ask if the resulting object is well-designed
relative to those intentions, and we can ask whether the guiding intention is a worthwhile one.

For example, it doesn't make sense to criticize "Have a Cigar"
for its lack of insight into the geopolitics of the U.S. Military's
1970 Cambodian incursion if there's no evidence that the song
was meant to address that topic. To appreciate "Have a Cigar,"
a listener must understand that it aims to say something about
the music industry of the early 1970s, not about America's role
in Southeast Asia.

So how, then, should we evaluate the activities of a group
effort? In thinking about the aims of "Have a Cigar," should we
think about Waters's aims on the grounds that he wrote the
music and lyrics? Or should we think about the *group's* aims,
since the group included it as part of a group project? If we evaluate an individual's behavior by reference to the individual's

intentions in a given situation, where do we find the intentions that guide our evaluation of a group project?

To be more specific, suppose we agree with Gilmour that Pink Floyd's *Atom Heart Mother* album is "shit," the group's "lowest point artistically."[12] But how can this music be an embarrassment to the *group* unless there are group intentions in terms of which it is evaluated? Do these intentions differ from those of the four individuals who constituted the group when *Atom Heart Mother* was created? Or do we have to understand the intentions of the different individuals, and evaluate the album accordingly?

The philosophical problem is how to consistently endorse three ideas. First, any plausible theory of evaluation should endorse the idea that *Wish You Were Here* is better than *Atom Heart Mother*. Second, these albums were created by collective activity. Third, our evaluation should take notice of relevant intentions. The complicating problem is that only minds can form intentions. There is no "group mind" attached to Pink Floyd, so the group cannot have intentions informing the creation of Pink Floyd albums. In other words, it seems impossible for there to be *group* intentions over and above the intentions of distinct individuals who contribute to a project. This fact accounts for the great temptation to point to just one individual as the creative power in each stage of Pink Floyd's history (Barrett, then Waters, then Gilmour).

So we face a choice. On the one hand, we can endorse the idea that intentions always belong to specific individuals. According to this position, "agency individualism," a legitimate evaluation of *Atom Heart Mother* limits the relevant intentions and aims to the ones held by the distinct individuals who were members of Pink Floyd at that time.

On the other hand, we might decide that *Atom Heart Mother* reveals the first step in a larger Pink Floyd strategy. For example, the side-long track "Atom Heart Mother" is a crude prototype for what the group does so much better with "Echoes." Yet it might turn out that none of the individuals was thinking about "Atom Heart Mother" and "Echoes" in this way. We might want to say that "Atom Heart Mother" is better than Gilmour thinks it

---

[12] Quoted in Johnny Black, "Pink Floyd," *Mojo Magazine* (November 2001).

is, because it is an important developmental step in moving toward something better, namely "Echoes." To maintain this interpretation despite the lack of agency individualism, we must attribute a group intention to Pink Floyd. To distinguish it from agency individualism, let's call it "collective agency." Unfortunately, we cannot endorse collective agency unless we can explain how a group or collective can form intentions that cannot be equated with those of the individuals in the group.

Either way, we have a big problem. If intentions must be assigned to specific individuals, then Pink Floyd cannot have a group legacy. If an evaluation of *The Piper at the Gates of Dawn* is an evaluation of Barrett, and an evaluation of *The Wall* is an evaluation of Waters, and an evaluation of *Lapse of Reason* is an evaluation of Gilmour, then we've eliminated the possibility that our opinion of either *The Wall* or *Lapse of Reason* can have any bearing on *Piper*. We might as well ask whether *Lapse of Reason* reflects well on the Rolling Stones, or whether the *Echoes* compilation is a good overview of King Crimson's career![13] To make sense of the idea of a Pink Floyd legacy, we seem to need an ongoing entity with intentions. But it's tempting to say that groups can't have intentions and that we need a person to be there every stage furnishing intentions. However, no one thinks that Pink Floyd albums should be judged by reference to Nick Mason's intentions. After all, no one answers the question "Which one's Pink?" by pointing to Mason. Yet he is the only individual who participated in the creation of every album.

A Smile from a Veil? Hypothetical and Actual Intentions

Even if we select the first alternative and say that individuals are the only sort of thing to which we can attribute intentions, we do not have to evaluate the albums in terms of the actual intentions of individuals. There are two reasons in favor of this proposal (and many philosophers find them convincing). First, intentions are often obscure or unavailable to us. Yet we evalu-

---

[13] There are critics and fans who regard *Piper* as Barrett's record and who think that Pink Floyd ceased to exist when Barrett left the group. See John Cavanagh, *The Piper at the Gates of Dawn* (33 1/3 series) (New York: Continuum, 2003), p. 122.

ate them anyway. Second, songs and performances can have properties that their creators did not intend. Some of these unintended features contribute in positive ways. If we restrict our positive evaluations to actual intentions, then we cannot praise the work for having these properties. Therefore we should evaluate works *as if* all of their positive and negative features were intended, by responding to a hypothetical artist who had complete control over all of its properties. Aesthetic evaluations should be based on hypothetical intentions.

For example, the musical "hook" of "Shine on You Crazy Diamond" is a four-note theme on Gilmour's guitar. In the context of the song, the theme represents the fractured state of Barrett's mind. Gilmour composed it more or less accidentally, while improvising. It was Waters's idea to couple Gilmour's "mournful kind of sound" with lyrics about Barrett's absence.[14] To regard "Shine on You Crazy Diamond" as a highly successful, unified long-form composition, we might prefer to approach it *as if* Gilmour had the same purpose in mind as did Waters.

Nonetheless, I reject the strategy of hypothetical intentionalism. I think that *actual* intentions provide the proper constraint on interpretation and evaluation.[15] First, there are many cases where hypothetical intentions will give us a more satisfying interpretation, and thus a more positive evaluation, yet we know perfectly well that we shouldn't interpret and evaluate it in that way. Obvious cases are slips of the tongue and mispronounced words. For example, it's very hard to enunciate some words clearly when singing. Jimi Hendrix's "Purple Haze" includes the line "Excuse me while I kiss the sky." As Hendrix actually sings it, many listeners have heard it as "kiss this guy." In some contexts, the mistaken interpretation is more desirable than the one that conforms to his actual intentions—taken as political statement raging against mindless conformity, "kiss this guy" is politically more potent than "kiss the sky." However, the actually intended words are the words, and they should be the basis for interpretation and evaluation. Likewise, someone who hears the

---

14 Quoted in Rose, *Which One's Pink?*, p. 43; originally from Nick Sedgewick, "A Rambling Conversation with Roger Waters Concerning All This and That," in n.a., *Wish You Were Songbook*, 1975.
15 My discussion is heavily influenced by Robert Stecker, *Interpretation and Construction: Art, Speech, and the Law* (Malden: Blackwell, 2003), pp. 42–50.

phrase "ordinary men" in Pink Floyd's "Us and Them" as "old and hairy men" has just got it wrong, no matter how much they think it improves the song. The actual trumps the hypothetical.

Second, hypothetical intentionalism tells us that we gain nothing by consulting interviews with Waters and Gilmour in order to get a better understanding of the music and songs. If actual intentions don't matter, then knowing what the musicians actually said cannot guide our interpretation and evaluation. However, I certainly think that I have a better understanding of *Wish You Were Here* because I've read interviews with Waters in which he clarifies his actual intentions. Actual intentions again trump hypothetical ones.

Let's take stock. *The Final Cut, A Momentary Lapse of Reason* and several other albums are only relevant to our interpretation and evaluation of Pink Floyd if they are intended to be treated as such. We cannot pick and choose based on the outcome that pleases fans the most, as would be allowed by hypothetical intentionalism. Actual intentionalism is more plausible than hypothetical intentionalism. But this conclusion returns us to the serious problem of how to attribute intentions to a group.

Like a Cardboard Cut-Out Man: Collectives as Individuals

My overall argument requires connecting intentions and collective achievements. The first step is to clarify the nature of intentions. An intention is a willing or a desire that a result will follow from an action that is being undertaken, together with a belief that the action will cause that result. (If I don't believe that a sponge can break a window, I can't intend to break the window by throwing a sponge at it.) Basically, an intention is a desire for something to happen as a result of one's actions. Intentions combine with beliefs and feelings to guide actions.

Let's suppose that "Shine on You Crazy Diamond" was not intended to be about Barrett when Gilmour first came up with the music. Waters added lyrics and he intended those lyrics to be about Barrett. If only one of four members of the group intended "Shine on You Crazy Diamond" to be about Barrett, how can the group, Pink Floyd, intend it?

There are two ways to explain how this song, which does not name Barrett, is about him. One is the theory of agency individualism. It says that only individual people can intend things. So agency individualism says that the song is intentionally about Barrett because an individual—in this case, Waters—intended it, and that's the end of it. Notice, however, that restricting intentions to individuals places all responsibility and credit on individuals. When we find an online blogger writing "I think 'Wish You Were Here' is Pink Floyd's best album," [16] we must deny that the blogger is literally saying anything about Pink Floyd, the group. Gilmour's musical theme has nothing to do with Barrett, and "Have a Cigar" and "Welcome to the Machine" were composed by Waters without any real involvement by the other members of the group. *Wish You Were Here* is a patchwork of achievements by various individuals.

The alternative theory endorses collective agency. It sees Pink Floyd as a distinct entity that has intentions that differ from those of the individuals who've been in the group. As a result, Pink Floyd can be evaluated collectively without concern for assigning responsibility to particular group members. It's possible for *Wish You Were Here* to be the band's best album, meaning that it is the best of those for which the group, Pink Floyd, is collectively responsible. We do not have to believe that all four *members* of the quartet were simultaneously operating at their best in order to say that *the group* was at their peak.

But our earlier discussion of Locke shows why collective agency faces a big problem. Collectives do not have a straightforward criterion of identity, because they lack something relevant that only individuals can possess. They lack the sorts of mental states that generate personal identity. So if intentions are mental states accompanying beliefs and feelings, then the group Pink Floyd can't intend anything. Pink Floyd is a collective, but collectives don't have minds. And because collectives don't have minds, they lack states of mind. So collectives can't intentionally do things that are subject to praise and blame.

But this argument against collective agency is less compelling than it might seem. We tend to assume collectives don't have minds, after all, because we can't easily imagine a mechanism or process by which separate individual minds can come

---

[16] Posted by Nick on Sunday, August 13th, 2006, in response to "One Big Ass Overview of Pink Floyd," posted August 17th, 2005, http://www.myspace.com.

together or give rise to a collective mind. But that's a familiar circumstance. We think that an individual agent's intentions form as a result of brain activity, but we have little understanding of *how* the brain achieves intentionality. In this case, however, we don't deny that a person with a brain has intentions. So why should we deny that a rock band is a collective with intentions?

There is another reason why we might confidently speak of group intentions. As several philosophers have independently argued, the important task is not to identify the actual intentions, beliefs, and desires of a group so that, in turn, we may legitimately evaluate them. Instead, they argue, we must turn the situation around and see that we already believe that these intentions exist, if only implicitly, when we reasonably evaluate group actions.[17]

So if it's reasonable to evaluate a group's activity, then it's equally reasonable to believe in collective agency and collective intentions. It doesn't matter, in other words, that I have no good reason for thinking that the *individual* members of Pink Floyd came to any clear agreement about what they were trying to do with *Wish You Were Here*, for example. I don't have to worry about the four members of the group, only the group itself. Anyone can tell that the album has an admirable conceptual unity and reasonably takes it to be the product of collective action, so it's reasonable to attribute the success of *Wish You Were Here* to the group.

True, I've allowed that the words to "Shine on You Crazy Diamond" are Waters's words, reflecting Waters's intentions. Furthermore, these words have a lot to do with the album's conceptual coherence. But I haven't actually endorsed agency individualism as it may appear. For collective agency is compatible with the way that groups place responsibility on individuals to carry out activities on behalf of the group. So we can praise or blame Pink Floyd as a group in full knowledge of the fact that different members play different roles in bringing about the results that we admire or criticize. As members, different indi-

---

[17] The argument that follows is based on Copp, "On the Agency of Certain Collective Entities," and Deborah Tollefsen, "The Rationality of Collective Guilt," in Peter A. French and Howard K. Wettstein, eds., *Midwest Studies in Philosophy Volume XXX: Shared Intentions and Collective Responsibility* (Boston: Blackwell, 2006), pp. 222–239.

viduals have responsibilities to further the goals of the group even when, as individuals, they do not wish to do so. Knowing that *The Wall* had to be finished in time for the Christmas sales period of 1979, for example, Wright should not have made himself unavailable by going to Greece for a vacation. But because we can criticize individuals for what they do or fail to do within the group, it is tempting to suppose that we must *always* assign praise or blame to individuals each time we evaluate group activity. But there's no good reason to do that. Johnny Rotten may not even have known how many members were in Pink Floyd when he announced to the world that he hated them.

To Join in with the Game

We started with the question of whether there is a criterion of identity for Pink Floyd that will settle the question of whether, for example, the Gilmour-era group is "fake" Floyd. The central question is finding a principled way to decide which music made under the name "Pink Floyd" was made by Pink Floyd, the collective. Collectives always operate through individuals who are charged with acting responsibly on behalf of its intentions. The question, therefore, is who was charged with acting on behalf of Pink Floyd, the time each person was responsible for doing so, and whether those persons did in fact act responsibly. If there was a time when no person continued to have responsibility for acting on behalf of Pink Floyd, furthering Pink Floyd's collective intentions, then *that* is when Pink Floyd ceased to exist. Our criterion of identity, that is, lay in the dual requirement of being charged to act on behalf of the group's intentions and acting responsibly in that regard.

So what happens when a group member's individual intentions are no longer compatible with those of the group to which he or she belongs? Or when an individual acts irresponsibly relative to the group's intentions? Such things happen all the time. Suppose that I personally reject all of the goals set out in my university's official long-range plan. Unless I quit my job, when I'm at work I must *accept* the official goals by virtue of my position in the organization. As an employee, it's my responsibility to support the collective's plans. Should I act on my individual beliefs and sabotage what the university is trying to accomplish, the university would have just cause for terminating me. On the other hand, I might find it too hard to accept the goals, and I might quit. My department would then hire someone else to do my job.

There are many kinds of collectives, but two basic principles apply.[18] First, individual members of the group cannot nullify a group intention, decision, or plan. Second, no member can disband the group without the consent of every other member of the group. It sometimes happens that one person wields enough power or influence that he or she has the practical ability to suspend the group's activities or destroy the group. However, the group has the right to remove such a person from the group if she acts against the group's own interests. If you can't stomach *The Wind in the Willows* when that's been chosen by your book group as its next read, don't be surprised if, despite your objections, the group simply meets without you.

What is true of a loosely-organized book club is also true of a rock band. Waters may have had legitimate personal reasons for wanting to leave Pink Floyd. As the individual who'd guided the band during its greatest successes, he had every reason to think that a post-Waters group would produce weak music that would embarrass the Pink Floyd name. However, Waters had no power to disband Pink Floyd, and the other members had every right to replace him in any manner they saw fit. Indeed, once Waters saw that he could no longer function within the Pink Floyd framework, he had a personal duty to leave. Furthermore, in the absence of an explicit, shared agreement about what Pink Floyd was trying to accomplish as an organization, the remaining members were perfectly free to reject the working processes that governed the group when Waters was a dominant voice. Just as Barrett's departure did not automatically disband the group as long as the others wanted to continue, Waters's departure did not spell the end for Pink Floyd.

This does not mean, however, that the others were free to do *anything* and still claim to be Pink Floyd. From the beginning, the group was a group of musicians. Had Gilmour, Mason, and Wright employed "Pink Floyd" as the name for a company that restores vintage aircraft, this project could hardly count as a con-

---

[18] Margaret Gilbert, "Concerning Sociality: The Plural Subject as Paradigm," in John Greenwood, ed., *The Mark of the Social: Discovery or Invention?* (Lanham: Rowman and littlefield, 1997), pp. 17–36.

tinuation of Pink Floyd the rock band. The framework under which we are to evaluate success or failure would have completely changed.

In retrospect, the group's activities and intentions are pretty clear. Pink Floyd displayed the collective intention of creating original music and, in concert, presenting both new and old songs from their repertoire. When Gilmour decided to record *Lapse of Reason* and then to launch a tour in support of it, he was acting in keeping with the group's longstanding intentions. Waters had every right to refuse, but he had no right to deny Gilmour the opportunity to organize these activities on behalf of the group.

The fact that Gilmour had to find an alternative way to make Pink Floyd work (such as hiring lyricists) does not count against the continuation of Pink Floyd's identity. A similar self-governing enterprise by working musicians, the Vienna Philharmonic, was formed in 1842. Scores of musicians have joined and left, but its collective identity is unchanged. Because Pink Floyd has not allowed a new member to join since 1968, its organizational practices will prevent it from existing for 160 years, like the Vienna Philharmonic. But Pink Floyd can add to its legacy for many years to come. Pink Floyd performs any time Gilmour, Mason, and Wright decide to play together under that name, consistent with the group's guiding intentions, with or without Waters.

As for the *Echoes* compilation, therefore, it's an accurate overview of the real Pink Floyd.

12

The Dinner Band on the Cruise Ship of Theseus

MICHAEL F. PATTON, JR.

Philosophers have a long history of taking seemingly simple issues and making them very complex. As an example, some of us even call this activity by an overly complex name: Problematizing. To be honest, most of us think we're actually revealing the deep and interesting complexity that the demands of life have us gloss over, and we think that the world is a better place because of it. However, this can be frustrating for those just starting out and for the old pros as well. As bright a philosophical light as David Hume had a sort of breakdown at the end of his *Treatise*:

> The *intense* view of these manifold contradictions and imperfections in human reason has so wrought upon me and heated my brain that I am ready to reject all belief and reasoning, and can look upon no opinion even as more probable or likely than another . . . I am confounded with all these questions, and begin to consider myself in the most deplorable condition imaginable, inviron'd with the deepest darkness, and utterly deprives of the use of every member and faculty.
>
> Most fortunately it happens, that since reason is incapable of dispelling these clouds, nature herself suffices to that purpose and cures me of this philosophical melancholy and delirium . . . and when after three or four hours' amusement, I wou'd return to these speculations, they appear so cold, and strain'd, and ridiculous, that I cannot find in my heart to enter into them any further.[1]

---

[1] *A Treatise of Human Nature* (Oxford University Press, 1978), p. 269.

When Hume gets to the point where the lunatic has come off the grass and gotten into his head, he cannot carry on anymore. In what follows, I will use some examples from the history and music of *Pink Floyd* to explore some philosophical puzzles about identity, at least until I get brain damage. After all, the guys who make up *Pink Floyd* have been performing the songs they wrote together since 1965. I mean, some of them have been performing the songs they wrote and then others later performed those songs and some new songs they wrote after a couple of the first guys left. Along they way, it started sounding different, some members left and came back while others just left and finally they went out of existence. Then they played a concert in 2005, when four of them shared a stage for the first time in twenty-five years. Wait a minute, now I am confused.

Wot's . . . Uh the Deal?

Problems of identity across time, or diachronic identity, are as old as philosophy itself. Basically, the question is "When is it true to say that object a at time one is the same object as object b at time two?" Am I the same person as I was when I was twenty? Is the thing I climbed in Paris (Okay, I rode the elevator) the same thing as Monsieur Eiffel built in the second half of the nineteenth century? The story of Theseus's ship problematizes these questions, all of which have the pre-reflective answer of "Duh . . . yes!," by pointing out that we can describe cases where there are strong reasons to answer "no" or else run afoul of basic logic. Here's how the argument goes (at least the way it goes in my head):

Theseus leaves port on the *Trump Princess*, which promptly begins to disintegrate. Luckily, between the hold and the barge he is towing, Theseus has enough spare parts to repair absolutely anything that goes wrong with the ship. Also, being something of an environmentalist, Theseus stows all the damaged and broken parts in the hold or on the towed barge. As bad weather and poor construction standards dog Theseus and his crew throughout the trip, it finally happens that Theseus has rebuilt the *Trump Princess* entirely, part for part. Trust me, if a knowledgeable seaman does this carefully, it can be accomplished without the ship sinking. (I promise. Really. If you're worried about all the welding and electrical work and such, fine, I'll make it Huck and Jim's raft, but it isn't nearly as interesting.)

Anyway, Theseus finally makes landfall and starts waxing philosophical: is this the ship that made landfall the same ship as the ship that left port so long ago? To help him think about it, he makes a nearly exact duplicate of his ship in dry-dock out of the salvaged parts. Certainly the salvaged ship has some sort of claim on being *the* ship of Theseus—it is the collection of atoms (minus a few here and there) that actually did leave the port with Theseus and his crew standing aboard. But, the ship that made landfall has a claim to being *the* ship of Theseus as well. After all, Theseus and the crew never got wet or jumped to another boat at any point during their trip. At the most they had to step around some "pardon our progress" tape while a certain part of the ship was being repaired. So how can anyone really doubt that there was just one ship that underwent repairs but made the whole journey?

The philosophical problems get worse when you think about animate objects. Our bodies exchange atoms with the environment at an alarming rate. If you drink a sugary beverage while walking, within ten minutes, the carbon in the sugar you ingested will be exhaled as CO_2. Three days from now, more than one=half of the particles that currently compose your liver will be outside your body. And, finally, within a relatively short amount of years, your body will composed of a completely different set of atoms than it is now. So we are all ships of Theseus with a big metaphysical decision to make: do we survive the wholesale exchange of all of our parts, in which case the very appealing doctrine that I am the parts that compose me at any one time is false, or do we say that we do not survive the loss of a part, and thereby say goodbye to the appealing claim that we persist over time?

Decisions, decisions. It's certainly obvious to me that I am me right now, and since I don't believe in an immaterial soul or mind, I have to be the things that compose me. But it also seems to me that I was me six years ago, even though almost all of those atoms were dispersed into the biosphere long ago. Neither answer really satisfies me.

There are other moves to make in this debate—one can say that a person's identity inheres in a nonphysical spirit. Many religious traditions are consistent this view of things. Alternatively, one could adopt the so-called theory of temporal parts—the thesis that enduring objects are four-dimensional things, not three-dimensional things, that have their parts timelessly all at once. These views are oft-debated, and I have discussed the objections I have to these solutions elsewhere.[2]

What Do You Want from Me?

Pink Floyd has had many Ship-of-Theseus moments. They've changed members, agents, managers, musical styles, fan bases and record companies. So, if we can figure out what the hell is going on with the diachronic identity of Pink Floyd, maybe we can come up with something intelligent to say about diachronic identity in general—for ships, people, bands, and everything under the sun. Then we can all go off and put in *Dark Side of the Moon* and *The Wizard of Oz* at the same time and freak out.

I want to discuss several different ways in which we might identify and then re-identify Pink Floyd. As we shall see, many of these categories overlap in some way or another, and this fact may provide a clue for the resolution of this puzzle that I will finally suggest. For the purposes of this exercise, I will consider five different possible sources of continued identity: Roster Identity, Stylistic Identity, Legal Identity, and Nominal Identity.

Band Roster Identity

What a mess this is. It's much harder than figuring genealogy, and includes nearly as many petty fights and squabbles as family life.

- For our purposes, the band called Pink Floyd started out with Bob Klose (guitar), Roger Waters (bass), Nick Mason (drums), Rick Wright (wind instruments), and Syd Barrett (guitar and vocals).

- These people were playing together up until the first album was about to be recorded, at which point Klose left

---

[2] "Probabilities and Temporal Parts," *Acta Analytica* 17:28 (2002), pp. 39–52; "The Officeholder View of Personal Identity," *Personalist Forum* 15:2 (1999), pp. 389–403.

the band to pursue photography. The remaining four constituted the band when *Piper at the Gates of Dawn* was released in 1967.

- Soon after this album began to get noticed, Barrett's much talked about problems led to the addition of David Gilmour on guitar and vocals.

- In 1968, Barrett left the band for good, and the line-up of Gilmour, Waters, Wright, and Mason remained constant until Wright was fired from the band in 1981 during the recording of *The Wall*.

- Next, Waters left the band in 1985, but Gilmour and Mason continued recording material as "Pink Floyd," prompting a lawsuit by Waters (more on this later).

- To cap it all off, in 1987, Wright rejoined the band.

Whew. It would be nice if we could just focus on the group from until 1968 until 1981 when the core four broke up with the departure of Wright. But, some people would not sit still for the exclusion of *Piper at the Gates of Dawn* from the discography, and I suspect no one would sit still for excluding *The Wall*, which was not complete when Wright was fired from the group.

Stylistic Identity

Let's now ask whether the band stays the same even though the style of music it composes and play changes. I think there are real questions here—consider the difference between the early, bluesy Peter-Green-era of Fleetwood Mac (the era in which they wrote and recorded "Black Magic Woman" in nearly the same arrangement that made Carlos Santana a star) and the post-Buckingham-Nicks-era that saw such monster hits as "Dreams" and the Clinton theme song "Don't Stop (Thinking About Tomorrow)." I'd be surprised to find someone who was able to pick these songs as coming from the same band if she was ignorant of the historical facts. An even more interesting (and more difficult) case can arise when we think of individual artists who drastically change their styles. Compare tracks from *The Freewheelin' Bob Dylan, Desire, Saved!, Shot of Love,* and *Love and Theft* and tell me that this seems like the same musical entity. It's made more difficult because we assume it is the same person, Bob Dylan, all the way through (but I'll get back to this point).

For Pink Floyd, it seems to me that the differences between the early Syd Barrett songs and the later Waters-Gilmour songs are immense. Take the first verse of Barrett's ode to his cats, "Lucifer Sam":

> Lucifer Sam, Siam cat.
> Always sitting by your side
> Always by your side.
> That cat's something I can't explain.

And compare that to the first verse of Waters's "Money":

> Money, get away.
> Get a good job with good pay and you're okay.
> Money, it's a gas.
> Grab that cash with both hands and make a stash.
> New car, caviar, four-star daydream,
> Think I'll buy me a football team.

The two could scarcely be more different. One is a drug-addled (or assisted) reverie about one's pets and, apparently, their litter box ("At night prowling sifting sand . . ."), while the other is a dandy (if overplayed) bit of social commentary. Yet both are *Pink Floyd* classics. The music the band made moved through four fairly distinctive phases: the psychedelic early sound so influenced by Barrett, the "classic" *Pink Floyd* sound from 1971 to 1975, the Roger Waters era (1976–1985), and the David Gilmour era (1987–1995). As different as the songs from these periods are, they all turn up on the playlist at the weekend *Pink Floyd* laser shows at the local IMAX theater. What's really going on here?

Even by the band's own admission in "Brain Damage," a change in musical style can trigger dramatic results:

> And if the band you're in starts playing different tunes
> I'll see you on the dark side of the moon

Well, then, I guess we're already there.

Legal Identity

From one point of view, the band is a legal entity. They have contracts with one another and the record label that determine, among other things, who gets what portion of the money. When the band changes members, as we have seen them do, the contracts get rewritten and life goes on. This seems pretty cut-and-dried, being all lawyerly and such. But as anyone who has filed a complicated tax return knows, just because something is defined by the law, that doesn't mean it is simple or even interpreted the same way every time. I recently had a tax attorney advising me on an IRA I had inherited tell me, "Well, Michael, understanding IRA law is more like arguing about art than about adding up columns of numbers." And so it happens that even when the legally-defined Pink Floyd is under consideration, there are disputes among the constituents of this composite entity. Take, for example, the incident in the late 1980s wherein Roger Waters sued to stop David Gilmour and Nick Mason from using the name "Pink Floyd." If the individual members of Pink Floyd cannot agree whether the band still exists, what hope have we of deciding? At the end of the day, to the legal system, Pink Floyd is the group that proffers the most convincing argument in court, both in the eyes of the band members and in the eyes of the record labels[3] and the others who own the rights to the music.

Nominal Identity

It's not even clear that we can settle the seemingly simple issue of what the band's name even is. The first mention of the words 'Pink' and 'Floyd' occurred when the original line-up assumed the name "The Pink Floyd Sound" at Syd Barrett's suggestion. The name was a reference to blues musicians Pink Anderson and Floyd Council whom Barrett had read about in the liner notes from a Blind Boy Fuller album. The band performed under that name and the name "Tea Set" for a time, and then settled on "The Pink Floyd." By the time they released *Piper at the Dates of Dawn* in 1967, the name had become "Pink Floyd."

---

[3] They've had four labels in the US and Europe during their career—Tower, Harvest, Capitol, and Columbia

Still, David Gilmour referred to the group as "The Pink Floyd" as recently as 1984. To make matters worse, in 1987, even though *A Momentary Lapse of Reason* was a project headed by David Gilmour and Nick Mason, Roger Waters filed a lawsuit to keep the name "Pink Floyd" from being used. Here's a case of an original member of the band suing one original member and one non-original member of the band, saying they don't exist anymore. Gilmour and Moore insisted they did exist as Pink Floyd, and the name lived on as the case was settled out of court. Despite the fact that they recorded one of the best-selling albums of all time in *Dark Side of the Moon*, I don't even know if the band members know what they were calling themselves. If they don't know, how do we have a chance of knowing what they're called? Let's just use a definite description—"The band almost everyone refers to as 'Pink Floyd'" and be done with it.

Wish You Were Here

So what are we to do about all of this? It seems that from every angle, there are problems with the claim that one and the same band, Pink Floyd, existed from 1967 until at least 1987. The line-up, style, name, and legal status of the band all seem unable to square with our intuitions that the band plays on.

Here's something that might get us out of this quandary. I call it the "Officeholder View" of personal identity. Suppose I am the amateur computer guy in my office. To several people, I am nothing more than that. So long as someone can work on the computers, they are happy. Clearly, it need not be me who is the computer guy for that office to be occupied. Thankfully, many of my relationships occur on a deeper level than the one I just described. I am the only philosopher at my college, I am a colleague to several other faculty members, I advise some student clubs, I am a husband and I am a full time herder of five quite unruly cats. At the moment, I hold all these offices, but that could change. I can easily serve in one office even as I cease serving in another. Were I to become a right-wing republican, I could imagine my wife (truthfully) saying, "You are not the person I married." Yet even though my wife would rightly impeach me as husband, my Dean would probably not feel the urge—I could (and probably would) be the same philosopher he hired. My department chair might decide I was still able to teach philosophy, but she might bar me from teaching *political* philosophy. I might get tossed out of my bowling league for political reasons and yet stay accepted by my investment club. In short, the various constituencies I move among are in charge of deciding if I am the same person in the context they socially create and maintain. I simply do not get a vote.

In his moving memoir, *The Diving Bell and the Butterfly: A Memoir of Life in Death*, Jean-Dominique Bauby gives us a glimpse into this sort of situation from the other side of the looking glass. Bauby writes about his experiences with what is called "locked-in syndrome." The syndrome is caused in this case by a stroke low in the brain stem. In cases like Bauby's, the subject is paralyzed to the point of being unable to speak or voluntarily move much of anything at all. But all cognitive function is left intact. In many cases, the ability to blink on command remains, and blinking did, in fact, become Bauby's means of communication. Visitors would recite the alphabet and stop at the letter that he responded to with a blink, record that letter, and repeat the procedure until a sentence (or enough of one) became clear.

The process gets very confusing and frustrating, especially for the person blinking to communicate. It is like playing charades about everything, but worse because you can't use the canonical time-saving moves to set context, like pantomiming a movie camera or the reading of a book in particular. Bauby notes that this constriction of communication eventually changed his personality. Before his stroke, he was the editor-in-chief of the French-language version of the fashion magazine *Elle*. He was a witty, urbane socialite who was well known and well liked around Paris. But his paralysis eventually reduced his willingness to try to engage people as he would have in the past, and his ability to think on his feet. "The keenest rapier grows dull and falls flat when it takes several minutes to thrust it home," Bauby writes. "By the time you strike, even you no longer understand what seemed so witty before you started to dictate it, letter by letter.[4]

---

[4] *The Diving Bell and the Butterfly: A Memoir of Life in Death*, Jean-Dominique Bauby (New York: Vintage, 1997), p. 71.

For much of his memoir, Bauby describes the fading away of what he takes to be the core elements of his personality, his self, but all the while he calls whatever remains "me." This rang true when I read it, having lived for thirteen years with a brother in this same condition. My brother Josh went through almost everything Bauby described, and we went though it with him, as we kept him at home.[5]

With us, however, Josh remained the "same person" for all of those years. But this was not true for other relationships Josh had. These became attenuated as time went by, as Josh's friends transferred their friendships to my family members or else remained committed to what had been their relationship with Josh *before* his stroke. It is telling that almost all the discussions returned to events earlier in Josh's life. This isn't very surprising, since Josh didn't do all that much these days, but it was a consistent pattern. To me, Josh remained the same brother and son to his family and to himself, but he slowly ceased to be the same person at all to his former friends and even his fiancée. We chose criteria for sameness of person that let through even the most dramatic changes while everyone else had more finely-grained criteria.

Brain Damage, or Careful with that Axe, Eugene

If you're skeptical that judgments about when we are (or are not) the same person are usually taken out of our hands, here is another reason why this makes sense:

---

[5] One especially funny/embarrassing/interesting incident that unfolded over several days involved the blink method of communication. We had devised a system in which one blink meant "yes", two blinks meant "no" and eyelid fluttering meant "I don't know." Soon after we started using these shortcuts, Josh spelled out this message to me: I cant say I dont know sign too hard. I had no idea what he was talking about. My dad got the exact same message and checked Josh's O$_2$ levels. For the next few days, Josh spelled out the same message to everyone who would listen. He's start, and we'd all finish the message for him. It was exasperating for all of us. One night, after we'd all gone to bed, it hit me—I ran downstairs and asked "Are you saying that it is too difficult for you to flutter your eyelids in order to say "I don't know"? Josh blinked once and we laughed for a long time. A little punctuation, and we could have avoided all the madness.

Suppose I am subject to a series of minor strokes (or axe injuries) that successively incapacitates me. By this death of a thousand cuts, I lose my wit, my peculiar desires, my memories, my vocabulary and so on, up until the extinction of all consciousness.

At each stage of this erosion of what I would now call my self, I would answer, when question by philosophical types, that of course I still existed, that *I* was still here. This answer would emerge at every level of debilitation (because, I think, of the nature of self-reflexive consciousness), including those at which I could only nod or blink my assent or dissent to the question. But sitting here now, I know that *I* (now) am *not* that terribly disabled thing in the description and that I could never be it. My body might come to be in that condition, but here and now I will say it would not be me. As Derek Parfit has argued, when it comes to survival we care much more about higher cognitive functions, memories and dispositions than about the particular body or body parts we have (except those body parts responsible for those mental features).[6] So my scenario convinces me that I am not the best judge of whether I have survived a particular event or procedure in any nontrivial way. Maybe we should just say that while my body will construct a self with whatever cognitive resources it has left and consider it the same self as before, even if it has lost its memories of the past, other social groups are often quite properly more selective in this matter.

You could say that this is what happened to Syd Barrett in 1967 and '68, as, by most accounts, he gradually but definitely lost the attributes and personality characteristics that made him (if people like David Bowie are to be believed) the coolest guy in psychedelic London. For those who saw Syd only sporadically at the time, like Joe Boyd, the founder of the UFO Club and producer of the band's first single "Arnold Layne," the axe cuts seemed deep and sudden:

> After they'd signed with EMI [and begun recording *The Piper at the Gates of Dawn,* which Boyd did not produce], a few months went by when I didn't really see much of them at all. But we reached an agreement that no matter what happened, no matter how big they

---

[6] Derek Parfit, *Reasons and Persons* (Oxford University Press, 1986), pp. 255–56.

were, they agreed that they would come back in June '67 and play
the UFO Club. And sure enough, by June they were huge. There
were queues around the block and crowds outside the club and
everything. And there was no stage entrance, so the group had to
come in through the crowd to perform. So I saw them up close as
they came by, and I kind of greeted them as they came in. I said
hello to everybody, and Syd was the last one in.

That's when Boyd's own criteria for sameness of person led him
to immediately recognize Syd as another person altogether:

> And Syd, I would have to say, was a very, very different person
> that night in June from when I had seen him previously. He was
> very vacant-eyed, didn't really say anything. But he had always
> been very witty, made under-his-breath little sarcastic comments
> and funny little comments here and there. But none of that, that
> night. And when he went on stage, he just stood there, for long
> stretches, while the rest of the band played. It was very awkward
> and very disturbing to see.[7]

While idioms like "You're not yourself tonight" do convey the
fact that a person is behaving atypically, Boyd does seem to be
claiming real difference of person in this case. For Waters,
Wright, Mason, and the band's management who saw Syd from
day to day, he seemed to slip away more slowly but, sadly, inexorably. From their point of view, the final cut (so to speak) was
not another step in Syd's sad degeneration. For there was no
point at which Syd could suddenly no longer play guitar or write
songs (as his solo albums and occasional performances in the
early 1970s prove). Rather, the final cut—the moment when Syd
Barrett, member of Pink Floyd, ceased to be *that* person—
occurred in February 1968 when the other members of the band
decided it had occurred. "In the car on the way to collect Syd,"
for a show in Southhampton, Nick Mason remembers, "someone
said 'Shall we pick up Syd?' and the response was 'No, fuck it,
let's not bother.'"[8] Barrett, his friends, his bandmates and his
family members no doubt used different criteria to judge sameness of person, and the band's criteria told them that there was

---

[7] Joe Boyd, interview, "Syd Barrett: A True Rock Legend," *The Guardian* (June
11th, 2006).

[8] Nick Mason, *Inside Out* (San Francisico: Chronicle Books, 2005), p. 103.

no more Syd Barrett. As the office holder view of identity would have it, Syd didn't have a vote.

The Show Must Go On

So this is the position I suggest for our understanding of *Pink Floyd*: instead of insisting on a material criterion for identity, which could reside only in band roster, or some abstract criterion such as style, we should say that *Pink Floyd* is an office best understood along the lines of this officeholder view of identity. More properly it is a collection of offices, each filled or not by different people and their songs. To the die-hard fan of one sort, The Pink Floyd Sound is the same band that recorded all the other albums in the Pink Floyd discography. To another sort of fan, the real Pink Floyd is the band that had the run of albums that began with *Dark Side of the Moon* and ended with *The Wall*. To a third fan, Pink Floyd is the psychedelic band that ended when Barrett's influence finally wore off. And there are many other sorts of fans, each of whom is right in their context.

In the extreme case, *Pink Floyd* could be as long-lived as the Dresden Staatskapelle, the world's oldest orchestra. Founded in 1548, it has been composed of a host of different musicians, but still endures by our standards. While this is not as often the case with rock 'n' roll, *The Grateful Dead* shuffled many musicians through their ranks until Jerry died, and there is no reason to think he could not be replaced (whatever Deadheads might say) in principle.

What is the relevance of this reasoning to *Pink Floyd*? Just this: it looks like we have no way to comfortably say that one single thing lasted from 1967 until 1987 and that that thing was the band Pink Floyd. However, we can identify many different constituencies who will answer "yes" to such questions as "Is the band who released *A Momentary Lapse of Reason* the same band who recorded *Ummagumma*?" and that there are some (like Roger Waters) who will answer no. And similarly, I think we can handle just about any question that arises about the history of "the band," so long as we pay close enough attention to context and the interests of the parties involved. As for getting context- and value judgment-free answers, there aren't any, but that doesn't mean we can't all get along.

Absolutely Curtains

At this point, I've just got to stop thinking about all of this and go back to my simple, unreflective account. Pink Floyd is the band whose name appears on the spine of several of my CD's in the "P" section of my collection. I like them, and listen to them when I am in specific moods. And that's that, at least so long as I make sure that the lunatic is no longer in my head.[9]

---

[9] I would like to thank George Reisch for his very helpful comments and suggestions on an earlier version of this paper.

Perception, Non-Being and other Empty Spaces

13

Distorted View: A Saucerful of Skepticism

SCOTT CALEF

What do light shows, schizophrenia, psychedelic drugs, synthesizers, prisms, and Pink Floyd all have in common? Lots of things. But, in particular, they all remind us that what we regard as "normal" or "ordinary" perception is in fact highly contingent, almost arbitrary.

If I were tricked by the light into thinking there're paisley people on stage, I'd be seeing *something*, but not paisley people (since paisley people don't exist). I'd be seeing people who *look* paisley, but aren't. How things look is highly variable and dependent upon circumstances. If I were hallucinating on acid or mad, for example, I'd see the world differently. Or perhaps, I wouldn't see *the world* at all, though I'd have an experience rather *like* seeing. I hear footsteps running, planes exploding, dogs barking, vaults shutting and money cha-chinging. Or do I? Sound effects machines could imitate all of these noises so that I couldn't tell the difference. Prisms show that the visible wavelengths of light are only a fraction of the whole spectrum. If our sensory systems were differently constituted, we might see much more—or less—than we do.[1]

Pink Floyd is a philosopher's dream, for a more enigmatic and paradoxical group of music-making lads would be hard to find. With Pink Floyd, there's always something *more* than meets the eye—or ear. Theirs is a world combining and sepa-

---

[1] That what we see is in a sense "incomplete" is hinted at by the cover of *Dark Side of the Moon*, where the "rainbow" is deliberately partial, lacking indigo.

rating the seen and the unseen. Visionary in every sense of the word, the Floyd on the one hand are identified with their innovative and gob-smackingly trippy light shows, spectacular stage sets, props, projections, inflatables and iconographic album art.[2] And yet, for a band so bound up with film projects, visual effects, and explorations into the multimedia possibilities of the rock performance, they continuously suggest the unseen—what is hidden, absent, mysterious or imperceptible. Consider the album titles: *Saucerful of Secrets*; *Obscured by Clouds*; *Dark Side of the Moon*;[3] *Wish You Were Here*; *The Wall*.[4] This is one reason why the early Floyd were revered as not only "London's farthest-out group," but the consummate "Space Rock" band. Although Waters, in particular, came to reject this association, the Floyd took their audiences on a wild ride into outer as well as inner space. The band sonically evoked the everlasting void—the cold emptiness and invisible darkness which, though nothing, separates everything from everything.

To me, this is part of the real paradox of Pink Floyd, one that points straight to an ancient philosophical conundrum. What's the relationship between the seen and the unseen, the perceptible and the imperceptible? In this chapter, I want to explore the vagaries of perception, using Pink Floyd to illustrate—and perhaps begin to resolve—some fundamental philosophical problems about appearances and reality.

Random Precision

Philosophers have often argued that we don't perceive the world directly, but only indirectly. When we see the world, reflected light from the surface of an object enters the eye and stimulates the optic nerve. Those impulses are interpreted by the

---

[2] Their interest in and talent for visual impact is perhaps understandable, since the founding members were architecture students and a painter.

[3] And remember, "There is no dark side of the moon really. It's all dark." Here that which is never on view—the side of the moon that always hides its face—doesn't exist. So it is twice removed: On the one hand, we can't see it. On the other, it doesn't exist to be seen (though we commonly think it does).

[4] *The Wall* operates on two levels. It is both an impenetrable barrier keeping prying eyes at bay, and also, metaphorically, a psychological mechanism that shuts out, hides, isolates and disguises.

brain consciously as, say, a cow, moon, saucer, or cloud. We hear when sound waves produce vibrations of the inner ear which are decoded into the sounds of slide guitar, sea birds or Syd Barrett singing.[5] The point is, whether dealing with visual or auditory experiences, myriad very complicated electrical, chemical and physiological events are triggered by sensory input resulting eventually (but very quickly) in a conscious experience. So, what we call "seeing a flying inflatable pig" is really a construction in the nervous system caused by neural processing of environmental stimuli. But since the *experience* is in my head[6] and the pig is over Battersea Power Station, and since my head is much smaller than the forty-foot pig (which can't very well enter my eye and take up residence in my brain), what I am immediately aware of is not the pig but some kind of internal *representation* of the pig. What's in me—and all that I'm actually aware of—is a kind of picture or idea of a pig. On that basis, I *infer* the existence of a soaring swine over Battersea of which the mental image is presumed to be some kind of copy. I don't see the pig directly, but only indirectly via its likeness in consciousness.

Here's an analogy. Suppose you have cheap seats at a Pink Floyd show. You can't really see Nick Mason's face "directly" since you're too far away. But you can see it on the circular projection screen suspended above the stage. You see Nick—it certainly isn't Roger or Dave—but only indirectly via the telecast image. What you see of Mason is mediated via the projection. In a sense, that's how it is all the time. The mind is a sort of screen where our surroundings are simulated. You've never actually seen Pink Floyd "in the flesh", even if you bought a ticket and attended the concert. You've only "seen" your idea of Pink Floyd; you've been watching a projection the whole time. "All you touch and all that you see / is all your life will ever be", but what is it that you touch and see? A little piece of your own brain. As "Echoes" puts it, "What I see is me."

---

[5] The album cover to *Meddle* pays homage to this theory, where sound is represented as concentric waves floating over a human ear.

[6] It does sound odd to say I have experiences in my head, but philosophers do sometimes encourage this way of speaking. Perhaps experiences aren't the kinds of "things" that can *be* anywhere. But even if the experience isn't in my head, it isn't over Battersea Station either!

And What Exactly Is a Dream?

Philosophers have often thought that this way of thinking leads straight to skepticism. This is because, according to this particular theory of perception offered by science and psychology, all we immediately perceive are our internal, mental representations. But if that's so, how do we know there's anything else that exists beyond or behind these representations? We suppose these ideas are caused by something external to the mind—say, a hovering pig—but how can we prove it?

At this point we might reason like this: Well, the perceptions must come from *somewhere*. They can't just pop into existence without a cause! And I know *I* don't cause them, because I have no control over them. True, I can shut my eyes, or turn the volume down on the stereo, but if I chose to open my eyes or leave the volume up, I can't help but hear "Sheep" or "Echoes" (if its playing), or see the Scarecrow if it's in my field of view. You can't just will yourself to see "any colour you like"! Descartes (1596–1650) observed, however, that dreams are nocturnal phantasms that aren't caused by external objects. Somehow, it seems, I am the cause of my dreams, though by means of an "unknown faculty" within me.[7] Moreover, while I'm dreaming I usually don't realize it, and am deceived. What's true of dreams might be true of waking perceptions also. Perhaps we're their source, but can't voluntarily control them because we generate them unconsciously. Julia may be the "dreamboat queen, queen of all my dreams," but does she even exist? And if she does, what about the "scaly armadillo" trying to "find me where I'm hiding"? Does it exist? Presumably not. But then, why think that the objects of waking perceptions are any different? We could be dreaming this whole scene.

Distorted View (See Through, Baby Blue)

Even if we think—on pretty flimsy grounds—that a world external to the mind and its perceptions exists, we've no reason to

---

[7] Descartes makes the point in Meditation Three of his *Meditations on First Philosophy*. See *Discourse on Method* and *Meditations of First Philosophy* (Indianapolis: Hackett, 1980), p. 70.

think that world is the way it appears to be.[8] We can't verify that the mental image of the pig is a true likeness of the pig prop outside the mind—supposing there is one—because we can't compare the pig-image to the pig-balloon. To do so, we'd need to examine our perception, examine the plastic pig, and compare the two to make sure the one depicts the other accurately. But examining the plastic pig is exactly what we can't do, since that just means acquiring more perceptions of the damn thing— more mental representations. And comparing one mental representation to another isn't going to get us anywhere if what we want is confirmation that we're reliably sensing something which isn't a *representation* at all![9]

This is why some philosophers took the causal account of perception offered by science and psychology to place a veil between the observer and the world, as if, ironically, experience prevented us from actually seeing anything. The sensory experience stands between us and everything else, much as the "fat old sun" might be "obscured by clouds". It's almost as if we can never see our hands because something like a film or membrane covers up and conceals our actual skin. The "sense data" that we're immediately aware of comes between us and the object we're looking at, almost as gloves hide the hands they protect.[10]

But this is not to say that science alone puts us in this skeptical position. Some fairly simple philosophical arguments lead us there also. John Locke (1632–1704) suggests that what we actually observe are the sensible qualities of things. What do I experience if I'm examining the album cover of *Dark Side of the Moon?* Certain colors, chiefly black, white and the "rainbow." I feel the smoothness, coolness, thinness, and flexibility of the cardboard. It smells like, well, whatever it smells like. It tastes faintly of nacho grease. (Gross, I know, but as a philosopher I'm

---

[8] Again, according to science the physical universe is composed of atoms and energy. But it certainly doesn't *look* like atoms! For example, atoms aren't colored, but just about everything I see is.

[9] Of course, the flying pig prop *is* itself a representation. It's an artistic representation of a barnyard animal!

[10] Ludwig Wittgenstein (1889–1961) writes: "It is as if we detached the colour-*impression* from the object, like a membrane." He goes on to warn: "This ought to arouse our suspicions." *Philosophical Investigations* (Oxford: Blackwell, 1968), Section 276.

sworn to truth.) If I swish it back and forth rapidly it makes a kind of flapping sound.[11] Now, the colors are colors *of* something; the tangible properties are properties *of* something. What are these properties properties of? Well, the album cover. But this makes it seem like the album cover is a substance or thing in which these visible, tangible qualities inhere. The colors of the album aren't floating around, unconnected to anything.[12] They are, as it were, embedded in or attached to an object of some kind. But since we only perceive the sensible qualities of the album cover and not the thing in which they inhere, we never actually perceive the record jacket. The jacket is what Locke calls the "substratum" of the sensible properties which we perceive. He knows that it must exist, but all he can really say about it is that it's a "something I know not what."[13] We can't describe it because to do so would be to mention its qualities, and as the thing underlying the qualities, by definition it doesn't have any![14]

One of Locke's philosophical successors, George Berkeley (1685–1753), tried to avoid this conclusion by insisting that only the sensible qualities really exist. There isn't some mysterious, intangible, unknowable substrate underlying the observable properties of an object, Berkeley insisted; there're just the sensible qualities. This led Berkeley to metaphysical idealism, the view that only minds and their contents—*ideas*, broadly construed—exist. After all, sensible qualities—colors, shapes, sizes, smells, textures, and so on—are experiences, and experiences can only exist in consciousness.

---

[11] A word to the wise: in my experience, if you want to try this at home, you should take the record out first!

[12] Maybe sometimes colors *can* "float around, unattached" to anything. Otherwise, it's "Goodbye, Blue Sky."

[13] See John Locke's *Essay Concerning Human Understanding*, Chapter XXIII, "Of Our Complex Ideas of Substances."

[14] One implication of this theory may be that, at bottom, everything is the same. If the substrate that is the album cover has no qualities, and the substrate that is my bike has no qualities (its basket and bell that rings and things that make it look good notwithstanding), how does the album cover *itself* differ from the bike? On the other hand, if, according to science, at the atomic level everything is pretty much the same, despite differences that manifest at the macroscopic level, philosophy may be no more peculiar than science here.

You Raver, You Seer of Visions

A third class of arguments casting doubt upon the reliability of sensation works by means of various thought experiments. Descartes noticed that asylums are full of deluded individuals who, though naked or dressed in rags, believe themselves to be kings. Others think they're made of glass or that their heads are gourds. They may stand onstage and simply detune their guitars instead of playing, staring blankly into space with a rapidly melting, obligatory Hendrix perm. These people obviously perceive the world much differently than most of us, and don't know that they're mad. But then, how do I know that *I'm* not mad, that the lunatic isn't in *my* head? Perhaps I'm only imagining myself to be a philosopher when in reality I'm confined in a straitjacket and padded cell. Or, Descartes mused, perhaps an evil genius or malevolent demon as powerful and clever as God is devoting his entire energies towards deceiving us even about what seems most obvious. Surely such a being could cause Descartes to hallucinate an entire reality which didn't exist. A more modern version of Descartes's argument inspired *The Matrix* by asking whether we aren't brains in vats whose nerves are being stimulated by leads from a supercomputer in much the same way they would be stimulated by reading a chapter in a book entitled *Pink Floyd and Philosophy*, though there is no such book (or, alas, author royalties). Maybe somebody out there's singing "It's alright, we told you what to dream" and "welcome to the machine".[15] Waters writes in "If", "If I go insane / please don't stick your wires in my brain." Maybe we are insane; we might have wires in our brain. In either case, things aren't as they seem. No wonder the band wrestled with paranoia. . . .

---

[15] Commenting on the song "Welcome to the Machine," Toby Manning writes: "Taking the voice of the omniscient 'Machine' the lyrics steelily and sardonically describe/create the life/fantasy of the rock star/Pink Floyd fan." *The Rough Guide to Pink Floyd* (London: Rough Guides, 2006), p.206. For Waters, the evil forces which distort our perceptions and control our dreams are largely impersonal and societal, such things as the education system, the music industry, and capitalist constructs in general—what Marx called the "social superstructure."

It Takes Two to Know

Some have argued that we can avoid these uncertainties by submitting our private perceptions to others for external corroboration. I catch a glimpse of what looked like a flying pig. That's odd. Did I really see what I thought I saw? Since "quickness of the eye deceives the mind" ("Green is the Color"), I decide to double check by asking you. If you saw it too, then I have additional reason to trust my senses. If you didn't see it, I can ask a few other people. If they all agree with you, then I might put my previous experience down to inattention or you adulterating my Diet Pepsi. The point is, it may be difficult to tell whether I'm deceived or mad or dreaming as long as I rely exclusively on my own resources. But (solipsism aside) we're not alone. Arnold Layne had a "distorted view." Barrett asks, "Why can't you see?" but gives the answer: "It takes two to know, two to know, two to know, two to know." The line points to the need for corroboration, even as the repetition provides some. It's largely the willingness to subject our own observations to verification by others that accounts for the power and success of the scientific method.

When corroboration from others isn't available—I'm home alone, it's 3:00 A.M., and I see an effervescing elephant in the corner—then at least we can look again, check more closely, and make sure we weren't deceived by "quickness of the eye" through carelessness, haste, or intoxication.

This takes care of at least one of Descartes's arguments. He argued that because the senses sometimes deceive us, perhaps they always do, in which case we aren't justified in trusting them, ever. This argument is flawed. The premise asserts that the senses are fallible because they sometimes mislead us. But we know that precisely because subsequent observations convince us that earlier ones were mistaken. But then, we have to assume that the latter observations are accurate, in which case we can hardly conclude that the senses are *never* to be trusted. In short, we couldn't know we were deceived by the senses unless sometimes we weren't. And in the case of external validation, if I decide I was mistaken because you didn't see what I thought I saw, I'm presuming at least that what *you* saw was correct. We can't all be wrong all of the time.

On the other hand, some have argued that Descartes's arguments from insanity and dreaming are just mistaken as to the facts. Descartes supposed that madmen don't know they're mad. This may, of course, sometimes be true. But not always. And even if some people don't know that they're mad, if it's *possible* to know one is mad, skepticism might be surmountable. And, some people *are* aware that their minds are slipping away. Many interpret lines from "Jugband Blues" as Barrett's self-diagnosis: "I'm most obliged to you for making it clear that I'm not here . . . And I'm wondering who could be writing this song."[16] It's as if he's saying, "there's someone in my head, but it's not me." In the interviews recorded for the spoken passages on *Dark Side*, Chris Adamson said "I've been mad for fucking years—absolutely years." Jerry Driscoll, the Abbey Road doorman, concurred about himself: "I've always been mad. I know I've been mad, like most of us. Very hard to explain why you're mad, even if you're not mad." Adamson and Driscoll (and possibly Barrett) break down the barrier between lunacy and normalcy. Though they might be speaking loosely or metaphorically, they suggest the possibility that insanity can be self-diagnosed and introspectively identified. Where that isn't possible, we might come to recognize our condition with the assistance of others—say, competent therapists and psychiatrists. Madness is accompanied by symptoms. If I lack the symptoms, I needn't worry that my perceptions are the effects of a deluded mind with a distorted view.

Something similar might be said of dreams. Is it true that we can't tell the difference between dreaming and waking life? We may not be able to do so while dreaming, but that's not because dreams are just like normal perceptions. It's because we often can't reliably reason, form judgments or make discriminations while sleeping. Once aroused, however, we can always tell that a dream has ended, if not instantly, then very soon. Gilmour sings on "A Pillow of Winds": "behold the dream, the dream is gone." If we can know the dream's gone, we must know the difference between being "in" a dream, and waking up. To borrow an example from Oxford philosopher J.L. Austin (1911–1960),

---

[16] Note once again the theme of confirmation, though perhaps with tongue in cheek. Does Barrett know he's slipping away mainly because *others* have made it clear?

there's a big difference between being presented to the Pope, and dreaming that I'm being presented to the Pope (or, between dreaming that I'm backstage partying with the band and *actually* being backstage partying with the band).[17] Moreover, for me, songs like "Set the Controls for the Heart of the Sun," "Remember a Day," and "See Saw" have a lovely, lilting, dream-like quality. But as Austin also points out, if we couldn't tell the difference between being in a dream and being awake, *all* experiences would have a dream-like quality, and so "the phrase would be perfectly meaningless, because applicable to everything. . . . If dreams were not 'qualitatively' different from waking experiences, then *every* waking experience would be like a dream; the dream-like quality would be, not difficult to capture, but impossible to avoid" (p. 49).

Wondering and Dreaming. The Words Have Different Meanings

Other philosophers have argued that the very existence of language gets us around extreme skepticism. For us to share a language and understand one another, we must suppose that we're using words in more or less the same way, and that the meanings of our words are shared in common. If you understand me when I say "I see the see saw", you must know what I mean by "the see saw." But if by "the see saw" what I mean is one of my ideas, and not something in the public realm, you can't possibly know how I'm using the word. It would refer to something only I can experience, and therefore you wouldn't have a clue what I'm talking about.[18]

But it gets worse than this. For if words have meaning solely by virtue of referring to items in consciousness and not in the world, neither can anyone know "what he means by the word himself; for to know the meaning of a word is to know how to

---

[17] J.L. Austin, *Sense and Sensibilia* (Oxford: Oxford University Press, 1964), p. 48.

[18] Waters plays with the ambiguities and uncertainties of language as applied to seemingly "internal" mental states in the Pink Floyd documentary *Live at Pompeii*. He there teases Adrian Maben, the film's director, during an attempted interview by replying to each question with counter-questions like "What do you mean, 'happy'?" or "What do you mean, 'interesting'?"

use it rightly; and where there can be no check on how a man uses a word there is no room to talk of 'right' and 'wrong' use."[19] We can't rely on memory to ensure that we're using the word consistently, because there's no independent way to verify that we're remembering correctly. Under such circumstances, whatever seems right, is right. Wittgenstein likens the situation to a man buying several copies of the morning paper to assure himself that what it said was correct.[20]

To further illustrate the difficulty of having a language where the words refer only to private sensations, Wittgenstein invites us to imagine the following: "Suppose everyone had a box with something in it: we call it a 'beetle'. No one can look into anyone else's box, and everyone says he knows what a beetle is only by looking at *his* beetle.—Here it would be quite possible for everyone to have something different in his box. One might even imagine such a thing constantly changing . . . the box might even be empty."[21] The box is the mind and "beetle" is the name of your private perception.[22] But, Wittgenstein insists, we can't say even this since "If you say he sees a private picture before him, which he is describing, you have still made an assumption about what he has before him." No wonder "Emily tries, but misunderstands"! Skepticism about the senses makes language impossible. And since philosophical skepticism is a theory expressed in language, if skepticism is true, skepticism is unutterable. The theory is self-defeating.

I'll leave it to you, dear reader, to decide whether the possibility of corroboration and the requirements of language do effectively relieve us of these doubts about experience. As for myself, I confess to misgivings. Maybe the moon *is* all dark and obscured by clouds. What's unknown, unseen and imperceptible will always "Eclipse" everything else. I like it that way. Ultimately, perhaps one's taste in philosophies is like one's taste in music—more aesthetic than scientific. If Johnny Rotten hates

---

[19] Anthony Kenny, *Action, Emotion, and the Will* (London: Routledge, 1963), p.13.

[20] Ludwig Wittgenstein, *Philosophical Investigations* (Oxford: Blackwell 1968), paragraph 265.

[21] *Philosophical Investigations*, paragraph 293.

[22] I decided to name my private sensation "cat" instead of "beetle" so I could work in another Pink Floyd reference: "That cat's something I can't explain!"

Pink Floyd, I can't prove him wrong. I'm not sure the skeptic can be refuted, either. For me, much of the appeal of Pink Floyd's music, especially their earlier work, lies in the childlike sense of wonder it conveys. Aristotle said philosophy begins in wonder, too, and this suggests one difference between Pink Floyd led by Barrett and, later, by Waters. For Waters seems more like one of those restless souls who will never be content until everything's figured out and the many ugly things in the world that we are "only dimly aware of" are definitively exposed: "I've looked over Jordan, and I have seen / Things are not what they seem."

But Barrett-era Floyd appeals to the skeptic in me. They remind us to abide in mystery, contemplate the uncanny, and feel the allure of the unknown. In *The Rough Guide to Pink Floyd*, Toby Manning insists that "Enigma is the essence of Pink Floyd's appeal. . . . something mysterious, something fascinating but elusive."[23] Just like philosophy itself. But then, what can I say? I'm a fan. I'm with the band, man.

---

[23] *The Rough Guide to Pink Floyd*, pp. vi–vii.

14

Wish You Were Here (But You Aren't): Pink Floyd and Non-Being

JERE O'NEILL SURBER

Philosophy is a very weird thing. It started, legend has it, with a trippy little poem by a Greek named Parmenides who lived more than two millennia ago. It described his ride on a cosmic chariot piloted by a goddess and her entourage of dancing groupies. Parmenides was led through "the gates of Day and Night" and allowed to see things in a way that few people are able—as they *really* are. The goddess tells him that there are only two paths. The first, the path of Being, leads to truth; the second, the path of Non-Being, leads only to error, confusion, and ignorance. If he stays on the path of Being, he will always walk in light, but if he strays onto the path of Non-Being, he (like most people) will find himself in darkness that can't even be thought or spoken. Finally, the goddess leaves him with something of a Zen koan to ponder: "Thought and Being are One."

Parmenides doesn't tell us a lot more about what he himself made of all this, but the history of Western philosophy begin-ning with Socrates and Plato has struggled to figure it out. Despite the Goddess's warnings about the dark abyss of Non-Being, philosophers have been unable to resist thinking about it and peering into it from time to time.

Pink Floyd is a very weird band. It started with a guy named Syd who styled himself a "Piper at the Gates of Dawn" and spent most of the 1960s surrounded by groupies. An orchestrator of cosmic soundscapes, Syd launched the vehicle first called "The Pink Floyd Sound" on a voyage of experiment and discovery that would take it far past the "Gates of Dawn" and into the furthest reaches of cosmo-sonic space. But Syd abandoned his ship at an early point, leaving the "controls set" but the captain's chair empty. And he left behind enigmatic koans for others to decipher, such as, "And what exactly is a dream / And what exactly is a joke."

Syd himself is no longer here to tell us what he meant by this, but the subsequent history of his band can be understood as a musical struggle to peer into the metaphysical depths of life and reality they found at the heart of the sun. Rarely will you find Floyd dishing up catchy hooks, tunes short enough for airplay, or predictable three-chord blues progressions; and never will you find them spending much time on the usual pop pablum of romance, partying, or self-hype. Their sonic universe is expansive, intense, and challenging. Their interests are truth and illusion, life and death, time and space, causality and chance, compassion and indifference. And like the philosophical children of Parmenides, Pink Floyd consistently explored the shadowy 'anti-thought' of Non-being woven through all we touch and all we see.

The Philosophers' Struggle with Non-Being.

The story of Non-Being in European philosophy plays out in a prologue and four acts. It runs like this:

PROLOGUE: After Parmenides's stern warning, Plato makes a mighty effort to remain on the "path of Being" and avoid the "path of Non-Being" by positing a realm of unchanging, eternal, thought-like 'Forms,' but begins to stumble along the way in his later dialogues like the *Sophist* and the *Parmenides.*

ACT I: (*enter Aristotle*) "Non-Being" isn't a specter or shadow haunting Being at all. It's just "*logical negation,*" a feature of the way we talk about things, nothing more than that little word "not" that we sometimes throw into sentences when we want them to say just the opposite of what they say without it. "Nothing to get hung about," as a famous thinker later put it.

ACT II: (*enter Plotinus, Augustine, and the Neo-Platonists*) Just a minute, Aristotle; to say that Non-being is only a matter of the way we talk is a cheap trick, a superficial finesse. Surely Non-being is a serious matter and counts as some aspect of what is, of Being; it can't just be a bit of simple wordplay. When we talk about 'Non-being', what we really mean is that something is less than it might be, that it falls short of absolutely full or perfect Being (or maybe even 'God'). To make this clear, we'll say, from here on out, that Non-being is *"privation,"* that it is Being *"deprived"* of something that would make it whole. It's not "anti-Being" in any way; it's just "lesser Being."

ACT III: (*fast forward to the nineteenth century, enter Hegel*) Sorry, but after all these years, you've got it only partly figured out. Both you Aristotelians and you Neo-Platonists failed to realize that everything—including language, thought, and the world itself—is a *process*. Everything is always in a process of being what it is and becoming something that it's not. This *is* a feature of language, as Aristotle says. But it's not *only* about language. And you Neo-Platonists are right that "privation" is one form that Non-Being can take. But it's not the whole story. Non-being is the force that drives all processes (and don't forget that everything is a process). If you've got Being, then you've immediately also got Non-Being; if you've got something that's 'the same,' you've also got an infinite number of things that *are not* it, that are 'different' from it. You can't have Being without Non-Being or Non-Being without Being, because it's all actually Becoming. You can call this a '*dialectical*' view if you want.

ACT IV: (*enter Kirkegaard, Nietzsche and a chorus of modern philosophers*) The kind of "old school metaphysics" that Hegel practiced fell out of favor. Once Kierkegaard insisted that "truth is subjectivity" and Nietzsche warned that we must "be true to the earth," philosophers took up down-to-earth issues arising from our daily crises and uncertainties, our encounters and conflicts with other human beings, and our place in a universe that is largely unknown, possibly unknowable, and often inhospitable. In light of these concerns, Hegel's great metaphysical balancing act between Being and Non-Being seemed too abstract and too neat and tidy to illuminate human concerns. Parmenides's old problem of the "dark side" of Being certainly didn't go away. Given the massive destructive forces unleashed in the twentieth century, beginning with the First World War and continuing to the point of the potential total atomic or environmental annihilation of the human race, this gloom could not be ignored. But Non-Being and its relation to Being would require a complete overhaul if philosophy were to remain relevant to the actual lives of human beings. Enter Marx and, in rock music, enter Pink Floyd.

Non-Being as Alienation

If there is one phrase to describe the concept behind Pink Floyd's great 'performance piece', *The Wall*, it can only be "alienation in the contemporary world." On a very literal level, its performance involves the gradual construction of an actual wall of large cardboard blocks which first obscures and then, by mid-show, totally physically divides the audience from the band (although, at various times, there are temporary 'glimpses' and 'escapes' from behind the barrier). More of a 'rock opera' than a typical musical concert, *The Wall* involves a fragmentary story-line about a rock musician named Pink, who is gradually driven into isolation and madness by the death of his father in the Second World War, a childhood dominated by an overprotective mother, then tyrannical and uncaring teachers, a wife who cheats on him, and finally his own drug-fueled career as a rock star. The main character was clearly based on autobiographical details of Roger Waters's own life (he was the primary creative force behind the production) along with references to the mental collapse of Syd Barrett. In the theatrical and sonic world of *The Wall*, each brick comes to represent some experience or event that drives Pink further into alienation from everything and everyone in his life and ultimately into madness.

In fact, the central theatrical device used in *The Wall* had numerous precedents including Antonin Artaud's "theater of cruelty," Berthold Brecht's "alienation effect," and some of the experimental operas of Alban Berg. None, however, achieved nearly the popularity or sheer visceral effect of Pink Floyd's production in creating an actual wall between artist and audience. Alongside the Berlin wall, perhaps, the album and its themes remain one of the best-known symbols of personal, social, and political alienation.

To understand alienation in relation to Non-Being, we go to one of Hegel's most famous critics, Karl Marx. According to Marx, Hegel's intellectual vision of Non-Being as a constant and universal counterpart of Being was an abstract result or symptom in the realm of thought of the real material and social conditions governing modern life under capitalism. To Marx, Hegel's concept of Non-Being that was constantly present in all thought was really an abstract counterpart of the real and constant human suffering—physical, mental, interpersonal, and political—that permeated a world built on self-interest, individualism, competition, and violence—a world in which the luxuries of the few were maintained at the expense of the poverty of the many. While many later thinkers diverged from Marx's attribution of this to economic conditions, the concept of alienation as an endemic scourge of psychological and social life in modern society became central to later movements such as Psychoanalysis, Existentialism, and the Frankfurt School.

Marx specified four kinds of alienation that provided the basis for virtually all later philosophical discussions. They appear throughout Pink Floyd's work, so we'll let the band lead us through them.

1. One of the most memorable songs on Pink Floyd's most popular album, *The Dark Side of the Moon*, is "Brain Damage"—"There's someone in my head," Roger Waters sings, "but it's not me." There could be no better summary of what Marx means by "Self-Alienation." In fact, Marx regarded insanity—something Floyd returns to one way or another on most of its albums—as the most extreme form of self-alienation.

2. In "Welcome to the Machine," on *Wish You Were Here*, Floyd rages against the way that, from childhood, we are sucked into a world of material things that gradually come to define us and render helpless victims of "the machine." "You've been in the pipeline, filling in time, / provided with toys and 'Scouting for Boys,' / You bought a guitar to punish your ma, / . . . So welcome to the machine." Marx called this "Alienation of the Thing" to indicate that, in the modern world, all our "stuff" ultimately serves only to further estrange us from ourselves and others.

3. Probably the most prominent aspect of alienation in Pink Floyd is what Marx calls "alienation from other persons." This theme is at the core of *The Wall*, but it appears on virtually every Pink Floyd album in different forms. War, for example, is the most extreme form of alienation between persons. "Us and Them," on T*he Dark Side of the Moon*, is a song devoted to exactly this theme. "Us, and them / And after all we're only ordinary men / Me, and you. / God knows it's not what we would choose to do."

Later, *The Final Cut*, an effort conceived and dominated by Roger Waters, is devoted almost entirely to the various types of personal trauma and alienation resulting from war.

4. The most obscure aspect of alienation noted by Marx is what he called "alienation of man's 'species being.'" Roughly, modern human beings, who by nature are free and self-creating, become reduced to their "animal nature." They are not "living to work and create" as human beings should but merely "laboring just to live, to sustain life"—like animals. Pink Floyd's *Animals*, in a way reminiscent of George Orwell's *Animal Farm*, explores this kind of alienation. In "Dogs," for instance, Floyd sings, "You gotta be crazy, you gotta have a real need, / You gotta sleep on your toes, and when you're on the street, /You gotta be able to pick out the easy meat with your eyes closed."

Since these themes track so well with Marx's discussion of alienation, you might wonder whether the "pink" in "Pink Floyd" has another, perhaps unintended, political meaning. I wouldn't claim that the band maintains any very consistent or overt Marxist stance. But its best-known single, "Money," does seem to agree with Marx that, at the root of all these different types of alienation, is the capitalist "machine" that tends to convert all genuinely human values into the means of economic exchange. "Money, so they say / Is the root of all evil today."

Non-Being as Absence

Besides alienation, Non-Being also assumes another form that reflects "existentialist" rather than Marxist concerns. Here, Non-Being is confronted as absences experienced as loss, sadness, disappointment, aging, and death.

Among the existentialists, the French philosopher Jean-Paul Sartre employed the experience of absence, in his major work *Being and Nothingness*, to construe human consciousness as a type of "Nothingness" (maybe better written "No-thing-ness") embedded and engaged in a smothering, pre-existing world of opaque things lacking consciousness. In one episode, Sartre describes the familiar experience of entering a café to meet a friend Pierre who turns out not to be there. In reflecting on it, he wants to show that the entire ensemble of the café, with all it's various sensations, things, and persons, forms itself around, is saturated by, and derives its meaning from, something that "is not," is not present, that is, the "absent friend." He returns to this theme in discussing death, a sort of "permanent absence" of another person, the grief for whose loss can completely 'color' our own subsequent life and experience.[1]

I've already mentioned two "absences" that saturate Pink Floyd's music—the early "bail out" of their founder, Syd Barrett, and the death of Roger Waters's father in the Second World War. But there are many other references: to absent women friends, failed aspirations, unrealized political ideals, and, especially in the album *Obscured by Clouds*, to the loss of youthful joy and dreams as one grows older. As was Sartre, Pink Floyd is drawn to these experiences and, in particular, the "non-being" or "non-existence" of something that is no longer or, perhaps, was only a dream. "I caught a fleeting glimpse, / out of the corner of my eye," Pink sings in "Comfortably Numb." "I turned to look but it was gone, / I cannot put my finger on it now. / The child is grown, / the dream is gone." Being partly inspired by Syd, it's no surprise that this flash of nothingness in *The Wall* has something in common with the fleeting rise and fall Syd wrote about in "Jugband Blues," his final contribution to the band's recorded work: "It's awfully considerate of you to think of me here / And I'm much obliged to you for making it clear that I'm not here."

Existential Non-Being loomed even larger in the writings of the German philosopher Martin Heidegger. Where Sartre's nothingness often concerned individuals, Heidegger's was more cosmic. He took European history itself, the "history of metaphysics" as he called it, to be based upon a "forgetting of Being." Being was replaced by concern merely for the individual "beings" that make up what we call "the world." Being, of course, never really goes away. But, as Heidegger puts it, it "withdraws" in the face of a world of things, leaving us, especially after the domination of the modern world by science and

---

[1] Sartre, *Being and Nothingness*, (New York: Washington Square Press, 1953). See Chapter 1 for Sartre's discussion of Pierre.

technology, without any firm bearings, fundamental values, or "ground of our human being." Modern human beings live in a world where Being itself is an "ever-present absence," a potential basis for life's meaning that somehow always eludes us in its concealment behind the everyday world of material things, gadgets, and gizmos produced by modern technology. The result is the familiar and pervasive modern experience of anxiety, guilt, and loss.[2]

Were Heidegger to direct a film about modern life, Pink Floyd would obviously write the score. For their music registers this sense of modern *Angst*, of living in a cold and expansive universe from which any clear meaning is absent though still sensing that it could or even ought to have some meaning. *Obscured by Clouds, Wish You Were Here*, and other titles plainly point to this kind of "cosmic absence." *The Dark Side of the Moon* is literally cosmic, the song "Eclipse" taking in "All that is now / All that is gone / All that's to come / and everything under the sun." All of this "is in tune / but the sun is eclipsed by the moon."

Non-Being in 'Postmodernism'

The generation of thinkers after Sartre and Heidegger, often called 'Poststructuralist' or 'Postmodernist,' view 'absence' as dispersed throughout and saturating all products of human culture. Their approach regarded the entire world as made up of "texts," which they then understood as (more or less) loose "weavings" (from the etymology of the word "text") of words and phrases. Each of these were threads forming meaningful figures in a cloth, but separating and fraying at the edges and perhaps connecting to *other* weavings with their own figures, and so on.

A central idea of Jacques Derrida's was that these 'language-threads,' and in fact 'word weaving' itself, was a process of "*différance*." Among the things that Derrida had in mind by coining this new term (it sounds exactly like the French word "*différence*" but varies from it in its written form) is the ability of texts to mean different things depending upon the spaces, gaps, and punctuation that allow us to recognize one letter, word, or

---

[2] Heidegger's *Being and Time* (State University of New York Press, 1996) contains his assessment of Being and its forgetting.

sentence as standing apart from and "being different from" another. In particular, this meant that the basis of all language could never itself be articulated in the "smooth flow of spoken language" but only glimpsed in the form of writing or other non-spoken media. From a postmodern perspective, Being was not something "withdrawn" from or "absent" from words or things; rather, Non-Being in the form of *différance* was woven through the entire fabric of human language and meaning, constituting the very basis of its possibility.[3]

While Pink Floyd's work, at least thematically, seems more aligned with the 'alienation' and 'absence' approaches to Non-Being, there are elements of a postmodern sensibility in at least two aspects of their work. First, in reading and listening to their lyrics, one is often struck by the way in which lines seem to break off in 'mid-thought' or trail off into another idea, verses that often seem unrelated to what goes before or comes after, and even whole "concept albums" that leave us with questions about what, exactly, the 'concept' was. One could even mention how odd the punctuation in the written lyrics is and how the simple movement of a comma or period would change the whole meaning of the line or verse. Rarely does a Pink Floyd song tell a coherent story or express some single emotion or experience. Rather, most seem like 'loosely woven' collages of images, metaphors, and interrupted 'half-thoughts.'

A lot of rock lyrics read this way, but we can't forget the one thing that permeates the work of Pink Floyd and, more than anything else, defines them as a group: the music. Where most other bands neatly fit the songs to the music, the two forming a sort of autonomous and seamless whole complete with memorable 'hooks,' Pink Floyd tends to set lyrics within a broader 'soundscape' that often seems to have a life of its own. For instance, though not completely unique in this, Pink Floyd employs extended, stand-alone instrumentals which are never mere vehicles for showing off virtuoso licks but are planned and integral parts of the performance.

Also, Pink Floyd frequently experimented, like some twentieth-century classical composers, with non-musical sounds and

---

[3] A useful introduction to Derrida's philosophy is translator Gayatri Chakravorty Spivak's introduction to his *Of Grammatology* (Johns Hopkins University Press, 1998).

loops that produce an additional layer of experience or commentary on the songs themselves (certainly the most famous being the sound of the cash register in "Money"). The band devoted virtually an entire double-album to such sonic experimentation with *Ummagumma.* If not quite postmodern in their sensibilities, Pink Floyd was certainly at home with language and sound fragments—those heard throughout *Dark Side* are perhaps best known—that "float" indeterminately within a sea of other verbal material and musical sounds. These fragments may fail to present any clear meaning or coherent idea, but they play crucial roles in inflecting the overall meaning of the music.

Meet You on the Dark Side of the Moon?

We can be sure, I think, that neither Marx, Sartre, nor Heidegger ever heard or knew of Pink Floyd. Derrida, perhaps. And I doubt that the members of Pink Floyd spent too much time reading their works (though you never know about Syd and Roger). The point is not that these philosophers and these musicians may (or may not) have influenced each other. It's that they both addressed, in their own ways, the need to explore new ways of approaching, thinking about, and experiencing the old problem of Non-Being. In fact, when I first read these philosophers, it took me a long time to figure out what they were really up to, what their abstract concepts and special terms had to do with my own life and experience. But when I first heard *Dark Side of the Moon,* I immediately got it—at least, as far as there was an "it" there to get. Pink Floyd helped me better understand what the philosophers were up to. Hope it works this way for you as well.

15

It's All Dark: The Eclipse of the Damaged Brain

RANDALL E. AUXIER

All that You Love

Being has a hole in it. And the hole is your very self. Like many of you, I learned that tidbit of information before I was really ready for it. We feel like an orifice. That doesn't *have* to be bad news, but it can be and often is. It gets pretty dark down in there, and there is madness and death in the hole, but joy and hope originate from that same "absence." I wish I had understood the brighter side of it when I was younger.

But I was listening to Pink Floyd. I don't know if it would be apt to say I "loved" the music, or even really "liked" it. Somehow that doesn't capture the relationship. One can say "Pink Floyd is awesome," or "cool," but "I *love* Pink Floyd" seems almost perverse. We are in awe of this music, we respect it, we appreciate it, but it has not been made for love or fondness or affection. It's about black holes and dark sides and shadows; it's about hanging on in somewhat noisy desperation, but the noise has to be closely arranged for the maximum effect.

All that You Do

I can only put this in personal terms, but I think you've probably had experiences like mine too, and that they are surely still with you just as they are with me. With few resources for resisting the maximum effect, and no comprehension at all, at age twenty-one, I once listened to "Brain Damage" about forty times in a row, jerking the needle up as the first chord of

"Eclipse" slid in and setting it back; the last time I let the record play through to "Eclipse," mainly because I was too far gone to set the needle back by then. I did this repetitive exercise not because I really wanted to hear the song forty times, but because right then I didn't know what else to do. Staring at the album cover on the coffee table, in the sort of dim light that is so conducive to exploring the outskirts of consciousness, enhanced by whatever mind-altering substances I had on hand, anaesthetized, alone, and, frankly, heart-broken (the way one sometimes is, and can only be, at twenty-one). And I kept repeating to myself "this is impossible," with an intensity that only someone that age can gather. Which is to say, I actually meant it.

Many of you have been to this place, in your own way. Somewhere in the course of it, I came to the edge of the conscious world, as if a door opened in the psyche, and I peered through it, saw that I was, well, nothing to write home about; nothing before I was born, nothing after I die, and therefore nothing now. The darkness, the sheer nothingness of the void, the warm terror that is so far beyond worldly fear, and the sudden understanding that I did not *have* to choose the narrow path of my familiar habits of consciousness—all of this, and more, was behind the door that opened, somehow, through the music. I realized that holding my own little mind together, in the conventional and expected ways, was an effort I made every day, usually without noticing how much work it takes. And I also realized I didn't have to do that, that being sane and acceptable was actually a choice, not a requirement.

Like you, I have friends who stepped through that door; some came back and some never did. In my own case, I closed the door, quit the drugs, turned off the music (for many years) and went back to school. I mean, how can you have any pudding if you don't eat your meat? The music that had gotten me through the 1970s and into the early 1980s came to be associated with the scary door that opened, and so I turned off not just Pink Floyd, but also Yes and Led Zeppelin. It should have been clear enough, but I wasn't sure which music was the Mephistopheles opening the door, responsible for the visitation of the void. I have since come to understand that Zeppelin was not much more than a respectable roots band, that Yes always dwelt in the light. Pink Floyd was the problem. Well, no. *I* was the problem; Pink Floyd was the musical mirror I stood before in the dark and said "bloody Mary" forty times, until she finally showed up.

Years of gradual revelation about how consciousness works, and how it applies to my own history has cleared some of the murk. I don't understand it all, not by any means, but let me take you through a part I think I do get, if you want to go. It might be cool, although I doubt you'll "love it." I think you should cue up "Brain Damage" and "Eclipse" and listen to them now. This isn't a requirement, but it will help us occupy the same headspace. I also want you to avoid looking at the album cover for the moment.

All that You Touch, See, Taste, Feel

If you pay close attention to your own experience, it may dawn on you that your consciousness is always restlessly looking for something to fasten on to, and then when it does find something, it is never quite satisfied with whatever it has. At any given moment, your body is being pelted with sights and smells and feels and even tastes (yes, you taste even when you're not eating—for example, right now, I really want to brush my teeth—never mind why). In all that sensory confusion, you are paying *attention* only to a small part of what's available *for* your attention. When your eyes are open and the light is good, chances are that you will pay the most attention to what you are seeing, and then you will voluntarily put the rest of your senses into a supporting role.

Favoring your power of sight is perfectly voluntary on your part, and you can alter the weight you give to any of your senses at any given time. But the visual stuff is so much more interesting and powerful to your momentary consciousness—draws your attention so much more seductively—that you may need to close your eyes or dim the lights before any of the other senses can be in command for very long. This is the reason we don't listen to Pink Floyd in bright light. To do so is simply wrong. We want the ears to be in charge, and we want the sound to tell us what the light *means*. We want the ears to tell *all* the other senses what everything means. And that can be done. Pink Floyd is not background music. It demands center stage. With sufficient openness and also discipline, we can even have sounds drive the meaning of all the other senses and even our interior feelings and emotions.

But here is something that may not have occurred to you. There's such a thing as an aural or auditory "image," as distinct from a visual image. I am not talking about the visual images that may be *inspired* by sounds, those dancing color patterns, or the memories of places we have seen, or various album covers, that spring into consciousness when our eyes are closed. I mean the auditory image *itself*, the way we experience the music so that the *sounds* make sense, have a pattern and an order that we can understand. You can have an "image" of sounds. Try this: Imagine the melody to "Money" in your head right now. You may also be visualizing David Gilmour singing it, but leave that aside. Just imagine the song. What is going on in your head is not made of sound waves, and it is not visual. You sort of "hear" the song in your head, right? You know you aren't actually hearing it, but somehow it is there. That is an auditory "image," because you are *imagining* it. It is very different from a visual image.

The same is true of all our senses; they all give birth to images of different sorts. You can imagine what a fresh cut lawn smells like, and a rotting corpse, and cookies baking, without actually smelling these things. That is your olfactory imagination, and the result of the effort at imagining produces images. And you "can just taste" those cookies before you eat them, can't you? We often use our power of making tasty images when cooking, especially when choosing combinations of spices. So remember, not all images are visual pictures.

All You Create

Visual images are spatial. When we are conscious of visual images, they have a top, a bottom, a left, a right, a depth, and an imagined distance from us—these are all spatial dimensions. Follow me in a little experiment. Do not look at the album cover, but picture before your mind the cover of *Dark Side of the Moon*. You know it well, the prism enveloped by blackness, the ray of light on one side, the refracted spectrum on the other. You *know* approximately where in the field of black to situate the prism, you know roughly which direction the tip of the prism points.

But are you altogether certain? Is the prism off to one side by just a little? Is the prism a pyramid or just a triangle? Is it tilted just a bit? This is all about spatial order. Are you sure about *which* side has the ray of light and which side is the refracted spectrum? Try imagining it both ways and see if you can decide which is "correct." So long as you are trying to re-create in imagination the album cover you have seen so many times, you will be working with a kind of consciousness that is really visual memory, but you also will experience a certain freedom to alter and vary the image right now; yes, you are *trying* to *re*-create it, but in truth, you are *creating* it, which is the only way you can actually remember anything. The image is yours to alter as you wish, and there is no right and wrong about how you imagine it unless you choose to judge your image against another one (which you don't have to do).

Some philosophers call this power to create images the "spontaneity" of consciousness. That sounds more sophisticated than saying "wow, man, the image just appears from nothing," but that's what "spontaneity" basically means: the immediate presence of whatever is present to consciousness. As you spontaneously make a visual image, you can move the image around, trying it now one way, now another. But the point is that you can situate the visual image in your mind spatially in most any way you choose, play around with it, invert the prism, change the colors of the spectrum, and so on. That is what I mean by *spatial* order in visual images. There are also limits to what you can do with a visual image—for example, you cannot simultaneously imagine the prism as *both* a flat triangle and as a pyramid; you can, at most, alternate between them. So not only is there spatial *order*, but there are rules or laws (and limits) that apply to the act of imagining visual images. These are mainly geometrical rules, by the way, because geometry is the general structure of space.[1]

---

[1] Here's something fun to do with your brain that your math teacher never taught you. First, take some drugs. Now, imagine a point. Now make it move in one direction. It becomes a line. Now, make the whole line move in one direction. It becomes a plane. Now make the whole plane move. It becomes a solid (it has has three dimensions). You are using your imagination to multiply dimensions. You can go beyond three dimensions if you really, really work at it, or if the drugs are good enough.

Auditory images exist in *time* in about the same way that visual images exist in space. That is, instead of up and down and left and right, you have mainly "before" and "after" when it comes to imagined sounds. Imagining what someone said or a melody takes you some time, whereas visual images seem to appear instantaneously. Both are spontaneous, but obviously "spontaneity" isn't the same thing as "instantaneity" (I made up that word, but I sort of like it). There are limits and rules with auditory images also. If I ask you to imagine the melody of "Money," you just cannot do it all at once. The melody takes time to imagine; within a certain range, you can speed it up or slow it down in your imagination, but you cannot collapse it into one instant or extend it to an hour (for one time through the musical phrase). If you try to make the image all at once, the song just disappears; if you try to extend it too long, other images intervene before you can finish it. And imagined time does not follow the same rules as physical time. You can imagine a melody, without distorting it, much more rapidly than you can physically create it singing it out loud. It would be cool to learn whether there is some sort of ratio of imagined time to physical time. No one has figured out a way to measure that, but there is some kind of relationship I'm sure. Anyway, the point is, we find the laws that apply to auditory images in the way *time* is structured (always with a past, a present, and a future).

All that Is Now, Gone, to Come

Most people are not trained to work with auditory images in the way we all habitually mess around with visual ones, but musicians learn to do this with auditory images—they *have* to learn it. They may not know how to explain it, but music unfolds over time, and that allows them some freedom and variation and creativity in the way they are remembering and anticipating what is in the music. To create music, to work with it at all, requires that one be able to, in imagination, arrange and re-arrange experiences in time. Musicians all know that temporal arrangement is the basic pattern of order in a piece of music—the "groove" of the piece. Choices of notes and chords come later and are built on the timeframe.

To give you an example of some features of this kind of temporal "order" (and it has many, many features): Sing to yourself in your imagination (hell, do it out loud if you want to) the opening line of "Brain Damage." You are singing "The lunatic is on the grass" (and I know you will say "grahhss," whether you are British or not). You may also be picturing your favorite image of a madman on your front lawn (for me it always starts out as Charles Manson, whose picture frightened me as a boy, and he's definitely coming for me, not walking away or sitting still), but that is *visual* imagery. I want to draw your attention to the fact that, as you complete the line you are singing, you now want to pause for a bit and then *repeat* it. You have an *urge* to do that, and it will be a *strong* urge. Interestingly, it is easier to stop yourself from repeating it out loud than to stop yourself from repeating the auditory image. Our control of our bodies is quite a bit easier than commanding our own consciousness. Consciousness is suggestible, but hard to control.

If you imagined the first line of "Brain Damage" (and you did, because I have you in my power), you will probably repeat it even if I tell you not to (so much for my delusions of omnipotence). If you sang it out loud, you will repeat it silently in your imagination, even if you don't sing it again. Why? "Well," you will answer "that's how the song goes." And I will say "that is precisely my point." The auditory image *lives* in these urges that *tie* the past (your memory and previous experience) to the future (your next experience), and in an orderly way—you know how the song goes, you learned it, and you remember it. If anyone starts you down that time-path, you will project into the immediate future the temporal sequence you learned, and you'll just take off down that path (like a friggin' lunatic). You almost can't help yourself.

I assure you, Gilmour and Waters are well aware of this little feature of consciousness. In writing the lyrics, Waters didn't *have* to repeat that first line at the beginning of each verse.[2] In writing the music, Gilmour didn't *have* to repeat the same melody when the words were repeated. So why did they do it? In a sense, every child knows the answer. Repetition is, perhaps, the most powerful weapon in a musician's arsenal for controlling your consciousness. By means of repetition, a

---

[2] I guess Waters was actually the *last* person who really *had* a choice about that.

musician can rob you of *almost* all of your freedom. Your desires and your next act of consciousness can be controlled by getting you to fix your will upon only a single possibility for the future. If you doubt for a single second that Waters and Gilmour are doing this on purpose, I invite you to sing "Us and Them" in your head. You are doing it because I suggested it, and now I *know* you are so totally echoing yourself. I want to point out that "Us and Them" comes right before "Brain Damage" on the album. You honestly think this isn't a conscious set-up? The boys know what they're doing. It is a gentle kind of brain damage.

A repeated line is the most quickly learned in any song. You probably sang the repeated lines in "Brain Damage" the very *first* time you heard the song. I know I did. We were shown the time-pattern with the opening verse, and then shown the slight variations—he's in the hall, they're in the hall, he's in my head, dammit, he's in my head—and then, tacitly, seductively, Waters sort of said "now boys and girls, repeat after me." And we do it. We almost can't help it. And once we have co-operated, he has us where he wants us. We're nearly compelled to listen to the next line to find out what the lunatic will do. Off down the path we go. The lyricist is quite powerful in terms of getting us going, but now he can't stop us, so he loses his power once he uses it—Waters is a bee who stung you, but the stinger is gone, and with it the bee. Of course Waters is a whole hive. Repeated melodies are also powerful, but not as much as repeated words. But when you repeat both words and melody, as in "Brain Damage," the power becomes hypnotic.

There's a lot to be said about auditory images. I haven't even scraped the surface, but if you understand that these images work with your memories, your expectations, your desires, and most importantly, your *will*, well, you know most of what you need to know about why you eventually opened the door to your soul and took the trip into the void (or at least I think I know why I did). That trip is about how past experience and present desire make the future—sort of, make the future before it happens, as an image we project and then live our way into—and music is probably the single most powerful way to penetrate a person's regular "defenses" against, well, mind-control, and take him where he didn't quite intend to go. Music pene-

trates every pore of the body, moves the body and consciousness wherever it will, and endows those who create it with an
incredible power.

Everything Under the Sun Is in Tune

Fortunately, it's difficult to make music *well*, and those who do
learn to make it well are themselves even *more* susceptible to
its power than those who simply listen. Waters and Gilmour may
have you in their control, but they are more *had* by what they
are doing than you are. The music itself takes the musicians
where *they* didn't intend to go. So there is a cosmic balance in
music, because only those who are most deeply moved by it are
able to create it, and being so deeply controlled by it themselves, they have little energy left for using it to control others.
Usually. Instead, they generally make music to express, please
and, paradoxically, *free* themselves (from everything except the
music), first from the *inside out*, and then from the *outside in.*

What I mean by this is that in a musician, the music *first*
exists inside, as a kind of urge for release, and that urge *then*
manifests itself as bodily movements (exercising the vocal
chords or moving the fingers on a fret-board). That is inside-out.
After that, the music is generated as sound waves, and finally re-
absorbed into the body (mainly the ears) as heard sound. That
is outside in. When the cycle is completed, there is a kind of fulfillment of release.

But while playing, there is a short lag-time between the onset
of the urge and the re-absorption as intelligible sound (even
after our ears hear it, it takes a little time for it to be processed
by the brain). To keep the music going, a musician has to generate new urges and act on them while absorbing the results of
previous urges. Thus, from the inside, a musician is always at
least a little bit *ahead* of what his body is hearing, while from
the outside, he is a little behind himself. When playing music,
your whole existence, physical, conscious, emotional, gets
extended in time, and more extended depending on how far
ahead of himself he can get with the urges, while still retaining
the meaning of the sound coming in. This is a total rush, by the
way, when the loop gets going and the durational lapse is
expanded successfully. Of course, if a musician fails, gets too far
ahead, the whole loop snaps back into the immediate present,

and he's likely played a wrong note and is staring stupidly at his fret-board. That never happens to Gilmour, of course . . .

The result of this temporal self-extension is the creation of a traveling time-loop that can expand our awareness of "now" to a few more seconds than in a normal act of waking consciousness. In ordinary activities, "now" probably lasts a couple of seconds at most, as the last conscious act perishes and the next act is anticipated. "Now" for a musician can last up to eight or ten seconds, depending upon how and what he is playing. When improvising in a band with others, the musician gets a maximally expanded "now." Playing something thoroughly rehearsed and memorized tends to shrink the effect to something that is fairly mechanical, and expanded in time only for as long as it takes for the urge to become a sound that is heard (which isn't very long). Having an expanded now is an attractive experience, and in the expanded interval, a door is opened, a trap-door in time itself, through which the musician escapes. What the door is like and where it leads depends on both the musician and the music itself.

That is why musicians play mainly for themselves, and only secondarily for those who listen. And that is why musicians are themselves among the most devoted music fans. Practicing music is not as much a discipline as a pleasure, even an *addiction* to temporal escape, for those who can find the trap-door in time. Gilmour and Waters know many such doors. Perhaps too many. They are almost too good at what they do.

Heaven help the world if some truly great musician (not our heroes in PF) were ever detached enough to use the music he creates to work his will solely upon others, for it turns out that a musician can, with talent and practice, funnel you through the trap door he chooses and eject you into whatever place he wants you to go—if you let him, and, as we already saw with the "repetition strategy," it is pretty hard to stop him if he knows how to do it. Our heroes know this bit of magic. And there are dozens of other strategies besides repetition. Prime among these is getting you to create for yourself the images, under the domination of the auditory time pattern (of memory and anticipation), but including, especially, the visual images as a supporting cast; this is crucial to making good music. Waters *needs* you to *see* the lunatic almost as much as he needs you to repeat the line. One type of image reinforces the other. Your body is laid open by the presence of the sound, and then re-organized temporally by its pulses and repetitions and movements, and then you start seeing things in your head that make the music seem like more than just sound. It's a limited kind of time-travel. So you use *your own* energy to create visual images (your own version of Charlie Manson), and work with the music, actively, to find a temporal expansion that is sort of analogous to the one the musician experiences. You generate successive urges of your own and then experience the images you create. But, make no mistake, your experiences are quite different from the musician's. The musician exerts a level of control over the character of the time-expansion that the listener does not.

All that You Beg, Borrow, or Steal

So you can create different *kinds* of images with your body, not just visual ones. When your ears are in the driver's seat, the other kinds of images your body is creating—all the way from the way the couch feels against your backside to the visual picture of the lunatic in your hall—will swirl and change with the music. All of this activity plays on your own powers of attention. Attention is weird. It's like a vortex. At every moment your attention casts about for something to focus on, and as soon as some enticing possibility presents itself in any of your modes of awareness, you zero in on it, like going down a space-time wormhole, and for a split second, everything else just disappears.

This act of "appropriation," in which your consciousness begs, borrows or steals something from the perceived world for its own private party, happens so quickly that it is easy to miss what is happening (unless you have, er, umm, slowed the process down with some sort of, umm, chemical enhancement, which I do not condone, of course). But what happens in that split second when you "attend" to something is that you get sucked into a vortex, like a descending spiral in time, and at the end of the slide, an "object" appears. Then, all the rest of your sensory information returns as the background against which the object of attention stands out. The reason you could not resist repeating the line from "Brain Damage" is that it drew your attention down a wormhole, and at the end of the time-slide, there was the same damn line again. So you said it in your head. This is like a hall of mirrors in time, and you could easily say the line over to infinity—or perhaps listen to the whole song forty times in a row, if you're dumb enough to try that.

This whole sequence of events we call the song "Brain Damage"—the lyrics, the tempo, the melody, the amazing surge when the drums kick in, the climactic line that gave the album its name—all of this can become the extended and complex object of your attention. Once the sequence starts, it seems almost as if it completes itself, and almost against your will (which is why it is difficult to turn off any good song in the middle, or, what is much more unusual, it is hard to turn off *Dark Side of the Moon* anywhere in the album—the whole album is one long experience).

To get a sense of this level of control, consider this: If you are listening to "Brain Damage," you just *yearn* for those drums to kick in even before they do, don't you? That's why Nick Mason and the boys made you wait an extra, excruciatingly sweet, swell of four beats for each drum entrance—just for the simple value of anticipation. Good musicians know all about building tension and release in your little brain. Do you not want to raise your arms and make drum motions in the air, as if to help Nick find those same drums in the same order just one more time? Do your lips not move spontaneously with the sound of Roger's voice so as to make a date for a future lunar rendezvous (with Syd or whomever you expect to meet there)? Do you not release yourself in combined despair and defiance, in a lofty bitterness at a stupid world that cannot understand?

Alright, step out of the vortex—Jesus, I'm falling into a trance just writing about this shit. And now I can't get that damned song out of my head (maybe I found the lunatic). Try something else, now: Release your attention for a moment, and just think of nothing in particular (and here, the chemicals can also help, which I still do not condone). Try to think of nothing. You will find that there is a certain restless feeling inside you. Your consciousness is squirting all over the place, begging for an "object," something to focus on, anything. And if you close your eyes just to deny yourself any visual information, your brain will start borrowing visual images from your memory, and you'll be hard-pressed to make it stop. But let's try to stop this for a moment if we can. There are a few ways to do it. The easiest way to make it stop is just to give in and think of something in particular, just one thing. That object won't last long, but at least it is more satisfactory than dealing with the perpetual motion machine of your attention deprived of an object.

All that You Say

There is a way to train and discipline your brain to be more orderly: imagine just one word over and over. This is why they teach you a "mantra" for meditation in many Eastern religions. Repetition of a single word or very short phrase can bring your attention into focus. One is taught to repeat the word every second or two at first, while attention is in its usual frenetic condition, and then slow the frequency as calm sets in. The regular wandering of attention is brought gradually under your control. It is like calming your own private little Jack Russell Terrier by quietly saying "good dog" until he stops bouncing off the walls.

It's a dicey idea to calm your attention by saying the equivalent of "bad dog" to yourself. Some mantras can be pretty destructive. From personal experience, I can report that hundreds of repetitions of "this is impossible" over forty repetitions of "Brain Damage" make for an unwise plan. Don't do that. If you think that *which* word-images you choose to dwell on in your imagination doesn't affect you, I would gladly convince you otherwise. And since I'm being so solicitous of your wellbeing at the moment, I also do no not advise you to use any Pink Floyd lyric as a mantra, for reasons that will soon become clear.

There are others ways, however, to set your attention at rest, or to "unify attention," we might say. For example, if you turn up the music loud enough, you can make all that restless inner activity subordinate to the simple act of hearing. You can listen to music like a mantra that comes in from the outside world *instead* of an auditory image you create for yourself in your imagination. When you do that, you are using your power of sense *perception* to overwhelm your other two main types of consciousness, imagining and thinking (or cogitation or *conception*). Imagining is the kind of consciousness we have been talking about before, with the images; *conceiving* is what you do when you work with concepts (which is why they *call* them concepts, I guess), like doing math in your head for instance. You might imagine the numbers, as visual images, but an image of "2 + 2 = 4" is different from carrying out the conceptual operation of addition. You can confirm that if I ask you to add 17 and 27 in your head. Picturing the numbers doesn't give you the answer. You have to *think* to get the answer. If the music is loud enough, it may be pretty tough to do even that much math. The point is that you *perceive*, in addition to conceiving and imagining, and it is hard to do more than one at a time. Your brain, however damaged, makes fast transitions among them, though, so you might feel like you can think, imagine and perceive all at once. In a sense you are doing all three much of the time, it's a question of which one has your attention, which is only one of them.

Whereas meditation, which is a kind of imagining, creates a type of *internal* and *voluntary* control (imagining masters perceiving and conceiving), perceptual sensory overload begets a certain *external* and *involuntary* control of your mental processes. In the first case, one gives the inner life, the inner dynamic, an upper hand by depriving the body of movement, the ears of sound, the eyes of light. That is, the outer world is subjugated to the inner power of the will, and your wandering attention is set on auto-pilot by the repetition of the mantra. It may not surprise you that this process, reducing everything to your own free will, makes you *feel* powerful. Unfortunately, you can't *do* very much while attempting it, except perhaps become enlightened.

When you use the over-stimulation of the senses to *silence* the inner life, giving your perceiving body *and your soul* to whatever external stimulation is the most powerful, you can't hear yourself think at all, and your imagination gets scattered or enslaved. It is not surprising that you are at your least powerful, and least able to feel the freedom of your own will, when you use the outer perceptual world to squash the inner one. Your attention is at the mercy of whatever you are perceiving, and the acts of imagination you undertake are barely voluntary. In the case of music, to use the inimitable words of Waters, "all that you touch, all that you see, all that you taste, all that you feel . . ." comes under the sway of . . . of what? All that you *hear*, of course. In all the obvious lyrical choices in "Eclipse," that word "hear" is conspicuously missing. No way is this an accident. Roger knows what you are and are not doing when you have his voice in your ears.

Everyone You Fight

There is a reason why the American government uses loud heavy metal music to torture the people it claims are our enemies. It isn't because they like Metallica. Rather, Metallica weakens the will, if you hate the music, or after a while it does that even if you like it. Ironically, the same music *seems* to strengthen the will of the soldiers who are pumping themselves up to kill, but that isn't really what is happening. The music actually cancels their sense of freedom not to do what they are doing, anaesthetizes their emotions, cancels their imaginations, and turns them into killing machines. And that is what they want, given what they are being ordered to do. The soldier's will doesn't disappear, but it is set upon one task only, the fight. It's curious to consider whether such a reduced will is "stronger" than a free one. Is the person who employs his free will not to strike back when provoked stronger or weaker than the person who cannot stop himself? The "detainees" at Guantanamo Bay often pray to resist the Metallica—this is a fairly powerful self-assertion of the priority of the inner life over the physical body. For some of them, perhaps it works. I hope it does.

In any case, I think you will see why the government doesn't choose Pink Floyd to torture people. They want co-operative, docile prisoners, not insanely detached ones who don't care whether they live or die. And if I were a soldier, I think I might choose Pink Floyd for battle *if* I wanted help in letting myself be killed, rather than help to survive. It is clear that the music itself, whatever one chooses, carries a total message about how to be . . . or not to be, if that is the question. And for Pink Floyd, that is certainly the question. I would not be surprised if this is among the most frequently chosen suicide music.

So the point is that perception can squelch imagination and conceptual thought, but either of the other two can also trump its rivals, under the right conditions. So you have these three main choices about how to be, if you choose to be at all: imagine, perceive, think. It's like your own private game of rock, paper, scissors. Clearly perception is your rock, conception is your scissors, and imagination is your paper. But I never understood how "paper covers rock" was really a victory. I mean, rocks can shred paper as easily as they shatter scissors, right? Metallica is "rock" music, and I don't think or imagine very much when I hear it. Perhaps "paper covers rock" depends on what is written on the paper. If it's the lyrics to "Eclipse" with a little prism against a black background, be careful. The rock is still under the paper, and it's waiting there to blunt your scissors if you try to think too much about the words.

All You Distrust

It is not an accident that those who follow Floyd also follow a common pattern. We turn down the lights and we turn up the volume. We turn it up until the inner world has no choice but to follow wherever the music may lead. *The Dark Side of the Moon* is one of the greatest collaborative works of art of the twentieth century. Part of the reason is that it forms an aesthetic whole, a total experience that puts us in a place of *externally* induced inner silence for forty-three minutes, a sort of comfortable numbness. There are many artworks that can accomplish the same end of creating a "whole experience," from Beethoven symphonies to Tarantino movies, which can hold us affixed to something external for long periods of time. Not all such experiences have the same effect. Some really get us going, but Pink Floyd does the opposite. It mellows us or paralyzes us.

All such experiences have external control, perception over imagination and thought, but clearly the external control is only one facet of the work of art. We can also silence our inner lives for hours on end watching television, and there is nothing "great" about *that*. Yet, the vortex of attention is exploited by artists of all sorts, good ones and bad ones, in order, presumably, to show us something meaningful or beautiful or perhaps even educational or profitable. Artists use a thousand devices to *get* our attention, and then we expect some pay-off from for having given ourselves over to their external control—for having trusted them with not only our time and our senses, but with our free will. We make ourselves vulnerable to artists when we allow them to take control of us, to offer their creations as possible objects of our attention. This is a way of opening the doorway to the soul, and hoping that something worthwhile will come through it. And some of us want the trap-door as well, those of us who truly *live* for aesthetic experiences (that includes every good musician and many music fans).

In a sense, I would say that a chef more than a musician is the *ultimate* artist in this way, because not only does a chef convince us to give away our time, our attention, and our senses, but in this case we actually consent to put the artwork into our bodies and have it become a part of our own physical being. This is an astonishing act of trust, when you think about it. But the music we hear and the sights we see become part of our bodies and part of our memories also. There is no going back once you have seen or heard something—you cannot "unsee" or "unhear" it (remember that the next time you pass by an automobile accident, or have the urge to say "I hate you" to someone you love).

When it comes to experiencing artworks, we reserve a special level of attention, and with it a heightened level of vulnerability to what we will experience, and so there is a special kind of trust involved. For that reason, music requires us to expose ourselves. Do you trust Gilmour and Waters? Would you want your daughter to date them? Yet, we are so very vulnerable and they are so very seductively good. Yes, we trust them. What can we say? We like living dangerously, don't we? What if the dam breaks open many years too soon, like, when we're twenty-one?

Everyone You Meet

In what I have said up to now, I have been drawing on a theory by the French philosopher Jean-Paul Sartre (1908–1980), so you should probably meet him. He's dead of course, so you'll have to settle for meeting his theory. But I don't want to weigh you down with a bunch of crap that would be boring, and yet, I do need to be a little more explicit about what is going down here.

Nearly everything I have been doing to your head is called "phenomenology," which is a pretty sassy method of doing philosophy. There are different ways of doing phenomenology, and some of them are, well, a trip. Sartre frankly makes my head explode with dark forebodings, takes my thoughts where they didn't intend to go, sort of the way Pink Floyd takes my imagination through unforeseen trap-doors. This is not to say that Sartre is cooler than Pink Floyd, but I have a feeling the boys in the band may have read some Sartre along the way. I'm not fishing for a compliment, but if you kind of dig what's been hap-

pening up to now, you could check out some of the books I've
been using. Here is the obligatory footnote.[3]

I can't tell you much about Sartre here, but I can give you a
sense of the dude. He was a hero of the French resistance in
World War II, a controversial radical all his life, and he could
really write. They gave him a Nobel Prize for literature, but he
told the Swedish Academy to stick their prize where the sun
doesn't . . . race around to come up your behind, if you get my
drift. I admit I think it is kind of groovy to turn down a Nobel
Prize. I mean, I would accept the prize, and I have nothing
against the Swedish Academy, but it takes some serious balls to
say "your prize is bullshit" when it's *that* prize. I repeat, I would
take it, in case any members of the Academy are reading this
. . . I haven't earned it, but I don't want to lose my shot just in
case the Academy likes PF.

I brought this up before, but now I'm back to it. Sartre said
(and I think he was right) that when we form an image, whether
visual or auditory or olfactory or kinesthetic or some combination, we simultaneously "believe" something about the image
we form. You can't form an image without believing something.
I think that is damned interesting—I finally understand why I
clapped my hands when Tinker Bell was dying in Peter Pan. I
do believe in faeries, I do, I do. At least I did. You clapped your
hands too, asshole, so stop trying to be so grave about everything just to seem so all-fired laid back. You didn't kill Tinker
Bell. I'll bet Syd Barrett didn't clap. So Sartre calls this belief
thing the "positional act" of consciousness. In a sense, we
"believe" an image into existence. But before we get to *what* we
believe, I need to tell you something kind of freaky.

Sartre thinks that images are not something *in* your consciousness, the images *are* your consciousness. When you pay

---

[3] Primarily I am using Sartre's *The Psychology of Imagination* (New York:
Citadel Press, 1991). This was first published (in French of course) in 1940, and
a lot of stuff has been learned about how the brain creates images since then,
but I think the core of Sartre's theory is still intact. Also check out
Imagination: A Psychological Critique (Ann Arbor: University of Michigan
Press, 1962). This is far less exciting and was written three years earlier when
Sartre was figuring out what was wrong with everyone else's theories. For a
really wild ride see Sartre's novel *Nausea*, which is frankly a lot like listening
to *Wish You Were Here*, and the protagonist, Roquentin, reminds me of that
dude who is on fire on the cover.

attention to something, steal a piece of the world for yourself, it isn't the thing *outside* your body (like a tree or a Pink Floyd song on the sound system) that has your attention, it is your *own* imaginative activity you are paying attention to. This isn't hard to understand when you think about it. Trees are made of, like, cellulose and water. When you see a tree (that is, perceive it), it's not as if actual cellulose is flying through the air and entering your body. "No," you say, "light is entering the body." Yes, but not the *same* light that's over there bouncing off the cellulose. The little photons are communicating with each other and sending a certain wave-particle pattern your way, and it affects your body, but the light isn't exactly entering your body either; it has to be changed. Your body turns the energy in the photons into nerve impulses and electrochemical reactions. Your image (apparently) comes from those reactions, not directly from cellulose or light.

The same is true for sound. You are not hearing the record or the CD or even the band at the Pink Floyd show. Sound waves are getting turned into electrochemical reactions by your body. But here is where things get freaky. How the hell, pray tell, do a bunch of electrochemical reactions inside your body create an image that refers to just *that* song, or just *that* tree? They're just ordered reactions, and they are *yours*, not the world's. And they may serve to generate the image, but the image you are paying attention to is not *made of* electro-chemicals—at least its meaning is not, and I see no reason to think the image itself is "made of" those. Even if it is, you don't have to study body chemistry to understand your images, so I don't see how it helps anything to say that my visual tree image is made of such and such a reaction, while my auditory image of the PF show is made of this other reaction, and so on. I mean, BFD.

When I say Pink Floyd is spacey, I'm not trying to say "I prefer this collection of electro-chemical reactions to the ones I call KC and the Sunshine Band." There is a lot more to images than electro-chemical body processes. It has been a bit of a mystery among philosophers for quite a while as to how the images in my consciousness have meaning and reference to things like trees and rock bands, to which they have only the vaguest similarity in physical structure. So how do the images do that?

Sartre thinks it doesn't make much difference, ultimately, how we answer that question, since our answer can only be probable at best. But there is something we can know with absolute certainty, he claims: that we are paying attention, in every case, to the *image*, directly, not to the tree or the band. In fact the image just *is* our consciousness. Screw the perceived object, we'll never know exactly what it is, and we don't really care about it. We want our daisy-chain of images, and as long as we get them, we can pretty much tell the cold cruel world to go piss off. And Sartre says we can know *everything* there is to know about the images we make because, well, we made them. There isn't one thing in your image, even of a perceived object outside you, that you didn't put into it yourself.

The down side of this is that you can't learn anything you didn't already know from an image. The up side is that you can be certain about the image itself. That isn't much of a victory in the land of knowledge (I mean, so what? We *do* know what we know, at least when we know it well enough to create it), but it is your very own creation. Your images are your special gift to yourself that no one else can give you (never mind that you stole them from the world). You might as well be proud of your little images, since no one else will be, and they contain all you know (which isn't very much or very interesting in the grand scheme of things, as Waters and Gilmour constantly remind us).

All that You Give

So let's say you and I are listening to *Dark Side of the Moon*, with the lights low and the volume high. In one sense, we're listening to the "same" album, even though the sound waves hitting your ear drums are not precisely the same *individual* waves that are hitting mine. I'm over here and you're over there. The waves have the same form, almost. I mean, the acoustics may be better where you are sitting, worse where I am sitting (because you stole the best seat, which makes you an asshole in my book), and the shape of the room affects the sound waves. But even if the sound waves were utterly indistinguishable, you and I would still be hearing different music, even if we are stealing from the same sonic cookie jar.

Let me make it more concrete. I happen to be a musician, and let's say for argument's sake that you're not (because I want to feel superior to you, to punish you for taking the seat I wanted, and I'm writing this and you're merely reading it, so I get to decide). When I listen to "Brain Damage," I attend to all kinds of things you probably don't even notice. (Now imagine the spooky laughter from "Brain Damage"; I'm doing that.) We bring different histories into the room, different sets of expectations about music, different levels of physical sensitivity, and different powers of imagination. Okay, your images may be better in some ways, but I prefer my own auditory images.

So when my body and my consciousness go to work on the music, I give myself auditory images of a sort that are certainly *different* from those you give yourself, and they may even be *radically* different. And we can both vary the ways we make the images, even in the presence of the "same" sound waves. I can approach "Brain Damage" in a spirit of resignation, if I want to; then, with an act of will, I can move to a feeling of strong resolve not to let the bastards rearrange me till I'm sane. When I shift from one way of giving myself the images to the other, the auditory image I am creating for myself shifts accordingly.

I also hear the bass line first and foremost because I happen to be a bass player, and I can construct my image of the total sound from that starting point, and I usually do (although not with Pink Floyd because the bass lines are boring and monotonous, but that is intentional on their part, of course). So perhaps I start from the keyboard sounds and work my way out in constructing the aural image. If you are not a musician, you may not have these options for building your own aural image, but you may have other choices that I do not have (and would not want of course). We both have habits in the way we make our images, but we also have options—spontaneity again, freedom.

All You Destroy

So what? Well, here is the key to how Pink Floyd took me, and probably you, through the trap-door and out into the abyss. In order to construct your imaginative consciousness, you have to, in Sartre's terms *annihilate the world* of perception. So all those sounds hitting your ears are getting whacked, and your body is substituting a *different* electrochemical type of order for the sonic order. Now, electrochemical reactions work differently from sound waves. This difference is far more complicated than the reduction of sound waves to electrical impulses like your telephone does. The point is that you use the stuff going on inside your own body as an "analogue" to what's going on in the perceptual world, to use Sartre's word.

That's right. Your body is a sort of short-delay analogue playback unit. It does not take long to convert perceptual energies into the stuff you make your consciousness with, but it isn't instantaneous. There is a slight delay.

And do you know what is happening during that delay? You are annihilating the perceptual world. Perceptual energies are like the specimens that crime labs have to destroy in order to analyze them. You can't really use photons and sound waves without destroying them in the process. You destroy what you are physically hearing in order to imagine it just afterwards, and you are paying attention *not* to the stuff you hear, but to the stuff you created to *replace* the stuff you heard.

Nobody knows what consciousness is "made of" although it seems to be some sort of subtle arrangement of energies that, as far as we know, only exists on the back of electrochemical brain and nerve activity. But that energy is so very subtle and so highly ordered that it might even be subject to quantum weirdness—for example, consciousness might be able to travel more quickly than the speed of light, and might affect things in the universe without any measurable space-time relation. There's no good evidence for saying consciousness is *just* physical energy, in the way we currently understand the word "physical," only that as far as we know, it doesn't occur *without* physical energy. Maybe it can, but we don't have any convincing evidence that it does.

But here is the point: your *body* is a weapon of mass destruction, and the stuff it is hell bent on destroying is all the types of stuff you perceive. It's like a massive invasion of the body-snatchers, as you suck up Pink Floyd sounds and turn them into, well, some very subtle stuff that you then pay attention to. And there is not one thing you pay attention to that you didn't snatch, destroy, and substitute.

While Sartre was ticking away the hours that make up a dull day, he wondered about something that *never* would have occurred to me. He asked himself, "well, Jean-Paul [this is how he addressed himself when he was thinking], *how* do we carry out this act of annihilation? Is it just *one* way, or are there several?" Damned if he didn't come up with an answer, which is part of the reason he got famous enough to turn down a Nobel Prize. This is how he puts it:

The image also includes an act of belief, or a positional act. The act can assume four forms and no more: (1) it can posit the object as non-existent, (2) or as absent, (3) or as existing elsewhere; it can also (4) "neutralize" itself, that is, not posit its object as existing.[4]

This is fairly tricky, but it's the whole key to the Pink Floyd trapdoor. One of the bizarre things about images is that the perceptual object does not *have* to be present for you to make one. You can hear "Brain Damage" *without* the sound waves, basically because you have heard the song before and you carried out the required destruction, and made the substitute, and you still *have* the substitute, implanted in your body-memory. If you haven't heard the song, you cannot imagine it. But having heard it once, the image pattern you gave yourself then is all yours. The more you repeat the action of destroying and substituting, the easier it is to recreate it when the song is not playing.

So the destruction of the perceptual energies needs to happen at least once, but—and pay close attention here because things are about to get even creepier—after *that* your imagination can do the work of bringing the image up with *any* perceptual information at all, even just the energies inside your living body, which you also perceive. Once you have the pattern, you can make the image of the song out of *anything* you happen to be perceiving. That's because the song you *paid attention to* was never "the song," itself, but your own imaginative creation, done in the presence of the song. You are a very resourceful little cuss, if I do say myself, using your own digestive processes, for example, as material for singing Pink Floyd songs in your head. All that you eat . . . can become Pink Floyd songs.

The constant in all this is that you are still destroying stuff in order to make other stuff to pay attention to. And you can destroy it in *exactly* four ways, Sartre says. I am not sure I buy the claim that there are exactly and only four ways to demolish my perceptual experience, but we won't go into that. Sartre was smarter than I am and certainly smarter than you are, reading your Pink Floyd book with your oh-so-damaged brain cells, so we'll just trust him for now. What are these four destructive acts in which you are constantly engaged? Let me move by concrete example.

---

[4] Sartre, *The Psychology of Imagination*, p. 16. I added the numbering.

The Sun Is Eclipsed by the Moon

First, turn the page back and look at the "four possibilities" again from the Sartre quote. You are not listening to "Brain Damage" at the moment, but now imagine it anyway. The sound waves are not here, but the song *exists*, right? So it isn't annihilation number (1). You are not saying to yourself "this doesn't exist." We will return in a minute to number (1).

So is the song just absent (2), or is it definitely elsewhere right now (3)? What do you *believe* about it when you imagine it? The song is almost surely playing somewhere right now (that must be weird for the boys in the band, to know that somewhere on Earth all the songs on *Dark Side of the Moon* are probably playing, 24/7/365). But that wasn't relevant to you when you formed your belief about it just now. You weren't thinking about that. It wasn't number (3) when you made the image, although *now* it may be (3), since I suggested that you think about the song as perpetually playing elsewhere. But that is not what you believed a minute ago when you gave yourself the image.

As far as we can tell, you have to believe one of the four Sartre gives us, and only one, in order to imagine something. Imagination will not occur unless you believe something, and it is your belief, your "positional act" that annihilates the perceptual stuff and substitutes the image. So in this case, a good candidate is that you "believed" the song simply to be absent, which is to say it *could* be present, but just doesn't happen to be. So you annihilated, let's say, your digestive energies and the light in the room (you need some stuff to annihilate, but anything will do) in the mode of "absent."

In the case of a song that exists in many, many recorded examples, this is an obvious way to do it. It's just contingently absent, I believe, and in so believing, I orient myself negatively in the world, and take a shredder to my perceptions, and make the auditory image of song. But in the case of making an image of a loved one who is alive (as far as you know), but not present at the moment, in order to think of her, you will annihilate your perceptions (perhaps, say, the pain in your left big toe, and the way the room smells) in the mode of number (3): "I believe her to be somewhere else," and presto, an image of your darling (with only a trace of foot odor left over; maybe you should have used other material for this precious image).

As you can quickly see, there is a *world* of difference between imagining a loved one who is believed to be elsewhere, number (3), and imaging a loved one who is dead—doesn't exist, number (1). You will not want to imagine a loved one whom you hope is alive (although you don't really know) in mode (1). That would disturb you. Allowing yourself to believe your beloved is dead in order to imagine her is dangerous stuff, and you will be superstitious about doing it. And you will choose number (2), absent, when she is in another room, and number (3), elsewhere, when she is far enough away as to require some time to bring her to your presence. Number (1) is, then, dangerous and disturbing. You only use number (1) when you are cornered. Most people prefer number (3), elsewhere, for their chosen belief about even the dead (whether elsewhere is heaven or hell seems to depend upon other judgments). But number (1) is quite a commitment, and commitment is scary.

Number (4) is odd. It is the mode we use when we need to believe *something*, but we can't decide whether it is (1), (2), or (3), and we still want the image. Sometimes when I hear a melody in my head, I don't know whether I have made it up myself or heard it somewhere else. Obviously it isn't number (1), since the damned thing exists in my head, and potentially in the air if I hum it out loud. But whether it is merely absent or elsewhere, I can't decide, so I let go for a moment and believe it in the neutral mode, which is kind of a meta-mode or a meta-belief; it gives me some place to hang out while I shuffle through the other three ways of destroying and replacing my perceptual world with something I find more interesting. Then I can have my image and eat it too, so to speak.

Okay, you're almost to the end, but you may not want to read further. Once you have, you won't ever be able to unthink the thought you're about to have. Don't say I didn't warn you, which is more courtesy than Gilmour and Waters showed to me. Here is the trap door.

Sartre said *freedom* is the most terrible thing we all face, because in the face of it we cannot escape responsibility for what we are. You are actually completely free to choose what to believe about not only the images you create in the *absence* of the object you are imagining, like the song "Brain Damage" that isn't playing at the moment. You can, if you choose, nullify, in *any* of the four modes, the objects that are *present* in your perception. You can believe that something right in front of you doesn't really exist, or is absent even though it *seems* present, or is elsewhere even though it *seems* to be here.

So let's say you are feeling really detached from your loved one. She can be sitting right in front of you, and you can still make her absent, elsewhere, or even non-existent—in other words, dead to *you*. People do this to each other all the time. It is this act that, when done from an attitude of cruelty, makes murder and slavery, and rape possible. You pretty much *have* to negate another person who is right in front of you, and do so selfishly and in defiance of your own perceptions, and self-satisfied with your own imagined substitution, in order to behave so monstrously. Or you may just subtly negate that other person, because she is gay, or black, or poor, or anything else you happen smugly to think justifies your little triumph over her. You say, "to me, you are absent," or "you might as well be elsewhere, because you are to me," or, "to me you don't exist at all, you are *nothing*."

But Pink Floyd doesn't do this and doesn't teach this and doesn't approve of it. Some music does, but not Pink Floyd. Because our heroes discovered that, when something is right in front of us, the beloved or anyone or anything, we can still refuse to believe any of these three negations, and just detach ourselves from any commitment about their existence at all. Perhaps you now see where this is going. We may say "I just don't have to decide about you, my love—whether you're absent, or elsewhere, or nothing at all; I am neutral about you."

There are many other *committed* but subtle attitudes we can adopt when we annihilate the presence of those we love and replace them with whatever we may desire or wish or will. Many of these annihilations are utterly benevolent—to see, for example, not the person your true love *is*, but who she most ardently *wants* to be, who she is trying to become. That requires a benevolent negation of her faults—not the ones that bother us, but the ones that bother her about herself. To imagine our loved ones in this way is a kind of encouragement, a kind of unselfish gift. These benevolent ways of imagining others are all quite familiar and concrete.

But Pink Floyd makes almost *no* use of these familiar attitudes of annihilation, in either their benevolent or the malevolent forms. They wish us neither ill nor well. It is not so much that they miss us, or love us, or hate us. Instead they use the neutral, uncommitted mode, number (4), to show us two rather disturbing things: (1) that it doesn't really matter which attitude or type of belief you choose, because as long as you have the option of neutrality, all the others really amount to the same thing; (2) the person you *most* destroy in annihilating your world is not others, it's yourself. You are condemned to destroy the world and yourself, and only free in how you choose to do it. You are still responsible for your choice no matter how you try to wriggle out of it, so why bother to choose?

There is no "better" or "more authentic" way to destroy yourself and create an illusion to believe in. And it makes no difference whether you see *yourself* as not really existing at all, as absent for a time, or as displaced; in the end you cannot really escape neutrality except by lying to yourself. The lunatic is in your head and he's not *you*, and no one else is *you* either. I didn't want to become aware of this "neutral" option, at twenty-one or now, and the only safety one can find is to flee into the three conventional modes of annihilation, and to try to use them benevolently. It may be a lie, but it's a useful one. Neutrality is very, very dangerous.

Isn't it amazing that *music* can be created that draws you, entirely without malice, inexorably, but by your own act of believing, straight into the abyss of meaninglessness? Now go listen to "Brain Damage" again and pay attention to what it really does to you. It neutralizes you, all the way down into the nothing that you are.

But it's your turn now. The sun is coming up and I've been dwelling in darkness long enough. I'm going to have a cigarette and a cup of coffee and see what images I can make from those. See you on the dark side of the moon, if I want to.

---

[5] I want to thank my friends, Jan Olof Bengtsson and Cory Powell for conversations that helped me think through this stuff and improve it.

The Art of Insanity:
Nietzsche, Barrett,
and Beyond

16

Wandering and Dreaming: The Tragic Life of Syd Barrett

ERIN KEALEY

Like most fans who discovered the Floyd after the '70s, my first experience of them was on the radio. In the years of appreciation to come, I saw *Pink Floyd: The Wall* a few times, reread *Animal Farm* to get the references on *Animals*, and even tried synching my copy of *Dark Side of the Moon* to *The Wizard of Oz*. But it wasn't only this middle-period Floyd that held my attention. I was especially intrigued by the tumultuous beginning years of "The Pink Floyd Sound" (as Roger Keith Barrett, known as "Syd", originally named the band after bluesmen Pink Anderson and Floyd Council) and, later, "The Pink Floyd," as they were briefly known before becoming, simply, Pink Floyd. Before the industry spotlight found them, they played London underground clubs and made a name for themselves as couriers of experimental and psychedelic sound and an outrageous light show.

1967 saw the Floyd's rapid rise to international recognition and Syd Barrett's destruction under the weight of fame and excessive use of LSD. In the Summer of Love, the Floyd lost their leader, although it would be many months before they replaced Barrett and released their second album without much contribution by him. But Barrett was the lyrical artist and alluring voice of the early Floyd. He first experimented with echo machines and feedback during live performances. He insisted that stage performances be as theatrical as they were musical. His music and his life were—and still remain—influential for many artists.

Barrett penned almost all of the Floyd's songs during his short reign, including the first two released singles ("Arnold Layne" and "See Emily Play"), all but one of the tracks on their debut album (*The Piper at the Gates of Dawn*), and a third single ("Apples and Oranges") before the release of their second album, *A Saucerful of Secrets*. While in the studio for their third single, Barrett wrote three other songs, one of which would be used on the second album ("Jugband Blues") and two that would be denied inclusion on the album by the other Floyd members, although they circulated among fans as bootlegs ("Scream Thy Last Scream" and "Vegetable Man").

All this happened in a little over a year. Then, Barrett would stare blankly at people without any recognition, suddenly act paranoid, and challenge the band's performances by not singing, strumming one chord over and over, or even just sitting on the stage as the others tried to carry the show. Eventually, the Floyd supplemented Barrett with his old friend, Dave Gilmour. But soon Barrett was no longer picked up for live shows by the others. He became more and more detached from them, spoke less and less, and was finally spoken about in the third person, as if he wasn't even there.

Storm Thorgerson, sleeve artist for the Floyd and another old Barrett friend, spoke of a number of catalysts for his breakdown. First, his father, who had encouraged his interest in music and bought him his first guitar, died when Barrett was only fourteen.[1] Second, Barrett attempted to join Sant Mat, an Indian religious cult. Upon meeting with the Master in London, Barrett was rejected "on the grounds that he was a student who should focus instead on finishing his courses." Thorgerson thought that Barrett never understood this euphemistic dismissal, so he felt "obliged to seek his enlightenment elsewhere—notably through artistic expression, and through chemicals" (Schaffner, p. 26). Finally, throughout the Floyd's touring and underground shows, Barrett was the most handsome and charismatic guy in the band, not to mention the only single one. He had no shortage of women throwing themselves at him, and Thorgerson remarked that this behavior

---

[1] Nicholas Schaffner, *Saucerful of Secrets: The Pink Floyd Odyssey* (New York: Delta, 1991), pp. 17–18.

toward Barrett was "a bit of an overload" and didn't help his "sense of reality" (p. 96).

Barrett's volatile and destructive behavior has been attributed to a variety of causes: the effects of acid, artistic protest, dementia, manic-depression, and schizophrenia. In his superb historical account, *Saucerful of Secrets: The Pink Floyd Odyssey*, Nicholas Schaffner contends that "*all* these factors—the drugs, the fame, personal and artistic differences, and some long-dormant disorder within Barrett's psyche—interacted with one another to increasingly nightmarish effect" (p. 78). I have always wondered if Barrett's downfall could be something deeper and darker than mere drug-induced psychological deterioration from the Floyd's seemingly instant fame. He created and played music with such passion that I would like to find a more philosophical way to understand his downfall, his apparent need to escape the music world and never return. He seemed to collapse just as he began to shine. The timing may have been more than coincidental.

Syd and Friedrich

Philosophy has had its share of crazy diamonds whose genius took the world by storm. An obvious counterpart to Barrett is Friedrich Nietzsche, the German philosopher born in 1844 in Prussia. Like many men in the family, Nietzsche's father was a Lutheran minister, but he died when Nietzsche was still young, leaving his mother to raise him. Nietzsche spent most of his days using his expertise in linguistics to examine and challenge the way his contemporaries approached philosophy.

Because of illness, Nietzsche's creative period was brief. It spanned from his first philosophical publication in 1872, to a temporary leave of absence in 1876 due to illness, to his 1879 retirement from academia, and finally to his collapse in 1889— a breakdown from which he would never recover. By 1900, the year he died, Nietzsche was only beginning to come to international critical acclaim. But he is now considered one of the most important philosophers of the nineteenth century, as well as one of the earliest and most influential existentialists.

Nietzsche spent the last decade of his life under the care of his mother, and then his sister, as he suffered from insanity induced by syphilis. His early brilliance, presenting challenging philosophical content in experimental styles, would shine on for generations, but his downfall in later life would forever cast a shadow on his creative vision. Although they were separated by almost a century, Nietzsche's creative life parallels Barrett's. His first major book provides an interesting philosophical account of how to understand both Barrett's artistic downfall and the artistic transition among his bandmates that led Pink Floyd to their hugely successful concept-driven albums and concerts. Nietzsche also gives us reason to hope that Barrett's life improved in his years of seclusion.

Nietzsche's *Birth of Tragedy*

The book is *The Birth of Tragedy from the Spirit of Music*, in which Nietzsche examines Greek tragedy. He explains that artistic beauty comes from the fusion of two opposing forces that exist in nature and are imitated in art. The forces are represented by the Greek gods Apollo and Dionysus. Greek tragedy, Nietzsche says, exemplifies a balance between the forces, a simultaneous artistry of dreams (inspired by Apollo) and intoxication (inspired by Dionysus). Neither element exists completely isolated from the other. Since Nietzsche does not limit his discussion to art, his theories and descriptions also apply to human behavior. A well-balanced tension between the two elements in our characters can ultimately create an ordered, Apollonian conquest of our dynamic, Dionysian passions.

Dionysus represents "the drive towards the transgression of limits, the dissolution of boundaries, the destruction of individuality, and excess."[2] The Dionysian element is unrestrained and unlimited dynamism. Apollonian structure provides us with illusions, like language, but Dionysian dominance creates illusions of illusions. The individual who succumbs to Dionysian dominance becomes intoxicated—but not necessary through drinking or taking drugs. Nietzsche's concern is intoxication that can result from any passionate activity through which one loses control, even an activity like dancing.[3] This state of drunkenness

---

[2] Raymond Geuss, Introduction to Nietzsche, *The Birth of Tragedy and other Writings* (Cambridge University Press, 1999).

[3] Arthur Danto explains: "Dionysianism cannot simply be identified with self-abandonment, ecstasy, frenzy, or madness, except insofar as art is able to

results in a loss of identity and individuality to the undifferentiated ocean of life.

If life is guided by this tension between Apollonian structure and Dionysian revelry, the musical career of Pink Floyd looks something like a tug of war with different sides winning at different times. With the production of their first single, "Arnold Layne," in February 1967, the Floyd officially became professional musicians. The song was about a transvestite who took to stealing women's clothes at night—"moonshine, washing line"—and got caught. When asked to explain his unconventional topic, Barrett simply stated that a lot of people dressed up in women's clothing, so the press simply ought to accept reality. Already tapping into the Dionysian element for successful art, Barrett wanted to lift the veil of illusion and present reality for the world to see.

The Floyd's early success resulted from Barrett's broad group of musical and literary influences, which "all percolated in the cauldron of his subconscious to re-emerge in a voice, sound, and style that were uniquely Syd's" (Schaffner, p. 35). Yet Nietzsche might say that Barrett "surrendered his subjectivity in the Dionysian process" (*Birth of Tragedy*, Section §5). Barrett's experience of stark reality shattered his individuality as he was inundated by the excitement of a Dionysian frenzy. Thus was born the band's first full-length album, *The Piper at the Gates of Dawn*.

Apollo and Dionysus in *Piper*

Language is an illusion passed down to us, which we cling to so that we can impose order on the world. Language creates symbols that only touch the surface of the reality which words attempt to express (*Birth of Tragedy*, §6). In *The Birth of Tragedy*, Nietzsche wanted to find out if "one could significantly achieve a Dionysian language with which to express Dionysiac thought" (Danto, p. 35). His stylistic experimentation with language and meaning exposed how much we take this forgotten ordering for granted. Barrett's stylistic experimentation with music and sound did, as well.

---

induce these states in its audience" (Arthur C. Danto, *Nietzsche as Philosopher* [New York: Macmillan, 1965], p. 50).

"Matilda Mother," for example, is about Syd's childhood and the innocent transcendental effect of being read fairy tales by his mother. He pleads for her to keep reading the lines that are "scribbly black and everything shines." Barrett looks back at the experience and sings that, "Wandering and dreaming / The words had different meaning." The language of Apollonian illusions brings to life the dreamy visions of a fairy story. But Barrett would wander off to discover what was beneath those visions. As he approached Dionysian intoxication, the words of the stories took on new meanings, and their control over the experience came to light.

Through his lyrics and instrumental improvisations that were even more expressive than words, Barrett may have actually created a Dionysian language through music. In "Astronomy Domine," he sings: "The sound surrounds the icy waters underground." In instrumental pieces, such as *Piper*'s "Pow R Toc H" and "Interstellar Overdrive," he left the illusions of language behind altogether.

Barrett also opened himself up to the spontaneity of chance with the *I Ching*, the Taoist Book of Changes. After tossing coins six times, a unique pattern can be consulted in the book for an ambiguous fortune from an oracle. Barrett wrote "Chapter 24" about the result of his turn. In the *I Ching*, Chapter 24 centers on change and return, two ideas that Nietzsche thought were very important for individuals and society.

Like "The Gnome," Barrett left the safe world of conventional shelter and "had a big adventure / Amidst the grass / Fresh air at last." In all of his new experiences of seeing the world around him, he asked, "Isn't it good? / Winding, finding places to go." You could say, though, that he embraced the Dionysian elements of life too tightly, and never found his way back to any workable balance. He could only temporarily negotiate the driving forces of dreams and intoxication.

Dionysus and Disintegration

If Barrett indeed found a Dionysian language in music, he increasingly lost his ability to communicate with people. Jenny Fabian wrote a popular 1969 autobiographical novel titled *Groupie*. The first chapter featured Barrett as "Ben" of the group "The Satin Odyssey." In late 1969, she was sent to interview

Barrett for *Harpers & Queen*, but it did not go well. By her permission, Julian Palacios presented her unedited thoughts of the time she spent with Barrett that day. Much of it was silent, as if Barrett had no language to express what he was contemplating. Fabian thought that Barrett must have been indulging a complex line of reflections in seemingly infinite succession. She mused about all the weird and innocent songs he had written for *Piper* when he suddenly looked at her and said, "Isn't it boring lying here all day thinking of nothing?" She was shocked, noting that Barrett had "already gone to where he was going. His mind had gone there, but his body was still functioning in the real world. . . . I don't know what he thought, I thought he was thinking millions of things. And then for him to say that!"[4]

Barrett's song "Bike," which closes *Piper*, offers a early look at what was happening to him. The song "seems to teeter on the edge of psychosis." Schaffner explains that upon entry into the "room full of musical tunes," "all hell breaks loose . . . the sound effects bear no discernible relation to the rest of the song's content, and thus sound all the more diabolical and demented" (p. 67). Lyrically, the song is about many gifts that Barrett offers to a girl—a bike he has borrowed, his cloak, some gingerbread men, and a "room full of musical tunes." Jim DeRogatis explains: "We never know if he gets the girl, since the last gift is a mysterious room of 'musical tunes' that swallows the singer whole in an impressive explosion of sound effects."[5] It sounds as if Barrett had finally lifted the veil of illusion to glimpse the destruction and chaos of reality underneath.

By the time Syd and the band recorded "Jugband Blues," (the only song he wrote on *A Saucerful of Secrets*), it looked as if this Dionysian chaos was threatening his very personality and individuality. He questions the illusions surrounding him: "And I'm wondering who could be writing this song ... And I love the Queen / And what exactly is a dream?" When one is utterly inebriated, Nietzsche explains, one cannot even walk or talk. Barrett's final weeks with the Floyd seemed just as paralyzed as he sank into self-obliteration. In his great exploration of Barrett's

---

[4] Julian Palacios, *Lost in the Woods: Syd Barrett and the Pink Floyd* (London: Boxtree, 1998), pp. 237–38.

[5] Jim DeRogatis, *Turn On Your Mind: Four Decades of Great Psychedelic Rock* (Milwaukee: Hal Leonard Corporation, 2003), p. 128.

life, *Lost in the Woods: Syd Barrett and the Pink Floyd*, Palacios attempts to describe Barrett's final performances in the throes of a mental breakdown:

> Thought patterns, stripped of structure, became frustrating, with ideas and theories analysed to the point of paralysis . . . Catatonia would alternate with exaggerated motion. . . . The once dazzling psychedelic wash of colours gave way to murky darkness as the stage act became reality. Standing stock still on the edge of the stage, Barrett's fantasy of the Scarecrow, if anything, seems prophetic, as if Syd foresaw his inevitable progression to catatonia with chilling clarity. (*Lost in the Woods*, p. 208)

On *Piper*, the scarecrow stands without thinking or moving, except when the wind blows his arms around. Barrett sang that the "scarecrow is sadder than me / But now he's resigned to his fate / 'Cause life's not unkind—he doesn't mind."

Barrett didn't seem to mind that much either. I wonder if he felt resigned to this character development in these intoxicated times, and if he continued to see the scarecrow as sadder than him. Regardless of Barrett's feelings, the other members of the Floyd collectively decided that he was irredeemable from his state of self-annihilation, so he was taken out of live performances. Aware of his downfall, Barrett wrote about his looming absence in "Jugband Blues," one of his last penned songs for the group: "It's awfully considerate of you to think of me here / And I'm much obliged to you for making it clear that I'm not here."[6]

A Parting of the Ways

Barrett was "not here" in a number of ways. In terms of Nietzsche's theory of tragedy, he continued his Dionysian life of art and asked to be called "Roger" in his later years. As Nietzsche explains, Dionysians crave constant fluctuation in life

---

[6] For those interested in the playfulness and charisma that Barrett brought to The Pink Floyd, most of the early "videos" are available on YouTube. The particular case of Barrett's "Jugband Blues" performance provides a stark contrast from his persona in earlier footage. Barrett barely moves, his singing and his guitar-playing provide the only motion. This performance, not to mention the lyrics of the song, foreshadows Barrett's bleak future with the band. He seems to have already lost his personality.

by "eternally impelling to existence, eternally finding satisfaction in this change of phenomena" (*Birth of Tragedy*, §16). Barrett spent his post-music years working on his paintings, creating them only to destroy them upon completion "to emphasize the transitory nature of his art" (Palacios, p. 291).

Barrett did not lose contact completely with the other members of the Floyd, who helped on his solo projects. His impact on the band would fuel much of the Floyd's subsequent music. The influence of Barrett's struggle has been documented by parts of *Dark Side of the Moon*, and songs such as "Wish You Were Here" and "Shine on You Crazy Diamond," and even by some of the events depicted in the movie, *Pink Floyd: The Wall*. Although the film serves as a semi-autobiographical account of Roger Waters's childhood, many of Pink's episodes mirror early Barrett exploits, like Pink's bloody shaving of all his chest and facial hair.

But these major Pink Floyd albums adhered to a more Apollian ideal. The tension was apparent early on when some members of the Floyd wanted to use their stage time to play shorter album tracks rather than the longer, experimental songs that were not as well understood outside Club UFO and the London underground scene. "To Barrett, however, music had always been an act of spontaneous combustion, and repetition was simply redundant" (Schaffner, p. 94). After Barrett left the band, the former architecture students who had witnessed Barrett succumb to Dionysian intoxication could not replicate the successful language of his artistic vision. They opted for a more formal, controlled style which was not possible for a Dionysian artist who had handed his subconscious over to the results of a Taoist oracle and who sought inspiration in the woodland creatures of fairy tales. As Shaffner puts it, "It was, in any case, not long before Pink Floyd's artistic ethos began to take a 180-degree turn, the anarchic spontaneity of the Barrett era giving way to meticulous and elaborate constructions in which little was left to chance" (p. 130). The production of album tracks and the lighting elements of concerts became much more well-structured as the Floyd gave up the freedom of improvisations.

You Legend, You Martyr

As Nietzsche explains, the fall and death of a mythic hero provides spectators with an affirmation of life through art. Barrett lifted the veil of Apollonian consciousness to give us a view of the Dionysian reality beneath. He reported to us through his music and, for a brief time, reflected for us the tension and unified interaction of the two driving forces of art and human existence.

As a tragic artist, though, Barrett unfortunately succumbed to the dangers of acting as a medium for us to learn about reality (*Birth of Tragedy*, §2). Watching Barrett on stage and off, spectators may have stood "quite bewildered before this fantastic excess of life" (§3). But Nietzsche would contend that Barrett gives us a reason to live. Like Greek tragic art, Nietzsche could view Barrett as making "life possible and worth living" (§1). Richard Schacht explains that Nietzsche thinks about Greek tragedy as not just some new wave in the realm of art, but as laying the "foundation and guiding force of an entire form of culture and human existence, which alone is capable of filling the void left by the collapse of 'optimistic' life-sustaining myths" (Schacht, p. 497).

During the "14-Hour Technicolor Dream," the all-night 1967 summer fundraising event for the economically-strained underground newspaper, *IT*, the Floyd took the stage late in the show and played as dawn broke. Barrett may have had temporary control of his artistic place in his Dionysian frenzy. As if he were generating Apollonian illusions for the entire crowd to experience indirectly (and, therefore, safely), his mirror-tiled guitar reflected the shining sun into the audience. Barrett seemed to be driven by the "same impulse which calls art into being, as the complement and consummation of existence, seducing [us] to a continuation of life" (*Birth of Tragedy*, §3). His music, to borrow Nietzsche's phrase, was at that moment literally "a transfiguring mirror" that helps us through our suffering existence (§3).

In Chapter 7 of Kenneth Grahame's *The Wind in the Willows*, titled "The Piper at the Gates of Dawn," Rat and Mole experience music in a spiritual song-dream, and the onset of forgetfulness leaves them with a dim sense of beauty. The dawn call of glad piping compels Mole to gaze upon the august god Pan. However, unlike Mole's encounter, Barrett would meet his demise "once he had looked with mortal eye on things rightly kept hidden."[7] He could not emerge from his experience

---

[7] Grahame, *The Wind in the Willows* (New York: Scribner's, 1917), p. 155.

of Dionysian intoxication, but Nietzsche gives us reason to hope:

> Here, when the danger to his will is greatest, *art* approaches as a saving sorceress, expert at healing. She alone knows how to turn these nauseous thoughts about the horror or absurdity of existence into notions with which one can live. (*Birth of Tragedy*, §7)

Hopefully, Barrett escaped the ocean of despair and rediscovered his shining discrete individuality through his private art. Hopefully, he found a balanced character in returning home — something like "the kind of girl that fit in with [his] world" did as he wrapped up his stellar debut album. He knew, however, from the *I Ching*'s Chapter 24 that "Things cannot be destroyed once and for all." Nietzsche agreed that, in music, especially, the spirit cannot be destroyed: "That striving of the spirit of music," he wrote, which "suddenly breaks off after attaining a luxuriant development, and disappears, as it were, from the surface . . . Will it not some day rise once again out of its mystic depths as art?" (§17).

. . . for Syd, 1946–2006.[8]

---

[8] Big thanks to Prog Rocker Dave Evans for his valuable insights on everything Pink Floyd. Our conversations and his love of music made this chapter as exciting to explore as listening to *Piper* itself.

17

Submersion, Subversion, and Syd: *The Madcap Laughs* and *Barrett* between Nietzsche and Benjamin

BRANDON FORBES

Of the many stories about Syd Barrett's dismissal from Pink Floyd in 1969, two in particular stand out. Before one of his final shows with the band, Barrett, evidently dissatisfied with his appearance, mixed some of the pills he was on at the time with some styling product and coated his unkempt hair with the concoction. As the Floyd churned through their set later on that evening, the heat from the stage lights caused the pills to melt, covering Barrett's face with the waxy residue of the mixture while he played on, seemingly oblivious to his transformation. As many observers claimed afterwards, it appeared as though his face melted off during the performance, disturbing both band and audience.

The second incident occurred after Barrett had been relegated to a "behind the scenes" songwriter for the group, banished from the stage no doubt for his many bizarre behaviors. During one of the practice jam sessions, Barrett brought a new song to the group entitled "Have You Got It Yet?" To the perplexity of the band, Barrett changed the chord progression and rhythm each time they attempted to play through the number, virtually creating a new song with each take. The group, unable to turn the song into a reproducible composition, eventually put down their instruments in bewilderment. It was one of the last times Barrett ever played with the band as a whole.[1]

---

[1] Both of these stories are recounted in Mike Watkinson and Pete Anderson, *Crazy Diamond: Syd Barrett and the Dawn of Pink Floyd* (Omnibus, 2006).

Are these merely two sad stories of a man in the midst of a mental breakdown? Maybe. But a closer look at Syd Barrett's two solo records, released in 1970 after he had been banished from the band, places them in a different light. By engaging some of the philosophical ideas suggested by both *The Madcap Laughs* and *Barrett*, and keeping these two incidents in mind, we can see a connection between Barrett's solo records and the works of German philosopher Friedrich Nietzsche (1844–1900) and German social critic Walter Benjamin (1892–1940).

Late Nights at the Apollo

Nietzsche's *The Birth of Tragedy* is a many-layered work, incorporating philosophy, philology, history, dramatic criticism, and music criticism. Since its publication in 1872, it has spawned a library of criticism. Important for our discussion of Syd Barrett are Nietzsche's ideas concerning the opposing mythical forces of Apollo and Dionysius, and not so much his complicated arguments regarding the evolution of Greek tragedy and the operas of Richard Wagner. Indeed, all of Nietzsche's arguments in *Birth of Tragedy* seem to build themselves on the relationship between the concepts of singularity and multiplicity and of individual and group, concepts which he associates with Apollo and Dionysius. These concepts also appear in Barrett's erratic, yet passionate work on *The Madcap Laughs* and *Barrett*, where the idea of submersion in the wily intoxicating powers of Dionysius (at the expense of Apollo) seems to be at play.

An excellent example of Barrett's submersion into this dynamic between singularity and multiplicity comes with the famous B-side from *The Madcap Laughs*, the stirring "Opel." Released on a compilation of the same name in 1988, despite the fact that it was recorded in 1969, "Opel" presents us with an example of Barrett's fanciful storytelling as metaphor for his own slow withdrawal from the world of individuality. "On a distant shore far from land," Barrett sings, he lives in a "dream in a mist of gray." His reality seems to be overcome with a sense of distance from normality, as his mind lies where "warm shallow waters sweep shells." The final two minutes of the song drive this withdrawal home, as Barrett eerily opines in a series of confessions that "I'm trying / I'm living / I'm giving . . . I'm trying to find you."

The sound of Barrett's slightly out of tune, jangly guitar strumming as it meets with these haunting confessions highlights his alienation, his distance from the people he can no longer find in his former, confident notion of self. In effect, the "warm, shallow waters" are submersing him into the primal unity of Nietzsche's Dionysius. But before we discuss the power of Dionysius, we need to engage Nietzsche's concept of Apollo, where the singularity and individuality Barrett seems to be losing in "Opel" are defined.

For Nietzsche, Apollo and Dionysius represent "the opposed artistic worlds of dream and intoxication."[2] It is Apollo, most well known as Greek god of the sun, who symbolizes the dream world of prophecy and appearances found in the plastic arts of sculpture, painting, and architecture. While we may think of the wild unconscious world of dreams as having similar effects to that of intoxication—a world where, as Barrett's "Octopus" relates, kangaroos can shout and grasshoppers can play in a band—Nietzsche is thinking differently. It's not the nonsensical elements in the dream world that oppose Dionysian intoxication, but the fact that these elements, like the plastic arts, are appearances. In other words, images in a dream are just that—pictures and representations of the world which, absurd though they may be, represent phenomena, and therefore connect the individual to the world around him or her through observation. These Apollonian appearances, like the sun, can overpower vision through static beauty, leaving the viewer in awe of his or her surroundings.

As the "image-creating god"(1, p. 21), Nietzsche argues, Apollo represents the principal of individuality, or *principium individuationis*, that allows a person to distinguish him or herself from the world. This Latin phrase is borrowed from German philosopher Arthur Schopenhauer (1788–1860), who used the term to identify how individuals can exist among the overwhelming multiplicity of existence. Nietzsche uses an example from Schopenhauer's tome *The World as Will and Representation* to connect Apollo's role as image-creator to the principle of individuality: Just as a lone man in a boat tries to

---

[2] *The Birth of Tragedy and the Spirit of Music* (Oxford World Classics edition), 1, p. 19. For all Nietzsche quotations I give the section number followed by the page number.

steady himself as he is rocked about by the terrible magnifi-
cence of the waves around him, so too does the individual
attempt to bulwark him or herself against the terrifying images
of the surrounding world.

A similar theme is at work in Barrett's song "Late Night," the
final cut on *The Madcap Laughs*. In this haunting song, replete
with slide guitar and an earnest delivery from Barrett, the memory of a lover's eyes pulls the singer away from the realization
that "inside me I feel / alone and unreal." It seems as though
this vision distracts Barrett from the painfulness of his own
growing alienation. For Nietzsche, Apollo represents this very
escapism that can be found in observation. In other words, the
frightening realties of existence, of being alone and doubting
your place in the world, can be avoided by focusing on a "pleasurable illusion"(3, p. 29) like the eyes of Barrett's imagined
lover. Nietzsche offers the popularity of the Olympian gods
with the ancient Greeks as an example of the power of Apollo's
"pleasurable illusion." Zeus and his fellow gods, Nietzsche
posits, were seen as joyfully reigning over the cosmos in a
humanlike manner which the Greeks could identify with their
own existence. Nietzsche argues that these anthropomorphic
gods represent the best form of theodicy, that is, the best way
to explain suffering in a world created by divinity. Thus, the
gods themselves must endure humanlike life, having dreams
and desires and not always being able to realize them.
Importantly for Nietzsche, this Olympian pantheon stands
opposed to the older, darker myth of the Titans, who had a
"divine reign of terror"(3, p. 28) identified with violence and suffering that was not as easy to stomach by a people too influenced by the powers of Apollo.

Lost in the Dionysian Wood

Embracing this role of suffering in the world is one of the
greatest differences between Apollo and Dionysius. Where the
beautiful imagery found in the material arts of sculpture and
the prophetic powers of the Olympian gods assured many
Greeks of their own individuality, it is Dionysian intoxication,
Nietzsche says, grounded in the primal power of music, that
submerges the individual into "a higher communal nature" (1,
p. 23) that is at one with the *true* realities of the world.

Nietzsche spells out the collapse of the *principium individuationis* this way:

> Either under the influence of the narcotic drink of which all men and peoples sing in hymns, or in the approach of spring, which forcefully and pleasurably courses through the whole of nature, those Dionysian impulses awaken, which in their heightened forms cause the subjective to dwindle to complete self-oblivion. (*Birth of Tragedy*, 1, p. 22)

This losing of the self sounds strikingly similar to Barrett's own story, where heavy drug use helped exacerbate an existing schizophrenic condition, sending him to teeter on the edge of "self-oblivion." Yet Nietzsche insists that such a move is necessary to awaken the Dionysian impulses that lie in the intoxicating power of music and a mythic understanding of nature, impulses which allow the creation of art. In fact, Nietzsche goes so far as to claim that "only as an aesthetic phenomenon are existence and the world justified to eternity" (5, p. 38). And this justification can only begin if the individual allows him or herself to become submerged in the primordial "unity as the spirit of the species" (2, p. 26), a move that unleashes a powerful creative force.

But what, exactly, is Nietzsche getting at by this concept of a "unity" behind the human species? Again turning to Schopenhauer, Nietzsche uses the idea of the will as something much more than a name for what is behind making a decision. The will is, in fact, the force that lurks behind all appearances in the world. It lies behind the façade of all phenomena as the "thing-in-itself"—a category Schopehauer borrowed from Immanuel Kant (1724–1804) who distinguished sharply between phenomena encountered by the senses and (according to Kant) the unknowable things in themselves underneath. Nietzsche, following Schopenhauer, identifies these noumenal, underlying realities with the will, and then attaches his notion of Dionysius.

This power of the will, and of Dionysius, is most evident in the intoxication of the dithyramb, a hymn that was sung in Dionysius's honor among many sects in pre-Socratic Greece. Nietzsche claims the dithyramb best reveals the unity of the world, the true essence of reality. "In the Dionysian dithyramb," he writes, "all the symbolic faculties of man are stimulated to the highest intensity" (2, p. 26) and this "symbolism of music utterly exceeds the grasp of language, because it refers symbolically to the original contradiction and pain at the heart of the original Unity" (6, p. 42). In this way, art becomes genuine and justified only in so much as it owes its origin to the Dionysian dithyramb. And the Dionysian dithyramb owes its origin to the primal power of the unifying will.

The power of Dionysian music, then, lies in its ability not only to stir the artist to great heights, which Apollo could do using the dream-image, but in the fact that through the dithyramb, the artist is submerged into the reality of human suffering that collects all individuals in the unity of the mythic past and thereby makes contact with the eternal. What Nietzsche means by the eternal is no doubt the "unmediated language of will"(16, p. 89) which brings about the music of "Dionysian rapture" (17, p. 91). Music is the expression of the artist submerged in the world of Dionysian intoxication, a world where, "in spite of fear and compassion, we are the fortunate living beings, not as individuals, but as a single living being, with whose joy in creation we are fused" (17, p. 91).

Barrett seems completely submersed in the Dionysian dithyramb throughout both his solo records. On "Octopus," fantastical natural imagery meets nonsensical phrasing as Barrett implores the listener to "please leave us here" to "close out eyes to the octopus ride." Then, addressing himself to this "us," he announces, "Isn't it good to be lost in the wood?" Clearly, Barrett desires to be left in the confusion of lost subjectivity, swallowed up by the primordial wood and submerged into the Dionysian world of this "octopus ride." The straining of his vocals on the chorus seems almost a ritualistic prayer to Dionysius, emphasizing his desire to be submerged in this mythic power.

On the fourth track on *Barrett*, entitled "It Is Obvious," this loss of individuality seems just that. Over a weak organ and a bouncy acoustic guitar line, he sings:

> Reason, it is written on the brambles, stranded on the
> spikes . . .
> Growing together, they're growing each other
> No wondering, stumbling, fumbling
> Rumbling minds shot together,
> Our minds shot together.

Not only is reason left caught in the thicket like an outer layer of clothing, shed in a hurry to the call of dithyrambic music, but individual minds are unified, growing into an intoxicated union. Again, the self and the beautiful appearances distinguished by Apollo are discarded in favor of the power of will found in Dionysian dithyramb. It is this Dionysian power, "with its original joy perceived even in pain," that is "the shared maternal womb of music and tragic myth" (24, p. 128).

Treading the Sand of Subversion

If the idea of Dionysian submersion reveals the creative power behind Barrett's art, the reception of this art by the public reveals the subversive nature of Barrett's solo albums. When we first think of subversion and Syd Barrett, the social and cultural subversion of the counter-culture movement of the 1960s, better known as "sex, drugs, and rock 'n' roll," comes to mind. The counter-culture aimed to subvert received social traditions and cultural norms regarding, among other things, sexuality, politics, drugs, and civil rights. In conjunction with the counterculture social movement, the technological advances in film and sound recording bolstered the explosive economic power of capitalism in the West as TVs, movies, and records became staples of mass consumer culture. This technology encouraged the counter-culture movement itself, incorporating elements of the movement's criticism into popular music and film. Whether or not this incorporation thereby negated the subversive character of the original movement is a question that lies at the heart of Barrett's work.

A great example of Barrett's early indulgence in the subversion of the counter-culture underground is found in the video for "Arnold Layne," the 1967 single that was Pink Floyd's first real hit. In the video the band is shown meandering across a windy beach with a male mannequin in female attire, and its quirky production, which includes both backwards footage and fast-forwarding, is non-linear and comically absurd. These visual images, nontraditional even in the way they are filmed, go with Barrett's playful lyrics to tell the story of a cross-dresser locked up for stealing women's clothing from drying lines. Talking about the subject of transvestites through popular music was unheard of at the time, and "Arnold Layne" clearly embodies

Barrett's early subversive tendencies. With the later release of *The Madcap Laughs* and *Barrett,* Barrett's work can be seen as expanding these subversive tendencies into a philosophically nuanced critique of both the ideological and the economic foundations of late 1960s and early 1970s capitalistic society.

Walter Benjamin's essay "The Work of Art in the Age of Its Reproducibility" is helpful for understanding what Barrett was doing on these albums. Composed in spurts throughout the late 1930s, the essay seeks to radically critique the capitalistic implications of technology and art. Benjamin was a socialist and cofounder of the radical Frankfurt school of criticism. Like his colleagues, he was horrified by the violent rhetoric and bold imagery of fascism that had emerged in the 1920s and 1930s. This "aestheticizing of political life," he said, was inherent in the fascist movement and could lead only to war (4, p. 269).[3] His hope behind writing "The Work of Art" was to create a socialistic critique of art's technological reproduction to help the masses see through attempts at aesthetic manipulation by both capitalists and fascists. Benjamin died in 1940 while trying to escape the fascism he argued against so vehemently. But "The Work of Art" has lived on and helps us make sense of Barrett's subversive sensibilities.

A Long, Cold Look at the Aura and Authenticity

Consider Benjamin's concept of the aura. Originally derived from the Greek term meaning spirit or breath, he defines the aura as the uniqueness or singularity of a particular piece of art. The aura can be "the here and now of the work of art" which marks it indelibly as a "unique existence in a particular place" (4, p. 253). But it can also refer to "the unique apparition of a distance, however near it may be" (4, p. 255), an idea Benjamin illustrates with a mountain range on a summer afternoon. "To follow with the eye," he says, "a mountain range on the horizon or a branch that casts its shadow on the beholder is to breathe the aura of those mountains, of that branch" (4, p. 255). In other words, the overpowering presence of singularity in an experience—not just

---

[3] All Benjamin quotations are from his essay as it appears in *Walter Benjamin: Selected Writings, Volume 4, 1938–1940* (Harvard University Press). I give the section number followed by the page number.

viewing a painting on a wall or experiencing a concert, but approaching nature itself—can capture its aura.

Another way Benjamin analyzes the "here and now" of the work of art is by its authenticity. This is "the quintessence of all that is transmissible in it from its origin on, ranging from its physical duration to the historical testimony relating to it" (4, p. 254). This quintessence, or essential nature, of the work of art emerges, then, in the work's history, including "the changes to the physical structure of the work over time, together with any changes in ownership" (4, p. 253). Think of Barrett's interlocutor in "No Good Trying" who owns a "sequin fan" and is trying to hide it from Barrett's gaze. If we imagine that this "sequin fan" was created by an artisan in the nineteenth century, and has been owned by various persons up until the character in the song, we begin to get a picture of what Benjamin means by authenticity. Unlike, say, the fan that Barrett could go buy at the corner supermarket which has been manufactured at a plant, the sequin fan of the song's unknown owner owes its creation to a specific individual and has changed hands over the course of time. Its aura encompasses the tradition of its existence, which has a unique origin in a specific point in time and, because of this history, it cannot be duplicated.

Compare that, Benjamin says, to products of modern capitalism, in which industrialization, the assembly line, and mass production take away the uniqueness of art's origin. Of course, Benjamin acknowledges, "the work of art has always been reproducible" (4, p. 252). Replicas of art and religious icons have always been reproduced to a certain extent as a way to make money throughout history—the history of forgery attests this much. But what distinguishes the capitalist mode of production is that it is specifically technological. Machines have become the reproducers of these works of art, not trained apprentices or artisans as in the past. Photography, sound recording, print reproductions, and cinematography all have contributed to the technology of reproduction that

> detaches the reproduced object from the sphere of tradition. By replicating the work many times over, it substitutes a mass existence for a unique existence. And in permitting the reproduction to reach the recipient in his or her own situation, it actualizes that which it reproduces. (Benjamin, 4, p. 254)

Thus, the sequin fan Barrett could buy at the supermarket, while having none of the imagined authentic tradition found in the one owned by the character in "No Good Trying," can still be recognized by the masses as art, despite the fact that perhaps a million more identical fans exist. Andy Warhol's pop art is a great example of this logic as it was played out concurrently with Barrett's.

This example hits upon an important point for Benjamin when thinking about the reproduction of art under capitalism, namely, the mode of perception of the masses. Thrown together by a common experience as workers within a capitalistic economy, Benjamin argues, two desires have driven the masses to participate in the market of art's technological reproduction. With their desire to "'get closer' to things spatially and humanly" and "their equally passionate concern for overcoming each thing's uniqueness," the masses have embraced the "transitoriness and repeatability" of the reproduction of the work of art over its "uniqueness and permanence" (4, p. 255). In other words, the destruction of the aura "is the signature of a perception whose 'sense for sameness in the world' has so increased that, by means of reproduction, it extracts sameness even from what is unique" (4, p. 256). Playing on Barrett's lyrics we can now say that, according to Benjamin, there's "no good trying" to find singularity in mass production, especially in art—the aura is "long, long gone."

If It's in You, Reproduce It for the Masses

The aura may have disappeared, but Benjamin does not argue for the destruction of machines or opine for the "good ole days." He acts the part of the realist—society cannot go back because there has been an irrevocable paradigm shift in the mode of production. He argues that though the "cult value" of art in ancient to early modern times, that is, the mystery of its unique aura, has been destroyed by the rise of technology, the result has been a kind of liberation. "Technological reproducibility emancipates the work of art from its parasitic subservience to ritual" (4, p. 256), he says, because art is no longer enshrined in holy secrecy and has become a tangible reality for everyone, regardless of class.

Thus, for the late 1960s fans of Pink Floyd, phonograph technology meant that the sounds of the countercultural revolution could be distributed to, and heard by, everyone with access to a record player or a radio—not just those lucky enough to go to UFO or elsewhere and experience Pink Floyd's concerts first-hand. "As soon as the criterion for authenticity ceases to be applied to artistic production," Benjamin emphasizes, "the whole social function of art is revolutionized" (4, p. 257). Instead of ritual, art can now emerge from the social and political space opened by mass technological reproduction. In this light, viewing "Arnold Layne" or listening to *Barrett* is a social event and a political experience made possible by a technology predicated on mass dissemination of art in commodity form.

What capitalism has done, Benjamin points out, is made everyone into a critic. As he puts it in regard to film camera, "the newsreel offers everyone the chance to rise from passer-by to movie extra" (4, p. 262). Each person can not only see themselves as becoming a part of a work of art, they can see themselves as a critic of that art, as well. Capitalism has also made everyone, at least potentially, an artist—much as the way Syd Barrett encountered The Beatles on radio, records, and film, and was inspired to write music himself. Technology allows art to engender art and opens up possibilities for social and political subversion by its wide-spread dissemination.

For Benjamin the socialist, however, this democratization of art and criticism leads to the crucial question I mentioned earlier. All this is made possible by an industry devoted to reproducing and distributing art purely for economic gain. And, any socialist would recognize, this results in unfair exploitation of those responsible for creating the commodities, even if these commodities are recognized as art, since capitalists keep the surplus value created by workers as profit for themselves. How then can countercultural art remain subversive once it has been incorporated and commodified within the overarching capitalistic system? In other words, is there anyway that Barrett's solo records, despite their manufactured distribution to the masses, are more than just a sell-out?

Yes. For while *The Madcap Laughs*, and even *Barrett* for that matter, are commodities marketed by the record industry, they have qualities that challenge the overarching logic of radio and record sales. While Barrett's record label saw his solo career after Pink Floyd as a way to capitalize on his eccentric cult of personality, the actual realization of Barrett's art is hardly a radio-friendly way to move units. The second half of *The Madcap Laughs* stands out here since Barrett's approach to recording is a far cry from Top-40 polish. On "She Took a Long Cold Look," the microphones capture the sound of Barrett turning pages of lyrics in the background as he stutters through the acoustic strumming. "Feel" features much of the same struggling chord changes and fluctuating tempos, but it is "If It's in You" that goes the farthest in challenging the very idea of recorded songs as commodities. After featuring some studio banter at the start, including a brief false start, the track features Barrett beginning to sing the first verse again, but stopping in mid-howl, his voice sharply breaking out of tune. By the time he gets to the third verse, he replaces his stream-of-consciousness verbiage with the strangely compelling repetition of "yum, yummy, yum," seemingly forgoing the need for precise diction.

Here is where Benjamin's concept of the aura can be seen as having its largest subversive appeal, albeit somewhat at Benjamin's expense. With the bizarre recordings on *The Madcap Laughs,* we can see this record not just as an attempt by the recording industry to exploit the creative capacity of a man on the verge of a mental breakdown, but rather as an exploration into the possibilities of re-engaging the aura in mass form. In this light, the studio banter, false starts, and off-key harmonies can be seen not as merely pitiable moments in Barrett's life captured for profit, but as essential moments of authenticity rife with possibility for political change. It is not Barrett's non-sensical lyrics or his compelling childish melodies that serve as the highest subversion (though they do challenge social norms) but rather the fact that Barrett's songs are committed to tape in their rawest form that offers the greatest critique of the capitalistic system.

Piper at the Gates of Dawn has a subversive character to it, also. But it is produced in such a way that radio-friendly singles easily present themselves. The raw, lo-fi moments throughout *The Madcap Laughs* disrupt this pop-song commodity formula specifically by re-introducing Benjamin's aura, by making the songs audibly inseparable from Syd himself, and those events— the turning pages, the false starts, the forgotten lyrics—that mark their authenticity. This gives the aura a fighting chance to reach the masses, despite its technological reproducibility, and subvert the market system in which the songs are commodified.

Benjamin argues that the aura is gone for good in our age of mass reproductions, but that doesn't apply to Barrett and similar artists. For the reproduced art itself reminds the listener of the grittiness and realness of the aura, which in turn suggests the reality of the listener's social and economic position. So this fundamental challenge offered to the capitalistic aesthetics of polished, marketable art by Barrett's eccentric records remains aligned with Benjamin's hope that technology and art would challenge traditional forms of class dominance.

"The Madcap Laughed at the Man on the Border"

When that bizarre mixture of pills and hair product created the illusion of Barrett's face melted off during a live performance, the truth behind that illusion was Barrett's losing his individuality as he submerged into the Dionysian, unifying power of music. For Nietzsche, this tragic moment of the loss of self is actually an internal necessity for the creation of aesthetically justified music. It is only in Dionysian submersion that the pain of existence can emerge in the form of a rapturous dithyramb, the creative, joyful power of which is captured in Barrett's solo records.

As our discussion of Benjamin's "Work of Art" suggested, Barrett's gritty recordings, replete with false starts, loose song structure, and off-key singing, serve the same purpose as the forever changing song "Have You Got It Yet?" By utterly refusing to be isolated and commodified, it challenged the very idea of commodifying music, much as *The Madcap Laughs* challenges the convention of the radio-friendly record. And since, as Benjamin points out, technological reproduction allows them to be disseminated widely, these challenges of Barrett's art may engage listeners far and wide, over and over again, laying the groundwork for subversive political possibilities of which we can only speculate.

There's a line in "Octopus" on *The Madcap Laughs* where Barrett chants that "the madcap laughed at the man on the border." While this no doubt served as the inspiration for the album's title, it offers a fascinating image of Barrett as *both* submersed in madness and laughing subversively at this man on the edge. On the edge of what, Barrett doesn't say. But it's easy to imagine this border not only between sanity and insanity, but between individuality and subversion. Submersed in Dionysius and subverting social norms, the Madcap still laughs.[4]

[4] Many thanks to Micah Lott and Aaron Cowan for their helpful comments in the creation of this chapter. It is dedicated to the young Dionysians: Allister Jane Lowery, Efrim Patrick Sievert, and Nolan James Cowan.

18

The Worms and the Wall: Michel Foucault on Syd Barrett

GEORGE A. REISCH

The constitution of madness as a mental illness, at the end of the eighteenth century, affords the evidence of a broken dialogue, posits the separation as already effected, and thrusts into oblivion all those stammered, imperfect words without fixed syntax in which the exchange between madness and reason was made. The language of psychiatry, which is a monologue of reason *about* madness, has been established only on the basis of such a silence. I have not tried to write the history of that language, but rather the archaeology of that silence.

—Michel Foucault, *Madness and Civilization*

Did I wink of this, I am
yum, yummy, yum, don't, yummy, yum, yom, yom . . .
Yes, I'm thinking of this, in steam
skeleton kissed to the steel rail

—Syd Barrett, "If It's in You," *The Madcap Laughs*

I've never been mad, but I suspect that *Dark Side of the Moon* is Pink Floyd's best effort to convey something of what it must be like. Especially if you're wearing headphones, the voices, snippets of conversation, giggles, and screams that appear and disappear or hover at the edges of the songs could well make you think "there's someone in my head, but it's not me."

The Wall is different. It's less about the experience of madness than the habits, institutions, and social structures that *create* or *cause* madness. Roger Waters tells us about these dangers

257

at the very beginning of the album. To those of us who venture onto "the thin ice of modern life," he warns,

> Don't be surprised when a crack in the ice
> Appears under your feet.
> You slip out of your depth and out of your mind
> With your fear flowing out behind you
> As you claw the thin ice.

What is this metaphorical weight that threatens to crash through the ice? It's other people—the "silent reproach of a million tear-stained eyes" that we are condemned to drag behind us.

Our modern understanding of mental illness is quite different. It's not a social but a medical and usually neurophysiological problem. The fact that various pharmaceutical drugs can be used to mitigate, or at least alter, symptoms of mental illness (or that taking too many recreational drugs might make you fall permanently off your bike) suggests that this view is correct, that madness is caused by "brain damage" of one kind or another. But Waters is not the first to take up the idea that this is not the whole story, or even the main story. At least in part, madness is social.

There Must Have Been a Door There When I Came In

Jean-Paul Sartre's most famous play, *No Exit*, looked at Hell in a similar way. Far from some literal, otherwordly place, like Hades or Dante's Inferno—unthinkable for the existentialist and atheist Sartre—Hell was a mundane and ordinary place accessible to all of us. As the play begins, Sartre's three characters are ushered in to a well-appointed sitting room with chairs and couches. They know they've each died and gone somewhere, but they are unsure exactly where. Soon enough, once they've made each other's aquaintance, Inez, Estelle, and Garcin proceed to make each other uncomfortable, then *very* uncomfortable as they chip away at each other's defences, egos, and guilty consciences. They torture each other, in other words, with mutual reproach, leading Garcin to realize that "all we were told about the torture-chambers, the fire and brimstone" was a lie. "Old wives' tales! There's no need for red-hot pokers. Hell is— other people!"

The French historian and philosopher Michel Foucault (1926–1983) offered the most compelling social account of madness. In the early 1960s, a few years before Syd Barrett and The Pink Floyd Sound dazzled audiences in London, Foucault dazzled the intellectual world in France with his dissertation on the history of madness. He rejected the common-sense, metaphysical categories we all inherit (usually by way of our parents and teachers) and suggested that madness is not an objective medical condition like a broken leg or scurvy. Rather, madness has a rich and varied historical life. Different kinds and forms of madness appear and disappear at different times in the past, allowing Foucault (and the legion intellectuals inspired by him to this day) to study the different intellectual, social, and economic circumstances and events that trigger these sometimes sudden transformations. With Foucault, the different types and kinds of people we tend to take for granted (the insane—and, in his later studies—the delinquent, the pervert, the soldier, the student, the medical patient) are in fact social and historical entities that could not exist outside their particular historical times. In this sense, Foucault's work in history is a kind of metaphysical inquiry into the ultimate existence of things, the *contingent* existence, he would argue, that we usually mistake as objective, timeless and permanent.

Which Colour of Madness Would You Like?

"Syd Barrett went mad," everyone says. But what exactly does that mean? In *Madness and Civilization*, Foucault identified three stages or eras which gave rise to distinctive kinds and types of madness. Taking the practice of confining the insane on ships or barges as a starting point, he characterized Renaissance madness as a kind of *unreason* that separated the mad from the sane.[1] But separation does not mean isolation. Madness was understood to play an important part in the world. Unreason is utterly inscrutable and foreign to our reasoning minds. But it could still inspire poets and artists to create, prophets to predict,

---

[1] Whether the practice of loading the insane of barges was real or legend is in dispute. One of the most common and perhaps fair criticisms of Foucault is that the historical facts he uses to assemble his philisophical claims are themselves legendary or doubtful.

or healers to heal. It was a mirror of existence, some thought, that warned of the end of times or the folly that humans were prone to. In some ways, that is, the early modern world was saturated with madness: "madness and the madman become major figures, in their ambiguity: menace and mockery, the dizzying unreason of the world, and the feeble ridicule of men."[2] Madness was something that kept us humble and, possibly, grateful.

Things took quite a different form hundreds of years later as the "classical" age of science, literature, philosophy, and reason began to take shape in the seventeenth and eighteenth centuries. The mad were increasingly excluded from culture insofar as their unreason was taken to mean, literally, nothing at all. Whereas madness was once "present everywhere and mingled with every experience by its images or its dangers," it was now feared and avoided as something more alien from life. Madness was now on display "but on the other side of bars; if present, it was at a distance, under the eyes of a reason that no longer felt any relation to it and would not compromise itself by too close a resemblance" (p. 70).

The practice throughout classical Europe was to *confine* the insane—originally in "houses of correction" or "hospitals" (p. 39). This was connected to the birth of a new kind of madness, one connected to the new economic and political realities of European life. "In the history of unreason, [confinement] marked a decisive event: the moment when madness was perceived on the social horizon of poverty, of incapacity for work, of inability to integrate with the group . . ."(p. 64). Madness begins to acquire fundamentally different meanings and connotations involving social, economic and political concepts that also apply to life outside the wall, outside the asylum.

Asylums ceased to be places to warehouse people whose heads were filled (or empty) with unreason; they instead became structured microcosms of ordinary, civic life, replete with rules, regulations, schedules, and, of course, physical restraints that were believed to help *morally* cleanse and purify the mad of their madness. They were "confined in cities of pure morality, where the law that should reign in all hearts was to be

---

[2] Michel Foucault, *Madness and Civilization* (New York: Vintage, 1988), p. 13.

applied without compromise, without concession, in the rigorous forms of physical restraint" (p. 61).

With the mad confined in asylums, many of our contemporary ideas about madness began to take shape. We began to understand the insane as individuals who could not operate without guidance or constraint within the structures and schedules of ordinary society. They were, in this regard, akin to children who require the guidance and restraints of the asylum. Just as we were all once children, therefore, we all might regress and lapse into madness (or, fall through the thin ice of sanity)— either suddenly or perhaps because driven to madness by life and events. Foucault cites a Swiss doctor who warns "wise and civilized men" that their good fortune is more precarious than they know: "an instant suffices to disturb and annihilate that supposed wisdom of which you are so proud; an unexpected event, a sharp and sudden emotion of the soul will abruptly change the most reasonable and intelligent man into a raving idiot" (pp. 211–12).

Morality and Physiology

Pink went mad. Syd Barrett went mad. Roger Waters himself recalled having a short-lived "nervous breakdown" during a recording session. "Something happened in my brain," he recalled, that "frightened the life out of me."[3] This idea that madness is all about physiology, about *the brain*, points to the third, and final stage of Foucault's history—the point at which our current *medicalized* understanding of madness takes center stage. This is the madness of psychiatry, of Samuel Tuke, in England, and Philippe Pinel, in France, reformers who are usually credited with rescuing our understanding of madness from notions of demonic possession or biblical sin. As Foucault sees it, however, this liberation of madness from dungeons and manacles was just another change or reconfiguration in madness's long and varied historical career.

The most striking feature of this modern, psychiatric conception of madness is precisely what connects it to Pink's story

---

[3] Waters discusses this in a video interview posted to youtube.com (at the time of this writing).

in *The Wall*—the *internalization* of treatment. Drawing on the notions that the mad are *morally* corrupt and ethically obligated to redeem themselves, as well as the modern conception of madness as a natural, curable illness, psychiatric madness calls for the insane to *participate* in their treatment. Just as the sane must tread carefully on the thin ice and continually try to *avoid* lapsing into insanity, the insane are required to follow their medical treatments, report accurately their conditions, and assist their doctors or attendants as much as possible in the hope of recovering out of madness.

Foucault cites a story told by Samuel Tuke about a "maniac, young and prodigously strong, whose seizures caused panic in those around him and even among his guards"(p. 245) in the asylum. Tuke flouted conventional wisdom and ordered that the patient's restraints be removed, whereupon he suddenly became nonviolent and thoughtful:

> He was taken to his room; the keeper explained that the entire house was organized in terms of the greatest liberty and the greatest comfort for all, and that he would not be subject to any constraint so long as he did nothing against the rules of the house or the general principles of human morality. For his part, the keeper declared he had no desire to use the means of coercion at his disposal. (p. 246)

The maniac, Tuke wrote, became "sensible of the kindness of his treatment. He promised to restrain himself." When he again became noisy or threatening to other inmates, he needed only be reminded that he might again be subject to "the old ways" and, shortly, he would calm down. In four months, the story goes, the patient left the asylum and was considered "cured."

With stories like these to guide it, Foucault suggests, the modern asylum became a theater of observation designed to assist the insane in monitoring themselves and reporting their experiences and behaviors to their controlling superiors. "Everything was organized so that the madman would recognized himself in a world of judgment that enveloped him on all sides; he must know that he is watched, judged, and condemned; from transgression to punishment, the connection must be evident, as a guilt recognized by all." With Pinel, the punishment in question was typically a sudden cold water shower from a faucet above their heads in their cells, a shower that "often disconcerts the madman and drives out a predominant idea by a strong and unexpected impression" (p. 267). Repeat when necessary, Pinel said, thus reinforcing the new psychiatric ideal: "the internalization of the juridical instance, and the birth of remorse in the inmate's mind," as Foucault puts it. "It is only at this point that the judges agree to stop the punishment, certain that it will continue indefinitely in the inmate's conscience" (p. 267). Madness thus became a medical and *moral* predicament for the patient—a state of mind, a state of conscience, and an attitude and perpetual vigilance toward oneself.

I've Always Been Mad. And Guilty.

The Wall is the story of a rock star coping with people and circumstances that he cannot bear because they are driving him crazy. Once Pink's finished the wall and is safely isolated inside, he realizes that he's "crazy, over the rainbow." As a madman, Pink is an ideal patient. He did not even need to be sent to an asylum or condemned by the authorities. He condemns and imprisons himself, brick by brick, in his personal asylum. And he is driven to do this, in part, by his impending sense of *guilt*. In "The Trial," he asks, "I'm waiting in this cell because I have to know: have I been guilty all this time?" His greatest fear seems to be that, in fact, he *did* let everyone down, that his Mother *had* to smother him with control; his teachers *were right* to make fun of him and his poetical aspirations; that his wife had *no choice* but to leave him. The "silent reproach of a million tear-stained eyes" that weighed on him, in other words, was his own creation, his own just deserts.

I have no idea whether Foucault himself saw or listened to *The Wall* before his death in 1984, but this mixture of madness and guilt at the heart of Roger Waters's story and screenplay would have been familiar to him. It bears out his own view that madness is now inseparable from the social, economic and *moral* history of the modern world. Pink is placed on trial not because of any particular event or offense, after all. He's on trial merely for being himself, for being human, for "showing feelings of an almost human nature." His cross-examining accusors are none other than the people he's most familiar with: his mother, his wife, and his teacher. The judge who decides that

Pink is guilty sentences him to endure exactly that which he has spent his life struggling to escape, namely, the judgments and reproaches of others—"tear down the wall!" and leave Pink "exposed before [his] peers". Like Sisyphus condemned forever to start again rolling his rock up the hill, Pink is now back where he started—exposed, guilty, and without any escape plan other than once again condemning *himself* to isolation behind, most likely, a new or reconstructed wall. ("Which is where . . . we came in.")

I have no idea whether Roger Waters ever read Foucault's history of madness, either. But his view of "modern life" as the crucible of madness—its ingredients being the demands of custom, expectations, codependencies, and psychopathologies (like the schoolteacher's wife's) of *daily, ordinary life*—joins Foucault's view of madness as an evolving by-product of civilization as it changes and evolves through time. The sane and the insane are closely linked, bound by similar demands, expectations, and experiences of what it's like to be a member of society, always glancing over their shoulder at each other and paying close attention.

What about the Worms?

All of which might seem to have nothing to do with the rise of "the worms" after Pink's trial. In the movie version of The Wall, especially, the rise of "the worms"—the goose-stepping hammers in Gerald Scarfe's animation, and skinheads rioting in the streets of London—has always left me puzzled. Even Roger Waters throws up his hands about whether and how all this fits together inside Pink's personal story.[4] How, exactly, does Pink's degeneration and his inability to cope with the demands of modern life and rock stardom lead to—either causally or logically—the riot of skinheads and animated hammers that "follow the worms" through the streets of London?

One thing we know is this: the worms help make Pink crazy. In "Hey You," "the worms ate into his brain." And before his trial begins, Pink waited safely behind his wall, "in perfect isolation,"

---

[4] See the interview with Waters included as a special feature on the DVD release of *Pink Floyd: The Wall.*

simply "waiting for the worms to come." At the same time, Pink's "surrogate band" has taken his place at the concert and whips up a racist fervor in a concert hall filled with skinheads. "Are there any queers in the audience tonight? Get them up against the wall! . . ." Soon, this frenzy bursts out onto the streets with orders to "follow the worms"—to "cut out the deadwood," "to clean up the city," "to weed out the weaklings," and find "the queens and the coons and the reds and the jews."

This fascist clampdown obviously points to the Holocaust in Germany and, like many of Waters's songs, to the Second World War. But it also points to England's imperial past: "Would you like to see Britannia rule again, my friend?" the lyric asks us. Yes? Then join the crowd, smash windows, set immigrants' cars on fire, and otherwise suppress, exile or execute all those suspicious foreigners or deviants who, according to the typical logic of fascist nationalism, have stolen Britannia's glory and ruined her empire. Do you want revenge? Do you want to make the guilty pay? Then "all you have to do is follow the worms."

So far as I can tell, *The Wall* provides little explanation about why Pink's insanity and these fascist worms go together like this. But Foucault sheds some light. Pink's madness, after all, emerges from the fact that he is constantly at war with *himself.* As a modern psychiatric patient, he is, in part, his own doctor trying to redeem himself, change himself, and to obliterate or confine those parts of himself that he does not like (or has been taught to dislike), does not understand, or cannot control. The rioting skinheads, then, are a version of Pink's inner struggle in a wider, social setting. They too are preoccupied with those sectors of society that they do not like, do not understand because of cultural, economic, or racial differences, and cannot control.

Fascism and insanity, on this view, are different versions of each other. Both Pink and the skinheads are obsessed with reducing differences and promoting uniformity and similarity throughout society. Foucault hints at this linkage when he writes of cities as metaphors for modern asylums that sit within a larger state. In these cities, the insane are expected to toe the line, to accept a single, dominant code of conduct that cannot be questioned or appealed. The essence of insanity, on this model is

> that moral city of which the bourgeois conscience began to dream
> in the seventeenth century; a moral city for those who sought from

the start, to avoid it, a city where right reigns only by virtue of a force without appeal. . . . (*Madness and Civilization*, p. 61)

Pink grew up in this city. That's why his schoolmaster was able to humiliate him merely by pointing out his "little black book" of poems. Most children do not aspire to write poetry and such idiosyncracies are easy targets for schoolyard bullying and teasing. Why should that be so, but for the fact that people are quick to resent those who deviate from their expectations about what is normal and virtuous? Pink's mother tormented him for a similar reason—what she saw as strict, motherly love was, for him, a network of rules, regulations, and constant surveillance that made it impossible for him to be different, to be the person he wanted to become. As Pink's trial showed, these expectations and demands operate as a powerful "force without appeal." This logic of fascism admits no exceptions. Not even confining himself behind a wall would satisfy the judge who sentenced him.

The rioting skinheads were just as uncompromising in their quest to "clean up the city" and make their society uniform and undifferentiated. Foucault calls this "the underside of the bourgeoisie's great dream and great preoccupation of the classical age: the laws of the State and the laws of the heart at last identical. "Virtue," according to this ideal, is "an affair of the state" (p. 61) and every individual who is somehow different, who plays different tunes, or does not accept the dictates of classical reason and rationality is a threat, an offense, to the prevailing rule of uniformity.

Art, Madness, and Syd Barrett

If both *The Wall* and *Madness and Civilization* point toward this conjunction of madness and fascism, then it's not surprising that both conclude with an apology, a defense of artists, in particular, as society's best hedge against the threat of fascism. In *The Wall*, it appears at the very end in the song "Outside the Wall":

All alone, or in twos,
The ones who really love you
Walk up and down outside the wall.
Some hand in hand

And some gathered together in bands.
The bleeding hearts and artists
Make their stand.

The ones that "really love" Pink—and presumably the rest of
us—are the "bleeding hearts" who celebrate differences and
idiosyncracies in culture and artists who create and cultivate
what is novel and different. Their love for Pink is genuine,
Waters seems to say, because they accept Pink's differences, his
peculiarities. Were there more of those in the world, it might not
be the awful, "fucking sad" place that it is.[5]

Foucault's apology goes further. He defends not only artists
but the *unreason* which hovers around and threads through the
history of madness. In a world where insanity has been medicalized and psychologized, in which the insane are now treated
as fellow citizens of our own social and moral universe, and
trained to understand themselves along those lines, there is ever
less opportunity for unreason—that which is truly foreign and
different—to erupt into our world. There are few "empty
spaces," that is, through which we can confront that which is
truly different, unfamiliar, and perhaps utterly incomprehensible. Unless, Foucault insists, it comes to us through art:

> Since the end of the eighteenth century, the life of unreason no
> longer manifests itself except in the lightning-flash of works such
> as those of Hölderlin, of Nerval, of Nietzsche, or of Artaud—forever
> irreducible to those alienations that can be cured, resisting by their
> own strength that gigantic moral imprisonment which we are in the
> habit of calling . . . the liberation of the insane by Pinel and Tuke.
> (p. 278)

Only works by philosophers, performers, and poets like
these, Foucault claims, can genuinely challenge the sensibilities
and attitudes we have absorbed from the modern life around us
and force us to take notice of them and what they are. This is
not to say that unreason lay *within* great works of art, displayed
or dissected within it. Unreason is forever beyond our grasp.
Were it not, then it would be just another species of reason,

---

[5] The inverview in which Waters uses this phrase is in *The Pink Floyd Lyric
Songbook* (London: Pink Floyd Publications, 1982), p. 12.

something we could understand. The unreason Foucault defends, therefore, is a madness that never connects directly to the world or our understanding but still "interrupts" us and thereby confronts us directly: "by the madness which interrupts [the world], a work of art opens a void, a moment of silence, a question without an answer, provokes a breach without reconciliation where the world is forced to question itself" (p. 288). In these rare cases, "the world finds itself arraigned by the work of art and responsible before it for what it is" (p. 289).

With unreason, in other words, Pink's story gets turned around. Instead of society putting the insane rock star on trial, it is madness that puts us on trial. It is mute and silent, but nonetheless powerful, influential, and provocative. For some, it cannot be ignored, because it makes them question themselves, their values, their conduct, their selves. In the world of Pink Floyd, of course, that madness would be Syd Barrett. This is not the madness in "The Madcap Laughs" and other post-Pink Floyd albums that Syd released. It's rather the way that Syd's absence created for his former bandmates as well as Pink Floyd fans something like "a void, a moment of silence, a question without an answer" that they would return to over and over during the 1970s. The band's relationship to Syd was precisely "a breach without reconcilation" that could not be simply answered, explained or understood. But it loomed over the band and seems to have inspired at least parts of every major album.

The heart of *Meddle*, for example, is "Echoes," the sprawling psychedelic opus built around the core idea of genuine communication, sympathy, and *collaboration* with others:

Strangers passing in the street
By chance two separate glances meet
And I am you and what I see is me.
And do I take you by the hand?
And lead you through the land?

On *Dark Side*, Syd lurks as the madman whose band began "playing different tunes." On *Wish You Were Here* he is the "crazy diamond" who finds himself "caught in the crossfire of childhood and stardom" and, soon, a lunatic, a "target for faraway laughter." In *The Wall*, that lunatic has gone inside Roger Waters's head: Pink is a rock star (like Roger Waters) whose father was killed during wartime and endured a hellishly cruel youth and education, and who (like Syd) became increasingly crazy, violent, and detached from the world and others. "I am you and what I see is me," indeed. Even *The Final Cut* nods to Syd as Waters dreams of a world in which "maniacs don't blow holes in bandsmen by remote control" ("The Gunner's Dream").

If Foucault is right that great art acquires its power from unreason, then we can perhaps understand something about the power and success of the band's great 1970s albums on the basis of their odd relationship to Syd. This is not to say that Syd, before his departure, bequeathed to the band any kind of musical roadmap or blueprint for his future ex-bandmates to follow. Gilmour, Waters, Wright, and Mason obviously and audibly cultivated their own considerable talents as songwriters, musicians, and producers in the wake of Syd's decline. But the band's best and most compelling work—from *Meddle* to *The Wall*—has at least indirect reference to Syd, madness, or Syd's madness, in particular. It may be coincidence, I admit. But it seems likely that the band's relationship with Syd was a creative spark behind some of its most popular and compelling work. The band's least compelling work, on the other hand—the solo albums and *The Division Bell* and *A Momentary Lapse of Reason,* which do not involve Waters—have much less reference to Syd. And that makes sense, too. For in the 1980s and after, Pink Floyd had become a set of distinct and often conflicting parties, so perhaps the unanswerable queries and interrogations that he and his madness once posed no longer applied. The band that was interrupted and put on trial by Syd's madness, the band that had started playing different tunes, was no longer the same.

19

Living Pink

STEVEN GIMBEL

I have a good friend who responds, "Pink," when someone asks, "How are you doing?" To be pink is not exactly to be depressed or angry. Those emotions tend to be connected with particular events or circumstances in your life. Pink is more a vague sense of inconsolable malaise, a feeling that something in the structure is broken—not something localized that can be fixed, but something deeper and pervasive in all of society. It is a sense of powerlessness, a sense that there is not even a point in being outraged since anything you did would be, as the old Yiddish saying goes, just pissing in the ocean. "It can't be helped, but there's a lot of it about." It's not just "hanging on in quiet desperation," but an intellectual's reflection on that desperation, desperately wishing that there was something that could be done, all the time knowing that the problem is endemic to the human condition.

Our treatment of choice when one of us was pink was repeated playings of the later Floyd albums heavy in Roger Waters's sarcastic pessimism—*Animals*, *The Wall*, and *Wish You Were Here*. The hope was that, like a booster shot, maybe, ingesting large amounts of Waters's cynicism would reduce the pinkness. I'm not sure if it ever worked, but it seemed to make sense at the time.

But you can't stay pink. You need to *live* and not just fritter and waste the hours in a world full of dogs, pigs, sheep, and, if "Have a Cigar" is to be believed, snakes. If contemporary life is as bleak as Roger Waters's lyrics paint it, what is to be done? How can we approach living in a way that makes sure we don't just snap one of these days and cut someone into little pieces? A good number of Pink Floyd songs can be seen as wrestling with answers to exactly this question. I'll look at five options— capitulation, medication, re-creation, emancipation, and resignation and exploration—in hopes that, in the end, Floyd can keep us from being pink.

Capitulation—Riding the Gravy Train

If the system is irreversibly broken and there is nothing you can do about it, perhaps the best thing to do is to take advantage of it. Sure, injustice sucks, but if it's not your fault that the system is how it is and you end up on the right side of the bargain, what's to worry? Why not cash in?

A thread throughout Roger Waters's lyrics concerns success and adoration. It's always a temptation to take your own PR seriously. Maybe you have fame and fortune because you deserve it and acquiring more would merely validate the fact that you deserve more. Seeking a materialist's refuge seems a reasonable response since "all you touch and all you see is all your life will ever be." So why not touch and see as much as you can?

But all of the attention given to it shows that capitulation is not a viable option. Karl Marx argued that such a life alienates people in four ways, all of which show up in various places in the works of Pink Floyd. First, there is alienation from labor. You are what you do. You are a painter if you paint. You are a musician if you play music. Your activity not only creates a product, but it also creates you. But when you are forced to sell your labor, you also sell off the ability to define yourself. But embracing the corporate culture leads to separating, if not eliminating you from your self.

Think about the opening of *The Wall*, "In the Flesh?" (the title of which includes the question mark for a reason) and concludes, "Is this not what you expected to see? If you wanna find out what's behind these cold eyes, you'll just have to claw your way through this disguise." The disguise, the mask is the price of grabbing the cash with both hands and making a stash. When you seek adoration, your work becomes separated from your mind, projected instead on what you think others want, and the person you present ceases to be authentically you, but rather is merely a mask. You get the money, but lose yourself.

But that's not all you lose because you not only create yourself with your labor, you create other things as well. If you're an artist, you create art. But when you sell your art in a corporate capitalist culture, you lose the product of your labor. It becomes sterilized, packaged, ready-to-wear, TV dinner art. Sure, being authentic got the whole thing off the ground, "It's a hell of a start, it could be made into a monster if we all pull together as a team." You can get rich and famous, be a big star, always eat at the steak bar and drive your Jaguar, but you will have opted for "a lead role in a cage." Your work is no longer *your* work.

The third sense of alienation is alienation from other people. When your primary goal is to cash in, other people are no longer people; to you they are now competition, consumers, objects to be used or defeated. "You've got to be able to pick out the easy meat with your eyes closed. And then moving in silently, downwind and out of sight, you've got to strike when the moment is right without thinking." Others are mere means, not full humans.

As if this weren't awful enough, you also become alienated from your own humanity. In reducing others, you yourself become a mere object unable to live the life of a full blooded human being. "Day after day, love turns grey, like the skin of a dying man. Night after night, we pretend its all right; but I have grown older and you have grown colder and nothing is very much fun any more." Our existence as a member of the human species itself becomes undermined and there you are in the machine, another brick in the wall.

Medication—I Can Ease Your Pain

If capitulation isn't a live option and the wall is too high to be brought down, maybe the best we can hope for is for is to become comfortably numb, to live without the pain. There are any number of ways to medicate ourselves: alcohol and other legal or illegal drugs. Perhaps the proper stance is "Don't worry, be happy" . . . or at least be numb.

Indeed, some are considering the sharp rise in prescriptions for antidepressants like Prozac and Zoloft to be exactly this sort of option. Pay no attention to why you are depressed, take these pills because "they'll keep you going through the show. Come on it's time to go." It's fine to be a functioning addict, as long as you are functioning.

Antidepressants are largely marketed at upper-middle-class, middle aged women who are stressed from every part of their lives. If anyone has the right to be pink, it's them. Should we stop to evaluate why women are twice as likely to suffer from depression or shall we just give them a note for the pharmacist? Is there something truly askew in modern life, are our priorities and commitments out of balance? Does any of this matter when your moods can be so easily regulated?

The mom in the Prozac ads is always happy: happy to be putting in so many hours at work, happy to be ferrying kids to soccer games, happy to be cooking and cleaning at home. She can do it all and never stop to think about what it all means. And so it is with any of us who find ourselves pink, who are uncomfortable with what it is that is going on around us. With the flash of a physician's pen you can now become one of the neuro-chemically well-adjusted sheep, "harmlessly passing your time in the grassland away; only dimly aware of a certain unease in the air." But, of course, we all know what happens to sheep, "with bright knives He releaseth my soul. He maketh me to hang on hooks in high places. He converteth me to lamb cutlets."

Re-creation—A Day When You Were Young

But ours is not the only way to see the world. In fact, we have all seen it quite differently when we looked out through our younger eyes. We can always look back to those happier times before we walked into the machine, before we were made into bricks by required conformity of formal schooling. Back when we really didn't need no education. The joyous innocence of childhood may be able to serve as guide, as in "Remember a Day" (from *Saucerful of Secrets*). "Remember a day before today, a day when you were young. Free to play alone with time, evening never came. Sing a song that can't be sung without the morning's kiss. . . . Why can't we play today? Why can't we stay that way?"

Why can't we stay that way, indeed?

Friedrich Nietzsche argued that children have small horizons, that their worlds are simple, and that is something we deeply envy in them. "This is why [an adult] is moved, as though he remembered a lost paradise, when he . . . sees a child, which as yet has nothing past to deny, playing between the fences of past and future in blissful blindness."[1] The carefree nature of childhood was the opposite of being pink. Everything was possible. Everything was magical. Because you had no past and were not ensnarled in the adult world, true happiness was possible. With nothing to remember, we are free to fill the vast open regions of our minds with dreams.

But alas, once we walk through the door, it closes and locks behind us. "Climb your favorite apple tree, try to catch the sun. . . . Why can't we reach the sun? Why can't we blow the years away?" We cannot blow the years away, we cannot go back into the garden. The old apple tree is no longer there. Nietzsche and Richard Wright both show that it is for the same reason. "And yet the child's play must be disturbed: only too soon it will be called out of its forgetfulness. Then it comes to understand the phrase 'it was,' that password with which struggle, suffering, and boredom approach man to remind him what his existence basically is—a never to be completed imperfect tense" (Nietzsche, p. 9). And so it is that Wright ends "Remember a day with the repeated word, "remember." It is memory that makes us long for those days of innocence, but it is also our memory that makes it impossible to return. We no longer exist in the realm of open possibility, we remember and we are what we have done. We are what we remember. And our memories have made us jaded and cynical. Try as we may, as rational, self-aware adults living in the real world, we can no longer partake of the innocent joyfulness of children, only admire it longingly."

Emancipation—You'll Lose Your Mind and Play

Perhaps it isn't possible to get along in real world as a rational adult after all. And if we are doomed by our memories to be adults, then maybe the best option is to cease to be rational, to cease to live in the real world, to simply create your own. Why not choose to live instead in a world that's a happier one, one

---

[1] Nietzsche, *On the Advantages and Disadvantages of History for Life* (Indianapolis: Hackett, 1980), p. 9.

whose animals are not dogs, sheep, and pigs, but rather good mice named Gerald, effervescing elephants, and several members of furry, but unnamed species that are prone to gather and groove with a pict? Whether it is through the use of psychedelic substances or by going insane, could the answer to living pink simply be living in a new world of our making?

You find insanity and psychedelic substances romanticized in many places in the earlier Pink Floyd albums, but they were surely not the first. In the those days, there was considerable hope for enlightenment through the use of psychedelic drugs, from creator of the substance LSD, chemist Albert Hoffman (now a member of the Nobel committee) who called it a "medicine for the soul," to Harvard psychologist Timothy Leary. There were some very smart people at the time who held out for the possibility of better living through chemistry. Pink Floyd certainly was at the vanguard of producing the soundtrack for those on their own trip. The hypersensitivity of those under the influence gave music an important role and Floyd's early music and stage show were devoted to helping out.

The romanticized notion of insanity goes back to antiquity with the madman having special creative powers, joy, and access to knowledge. We see references of this sort liberally spread throughout Floyd lyrics from "You'll lose your mind and play," in "See Emily Play," to "And if I go insane and they lock me away, will you still let me join in the game?" in "If," to "The lunatic is on the grass, remembering games and daisy chains and laughs," in "Brain Damage," to "Shine On You Crazy Diamond's," "Come on you raver, you seer of visions, come on you painter, you piper, you prisoner, and shine!" Sanity is limiting. Being pink might be the result of seeing the world through the distorted lens of those whose minds are constrained.

But, of course, there is the dark side. For every reference that romanticizes insanity, there are the "heads exploding with dark foreboding" as in the homicidal and suicidal references in the titles "Careful With That Axe, Eugene" and "Set the Controls for the Heart of the Sun." But, perhaps, the starkest warning of all was the example of Syd Barrett himself, whose use of LSD and his own problems with mental illness combined to leave him an empty shell, not the lovable childlike gnome we all wished him to be. The miner for truth was also a miner for delusion whose eyes no longer shone like diamonds, but were vacant, empty like black holes in the sky.

Resignation and Exploration—I'll Climb the Hill in My Own Way

Is there no hope? Are we trapped in this life surrounded by suffering? Yes, but that does not mean that we are hopelessly trapped in a life of meaninglessness. Albert Camus likens living to the Greek mythological character Sisyphus whose hubris condemned him to forever rolling a large boulder up a hill only to have it roll back down when he just about had it to the top. Over and over again, Sisyphus would roll that stone never able to make any difference. But the real torture, the tragedy of the story lies not merely in the futility of the effort, but rather in Sisyphus's full awareness of that futility. "If this myth is tragic, that is because its hero is conscious. Where would the torture be, indeed, if at every step the hope of succeeeding upheld him? . . . Sisyphus, proletarian of the gods, powerless and rebellious, knows the whole extent of his wretched condition: it is what he thinks of during his descent."[2] If anyone should be pink, it is Sisyphus. Like Camus, I imagine Sisyphus plodding down the mountain with long, heavy steps, but in my image his iPod is playing "Echoes."

Camus argues, however, that the torture fails. That with each step back down towards the waiting stone, Sisyphus gives his life meaning. By walking down the hill "he is superior to his fate." "I leave Sisyphus at the foot of the mountain! One always finds one's burden again. But Sisyphus teaches the higher fidelity that negates the gods and raises the rock. He too concludes that all is well. This universe henceforth without a master seems to him neither sterile nor futile. Each atom of that stone, each mineral flake of that night-filled mountain, in itself forms a world. The struggle itself towards the heights is enough to fill a man's heart. One must imagine Sisyphus happy" (Camus, p. 91).

Our work may be in vain, but it is *our* work, it is *our* life. There's no doubt that the world is full of pain, that those in power do not have the best intentions, and the large mass of

---

[2] *The Myth of Sisyphus and Other Essays* (New York: Vintage, 1960), pp. 89–90.

people are oblivious. In the same way, we find in "Fearless,""You say the hill's too steep to climb. Climb it. You say you'd like to see me try. Climbing. You pick the place and I'll choose the time and I'll climb that hill in my own way." It is not what waits at the top of the hill, but the climbing itself that gives us meaning and in finding your own way of climbing, the climb is made valuable.

But we do have one considerable advantage over Sisyphus, we need not roll our stone alone. We have others with whom we may share the load. We are not alone, but live lives embedded in those of others. *Animals*, for all of its dark cynicism, ends with hope that springs from care. "You know that I care what happens to you, and I know that you care for me. So I don't feel alone or the weight of the stone, now that I've found somewhere safe to bury my bone. . . . A shelter from pigs on the wing." The danger is not gone, the pigs are still a reality, but one does not feel the weight of the stone in the heart of another.

Perhaps, then, the solution to living pink is not to be found in any of the meditations in which we look for it. The answer is not there. But, then at the same time, maybe it is. Could the answer be in the search itself? Socrates famously said that the unexamined life is not worth living, but he never told us what it is we are looking for in examining that life. Could it be the act of examination itself, a searching that could not take place if it weren't for the pressing need for it? We should be contemptuous of the world as it is, full of sorrow and injustice, a world that will largely rebuff any attempt to change it. Those attempts will not be easy and they will not come without pain and almost certain failure. But it is in creating something in such a world that we triumph through scorn. We are pink, but not pollyanna. We understand the world we are in just as Sisyphus understands his punishment. But it is our world, a troubled world, but a world with those whom we can share love and care. And creating ourselves and our relationships in this world is an artistic act. It is not hope, but life through living. Living pink means living.

Selected Pink Floyd Discography

Studio Albums

Track lists refer to original UK releases of albums. For more extensive discographies, see wikipedia.com or the discography in Schaffner's *Saucerful of Secrets*, pp. 320–27.

The Piper at the Gates of Dawn, 1967

"Astronomy Domine"
"Lucifer Sam"
"Matilda Mother"
"Flaming"
"Pow R. Toc H"
"Take Up Thy Stethoscope and Walk"
"Interstellar Overdrive"
"The Gnome"
"Chapter 24"
"The Scarecrow"
"Bike"

A Saucerful of Secrets, 1968

"Let There Be More Light"
"Remember a Day"
"Set the Controls for the Heart of the Sun"
"Corporal Clegg"
"A Saucerful of Secrets"
"See Saw"
"Jugband Blues"

Music from the Film More, 1969

"Cirrus Minor"
"The Nile Song"
"Crying Song"
"Up the Khyber"
"Green is the Colour"
"Cymbaline"
"Party Sequence"
"Main Theme"
"Ibiza Bar"
"More Blues"
"Quicksilver"
"A Spanish Piece"
"Dramatic Theme"

Ummagumma, 1969

"Astronomy Domine" (live)
"Careful with that Axe, Eugene" (live)
"Set the Controls for the Heart of the Sun" (live)

"A Saucerful of Secrets" (live)
"Sysyphus Part 1"
"Sysyphus Part 2"
"Sysyphus Part 3"
"Sysyphus Part 4"
"Grantchester Meadows"
"Several Species of Small Furry
  Animals Gathered Together in
  a Cave and Grooving with a
  Pict"
"The Narrow Way Part 1"
"The Narrow Way Part 2"
"The Narrow Way Part 3"
"The Grand Vizier's Garden
  Party Part 1: Entrance"
"The Grand Vizier's Garden
  Party Part 2: Entertainment"
"The Grand Vizier's Garden
  Party Part 3: Exit"

Atom Heart Mother, 1970

"Atom Heart Mother"
"If"
"Summer '68"
"Fat Old Sun"
"Alan's Psychedelic Breakfast"

Meddle, 1971

"One of These Days"
"A Pillow of Winds"
"Fearless"
"San Tropez"
"Seamus"
"Echoes"

Obscured by Clouds, 1972

"Obscured by Clouds"
"When You're In"
"Burning Bridges"
"The Gold It's in the . . ."
"Wot's . . . Uh the Deal"
"Mudmen"
"Childhood's End"

"Free Four"
"Stay"
"Absolutely Curtains"

The Dark Side of the Moon, 1973

"Speak to Me"
"Breathe"
"On the Run"
"Time" / "Breathe" (reprise)
"The Great Gig in the Sky"
"Money"
"Us and Them"
"Any Colour You Like"
"Brain Damage"
"Eclipse"

Wish You Were Here, 1975

"Shine On You Crazy Diamond"
  (Parts 1–5)
"Welcome to the Machine"
"Have a Cigar"
"Wish You Were Here"
"Shine On You Crazy Diamond"
  (Parts 6–9)

Animals, 1977

"Pigs on the Wing (Part 1)"
"Dogs"
"Pigs (Three Different Ones)"
"Sheep"
"Pings on the Wing (Part 2)"

The Wall, 1979

"In the Flesh?"
"The Thin Ice"
"Another Brick in the Wall
  (Part 1)"
"The Happiest Days of our
  Lives"
"Another Brick in the Wall
  (Part 2)"

"Mother"
"Goodbye Blue Sky"
"Empty Spaces"
"Young Lust"
"One of My Turns"
"Don't Leave Me Now"
"Another Brick in the Wall (Part 3)"
"Goodbye Cruel World"
"Hey You"
"Is There Anybody Out There?"
"Nobody Home"
"Vera"
"Bring the Boys Back Home"
"Comfortably Numb"
"The Show Must Go On"
"In The Flesh"
"Run Like Hell"
"Waiting for the Worms"
"Stop"
"The Trial"
"Outside the Wall"

The Final Cut, 1983

"The Post War Dream"
"Your Possible Pasts"
"One of the Few"
"The Hero's Return"
"The Gunners Dream"
"Paranoid Eyes"
"Get Your Filthy Hands Off My Desert"
"The Fletcher Memorial Home"
"Southampton Doc"
"The Final Cut"
"Not Now John"
"Two Suns in the Sunset"

A Momentary Lapse of Reason, 1987

"Signs of Life"
"Learning to Fly"
"The Dogs of War"

"One Slip"
"On the Turning Away"
"Yet Another Movie"
"Round and Around"
"A New Machine (Part 1)"
"Terminal Frost"
"A New Machine (Part 2)"
"Sorrow"

The Division Bell, 1994

"Cluster One"
"What Do You Want from Me"
"Poles Apart"
"Marooned"
"A Great Day for Freedom"
"Wearing the Inside Out"
"Take It Back"
"Coming Back to Life"
"Keep Talking"
"Lost for Words"
"High Hopes"

Live Albums

Delicate Sound of Thunder, 1988

*P*U*L*S*E*, 1995

Is There Anybody Out There?, 2000

Major Compilations

Relics, 1971

A Nice Pair, 1973

A Collection of Great Dance Songs, 1981

Works, 1983

Shine On, 1992

Echoes: The Best Of Pink Floyd, 2001

Early Singles

"Arnold Layne" / "Candy and a
Currant Bun", March 11th,
1967
"See Emily Play" / "The
Scarecrow", June 16th, 1967
"Apples and Oranges" / "Paint
Box", November 18th, 1967
"It Would Be So Nice" / "Julia
Dream", April 12th, 1968
"Point Me at the Sky" / "Careful
with That Axe, Eugene",
December 17th, 1968

Syd Barrett Solo Albums

The Madcap Laughs, 1970

"Terrapin"
"No Good Trying"
"Love You"
"No Man's Land"
"Dark Globe"
"Here I Go"
"Octopus"
"Golden Hair"
"Long Gone"
"She Took a Long Cold Look"
"Feel"
"If It's In You"
"Late Night"

Barrett, 1970

"Baby Lemonade"
"Love Song"
"Dominoes"
"It Is Obvious"
"Rats"
"Maisie"
"Gigolo Aunt"
"Waving My Arms In The Air"
"I Never Lied To You"
"Wined And Dined"
"Wolfpack"
"Effervescing Elephant"

Opel, 1988

"Opel"
"Clowns and Jugglers"
"Rats"
"Golden Hair"
"Dolly Rocker"
"Word Song"
"Wined and Dined"
"Swan Lee (Silas Lang)"
"Birdie Hop"
"Let's Split"
"Lanky (Part One)"
"Wouldn't You Miss Me (Dark
Globe)"
"Milky Way"
"Golden Hair"

In the Flesh . . .

RANDALL AUXIER ticks away the moments of many dull days on a piece of ground in his hometown of Carbondale, Illinois, where he teaches the students of Southern Illinois University about the philosophy of time—and then gives them their pudding even if they haven't eaten their meat.

SCOTT CALEF is Professor and Chair of the Department of Philosophy at Ohio Wesleyan University. He has published in ancient philosophy, applied ethics, political philosophy, metaphysics and the philosophy of religion. He has also contributed to *The Beatles and Philosophy, Hitchcock and Philosophy, South Park and Philosophy: You Know, I Learned Something Today*, and *Metallica and Philosophy*. His favorite Pink Floyd song is "Astronomy Domine", though "Careful With That Axe, Eugene" and "One of These Days" are close runners up on account of their sentimental value and past romantic associations. He's still trying to figure out why ya can't have any pudding if ya don't eat yer meat, and how Freud would interpret the line.

CARI CALLIS lives in Chicago and travels to the Caribbean to spend time with her Rasta friends whenever possible. She recently shot a documentary about the Rasta healing garden of MacKenzie, without whose knowledge of the philosophy of Rastafari her chapter in this volume would not have been possible. She is a professor who teaches at Columbia College in Chicago and is a ragamuffin wannabe who would wear dreads if she didn't think they looked stupid on white people.

PATRICK CROSKERY first heard Pink Floyd's *Animals* as a double major in Philosophy and English at the University of Virginia. His best friend had both this album and *Dark Side of the Moon* on a single 8-track tape (don't ask) which Patrick listened to over and over again (as any true Pink Floyd fan will understand). He went on to receive his Ph.D. in Philosophy from the University of Chicago, and is now Associate Professor of Philosophy and Director of the Honors Program at Ohio Northern University. His research interests include the philosophical foundations of professional ethics and the implications of intellectual property for political philosophy.

DAVID DETMER is Professor of Philosophy at Purdue University Calumet. He is the author of *Sartre Explained* (forthcoming), *Challenging Postmodernism: Philosophy and the Politics of Truth* (2003), and *Freedom as a Value* (1988), as well as essays on a variety of philosophical topics. Drawing inspiration from "Money," he occasionally lectures in 7/8 time, only to find, invariably, that the students are listening in 4/4.

BRANDON FORBES has an MTS from Duke University Divinity School ('03). He currently works in marketing and communication for Cato Research and is a freelance writer. He has covered indie rock for a variety of publications, including *Other Magazine, Thirsty Magazine,* and *Gaper's Block*. Residing in Chicago, with his wife and two dogs, he longs for his native Southern climes where it's good to be lost in the wood.

STEVEN GIMBEL is Associate Professor of Philosophy at Gettysburg College. He is editor of *The Grateful Dead and Philosophy: Getting High Minded about Love and Haight* (2007) and co-editor of *Defending Einstein: Hans Reichenbach's Early Writings on Space, Time, and Motion* (2006). He has written articles on the foundations of relativity theory, the history of mathematics, the notion of sportsmanship in the Kasparov–Deep Blue chess match, and the environmental ethic of the American Nazi Party. No longer does he consider "Relic" to only refer to a great album and his forehead is no longer obscured by hair.

THEODORE GRACYK teaches philosophy in Minnesota. He is the author of three books about popular music, *Rhythm and Noise: An Aesthetics of Rock* (1996), the award-winning *I Wanna Be Me: Rock Music and the Politics of Identity* (2001), and *Listening to Popular Music: Or, How I Learned to Stop Worrying and Love Led Zeppelin* (2007). He's waiting for Pink Floyd to release *Dark Side of the Moon II* so that he can watch the second half of the *Wizard of Oz*.

DAVID MACGREGOR JOHNSTON is an Assistant Professor of Philosophy at Lyndon State College. His scholarly interests lean toward aesthetics, phenomenology, and existentialism. As a contributor to *The Grateful*

Dead and Philosophy, he is becoming comfortable with his local reputation as "that stoner-music philosopher guy." He still has his first copy of *The Dark Side of the Moon*, and that TDK SA90 Tony gave him is somewhere in his mother's basement.

ANDREW ZIMMERMAN JONES lives in Indiana, where he works in the dark side of the education industry—math educational assessments. He also maintains the About.com Physics site at http://physics.about.com. He's a writer of various non-fiction pieces and fiction in the genres of science fiction and fantasy, more of which can be learned about at http://www.azjones.info.

ERIN KEALEY is currently in the Philosophy and Literature program at Purdue University and contributed to *The Beatles and Philosophy: Nothing You Can Think that Can't Be Thunk* (2006). As Erin makes her face up in her favorite disguise, she finds "existentialist" the most appealing. In her work, she is driven by the eternal questions: Is there anybody out there? What exactly is a dream? And, how can you have any pudding if you don't eat your meat?

EDWARD MACAN is professor of music at College of the Redwoods, Eureka, California. He is author of *Rocking the Classics: English Progressive Rock and the Counterculture* (1996) and *Endless Enigma: A Musicial Biography of Emerson, Lake and Palmer* (2006). He sighted his first pig on the wing at age fifteen and has been a Pink Floyd fan ever since.

SUE MROZ is an Artist-in-Residence in the Film Department at Columbia College, Chicago. She studied at the C.G. Jung Institute of Chicago before becoming an award-winning filmmaker. She now teaches Directing, Screenwriting, and Critical Studies, focusing on areas such as mythology, dreams, and the movies. It's official: She is now cooler than her brother.

MICHAEL F. PATTON, JR. is an obsessive audiophile who amassed a tremendous vinyl LP collection while working in a small record store in high school. A Pink Floyd fan since he was weaned off the Beatles at thirteen, he helped keep *Dark Side of the Moon* on the *Billboard* charts by inflating sales numbers back before all that business was computerized. He hopes that this is not considered a crime, or that the statute of limitations will protect him. Michael lives, loves, and teaches (though not necessarily in that order) in Montevallo, Alabama, where he is Professor of Philosophy at the eponymous University located there. He thanks his tolerant wife, Cheryl, and his sociopathic cats for all their help.

A few decades ago, **GEORGE REISCH** saw *Pink Floyd: Live at Pompeii* at a movie theatre in Basking Ridge, New Jersey, and has been a Pink Floyd fan ever since. He teaches philosophy at the School of Continuing Studies at Northwestern University, and has published articles and a book on the history, development, and demise of logical empiricism. He co-edited *Monty Python and Philosophy* (2006) and *Bullshit and Philosophy* (2006) with Gary L. Hardcastle and is the Series Editor for Popular Culture and Philosophy.

JOSEF STEIFF grew up with pigs, sheep, and dogs but now makes his home in Chicago, Illinois, teaching film and screenwriting at Columbia College. He is an award-winning filmmaker and the author of *The Complete Idiot's Guide to Independent Filmmaking*. Now loaded up on Joe's iPod, Pink Floyd is even more a part of his life's soundtrack.

JERE O'NEILL SURBER bought *The Dark Side of the Moon* on the day it was released, clamped on his stereo headphones (remember those?), and disappeared into cosmosonic space for about a week. Upon re-entry, he studied (what else?) philosophy—at Penn State and the University of Bonn. His primary gig since then has been at the University of Denver, with guest shots at such places as the Universities at Mainz, Leuven, and Oxford. His top numbers are German Idealism, Postmodernism, and Asian Philosophy. He's published or co-published seven books and a bunch of articles, including a chapter in *The Beatles and Philosophy*, but still can't figure out how to sound like Dave Gilmour on guitar.

Having written widely for academic and popular audiences on a broad spectrum of topics in rock music, **DEENA WEINSTEIN** is an unabashed Floyd fanatic, owning all but the Waterless Floyd albums in vinyl and CD. A professor at DePaul University in Chicago, she has taught a sociology of rock music course there for over a quarter of a century. Weinstein takes a multi-dimensional approach to the sociology of popular culture in her numerous publications including *Heavy Metal: The Music and Its Culture* (2000), "All Singers are Dicks," "Rock Critics Need Bad Music," and "Rock Protest Songs: So Many and So Few."

Index

actual intentionalism, 156
Adamson, Chris, 187
Adorno, Theodor, 117, 118
  on classical music, 99
  on mental illness, 102
  "On Popular Music," 96–98
  Philosophy of Modern Music, 96,
    99, 102
  on primitivism in music, 101–02
  on Stravinsky, 101–02
  on structural standardization, 98
  on twelve–tone music, 100
Aesop, 36
aesthetic evaluation, and intention,
    151–52
agency individualism, 153, 157
Alice in Wonderland (Carroll), 47
alienation, 61, 68
  from artistic authenticity, 78
  as self–estrangement, 62
  types of, 61–62, 272–73
Allen, Chesney, 67
Anderson, Jon, 4
Anderson, Pink, 169
Animals (Pink Floyd album), 4, 11,
    56, 61, 76, 77, 83, 89, 91,
    121, 126, 231, 271, 278
  alienation in, 73, 95, 196
  on capitalism, 72–73
  "Dogs," 36, 37, 72, 74, 196
  as dystopia, 36

emotion in, 87
empathy in, 41
  on false consciousness, 40
  hyper–capitalism in, 37–38
  as Orwellian, 35–36
  "Pigs (3 Different Ones)," 36,
    38–39, 87
  "Pigs on the Wing," 36, 64
  "Sheep," 36, 40, 78, 84
  thought experiment in, 36
antidepressants, critique of, 273–74
Antonioni, Michelangelo, 8, 52
Apocalypse Now (film), 26
apophenia, 47
Apollo, 234, 244–46
Aristotle, 31, 190, 192, 193
Aristotle's Plot Curve, 29–30
"Arnold Layne" (Pink Floyd single),
    xi, 6, 7, 173, 232, 235, 249,
    253
art
  controlling effect of, 216–17
  mass reproduction of, 253
  as mode of encounter (Buber), 134
  as mode of experience (Buber),
    134–35
Artaud, Antonin, 194, 267
artist, Romantic view of, 88
Atom Heart Mother (Pink Floyd
    album), 7, 8, 63, 113, 114,
    153

287

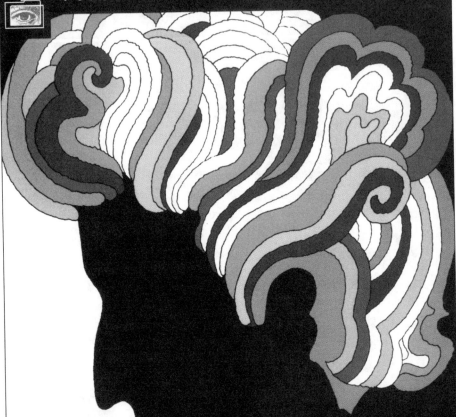

BOB
DYLAN
AND PHILOSOPHY

IT'S ALRIGHT, MA (I'M ONLY THINKING)

EDITED BY PETER VERNEZZE AND CARL J. PORTER